Because she entertained with the kind of grace that has inspired our collection, and because she was a valued member of the Austin Junior League, we dedicate this cookbook to Lou Neff.

THE COLLECTION
a Cookbook

Contents

Appetizers   1

Soups   23

Salads and Dressings   43

Entrées   75
  Light   75
  Beef   87
  Pork   109
  Lamb   116
  Poultry   121
  Seafood   136
  Game   144

Vegetables   153

Breads   195

Sweets   215
  Cakes   215
  Pies   230
  Cookies   243
  Candies   260
  Ice Cream   264
  Other Desserts   268

Etcetera   291
  Sauces   291
  Pickles   296
  Jellies and Preserves   298
  Other Condiments   303
  Butters   306
  Beverages   307

Index   316

Appetizers

Artichoke Balls

1	8 oz. jar marinated artichoke hearts, undrained	1	c. grated Romano cheese
¾	c. mushroom pieces	1½	c. seasoned bread crumbs
2	cloves garlic	2	eggs
1	c. grated Parmesan cheese		Salt and pepper to taste

Place in blender artichoke hearts, including liquid, mushroom pieces, and garlic; blend for 15 seconds. Mix cheeses, 1 cup of the bread crumbs, eggs, and seasonings; combine with artichoke mixture. Form into small balls; roll in remaining bread crumbs. Bake on greased cookie sheet at 375° for 20 minutes.
Yields approximately 50 balls/Freezes.
Mrs. Maury Hughes, Jr. (Phoebe Foster)

Chafing Dish Artichokes

2   c. butter
4   oz. blue cheese
3   14½ oz. cans artichoke
    hearts, drained

Heat butter and cheese, stirring until melted. Transfer to a hot chafing dish and mix in artichoke hearts. Spear with toothpicks.
Mrs. Roy M. Talley (Martha C. Green)

Artichoke and Cheese Canapé

½	c. grated sharp Cheddar cheese	Toast rounds
½	c. mayonnaise	McCormick Salad Supreme
2	T. finely chopped onion	seasoning

Marinated artichoke hearts,
   drained and dried with
   paper towel

Mix cheese, mayonnaise, and onion. Place an artichoke heart on a Triscuit or toast round. Spread filling on top. Sprinkle with seasoning. Heat under broiler until bubbly. Serve at once.
Serves 6 to 8/Freezes.
Mrs. Terrence Watt (Mary Avery)

Hot Clam-Cheese Dip

½ bell pepper, finely chopped
1 small onion, finely chopped
3 T. butter
2 7 oz. cans minced clams, drained

¼ lb. Cheddar cheese, grated
1½ t. cayenne, or to taste
3 T. catsup
1 T. dry sherry

Sauté pepper and onion in butter for 3 to 4 minutes. Add remaining ingredients. Stir in a double boiler until cheese melts; do not let water boil. Serve hot with crackers, melba toast, or potato chips.
Different from any dip.
Yields 3 cups.
Mrs. Jack Steinhauser (Cissy Wheat)

Lamb Riblets

4 to 5 lbs. lamb riblets
1½ t. seasoned salt
1½ t. garlic salt

1½ t. salt
1½ t. pepper
2 T. Worcestershire sauce

Cut riblets between each rib. Arrange on a broiler rack. Combine remaining ingredients and brush on lamb. Place lamb approximately 6 inches below heat source; broil, turning to brown on all sides. (Recipe may be made to here and completed later). Bake at 375° for 30 minutes.
Serves 10 as an appetizer/4 as an entrée.
Mrs. Larry Temple (Louann Atkins)

Jamaican Bacon

Thick-sliced bacon
Brown sugar

Cut bacon slices into thirds. Partially broil bacon and drain on paper towel. Sprinkle generously with brown sugar and return to broiler until crisp.
Mrs. Benjamin McPherson, Jr. (Marie Leopold)

Jalapeño Pie

3   canned jalapeño peppers,
    seeded and slivered
10 oz. sharp Cheddar cheese,
    grated, or ½ white Mexican
    cheese and ½ Cheddar
4   eggs, slightly beaten

Arrange peppers in a greased, 10 inch pie plate; cover with cheese. Pour eggs over cheese. Bake at 275° for approximately 40 minutes or until set. Cut into small wedges and serve hot.
Ideal for a large gathering as the pies may be half-baked, stored in the refrigerator, then rebaked and served hot.
Mrs. F.M. Covert, Jr. (Elizabeth Cartledge)

Devil Sticks

Thin-sliced bread
Butter, melted
Summer savory
Celery seed

Garlic salt
Paprika
Parmesan cheese, grated

Trim crusts from bread and cut each slice into thirds. Place the strips close together on foil-lined baking sheet. Brush the slices with melted butter; sprinkle with spices and cheese. Bake at 200° for approximately 2 hours.
Keeps indefinitely.
Mrs. C.N. Avery, Jr. (Lucille Sharp)

South American Appetizer

Bacon
Pitted prunes
Toothpicks

Cut bacon into thirds. Wrap around prune and secure with a toothpick. Broil until bacon is crisp. Drain on paper towel. Serve hot. To vary recipe, stuff each prune with a pecan before wrapping in bacon or substitute pitted dates or dried apricot halves for the prunes.
Mrs. Lem Scarbrough, Jr. (Alice Ann Rotsch)

Versatile Crab

1	8 oz. package cream cheese, at room temperature	2	T. finely chopped onion
1	T. milk	½	t. cream-style horseradish
8	oz. fresh lump crabmeat	¼	t. salt
			Dash cayenne

Combine cream cheese with milk; add remaining ingredients and blend well. Heat at 375° for 15 minutes or until hot. May be served over rice, toast points, split, toasted cornbread squares, in ramekins or pastry shells.

Serves 6 as an appetizer/2 as an entrée.
Mrs. W.T. Archer (Dorothy Newton)

Sautéed Shrimp

2	T. olive oil	¼	t. salt
2	lbs. large shrimp, shelled except for tail	¼	t. freshly ground pepper
			Juice of 2 lemons
2	T. butter	¼	c. dry vermouth
1	small clove garlic, crushed		

In large skillet bring olive oil to a simmer. Add shrimp; cook until golden brown. Reduce heat; add butter, garlic, salt, and pepper. May add more salt, as this is one dish that cannot be over-salted. When blended, turn heat to very hot. Add lemon juice and vermouth; simmer about one minute, stirring constantly. Serve as an appetizer or entrée.

Serves 8 as an appetizer/4 as an entrée.
Mrs. William H. Page (Lolla McNutt)

Artichoke Squares

2	6 oz. jars marinated artichoke hearts	⅛	t. pepper
1	small onion, finely chopped	⅛	t. oregano
1	clove garlic, minced	2	T. minced parsley
4	eggs	2	c. grated Cheddar cheese
¼	t. salt	¼	c. Italian style bread crumbs
⅛	t. Tabasco		Fresh parsley

Drain marinade from artichoke hearts and reserve; chop artichoke hearts. Sauté onion and garlic in marinade for 5 minutes. In a separate bowl beat eggs; add all other ingredients to eggs. Bake in a greased 7 x 11 pan at 325° for 30 minutes. Cut into 1 inch squares and serve hot as an appetizer. For a unique vegetable, bake in a smaller square pan; it doubles in thickness and may be cut into 8 squares. Garnish with fresh parsley.
Yields 77 squares/Serves 8 as a vegetable/Freezes.
Mrs. J. Dudley Youman (Sandy Geyer)

Cheese Toasties

1   c. butter, at room temperature
1   c. chopped green chilies, drained
Minced garlic or garlic salt to taste
½   lb. Monterey Jack, cheese, grated

1   c. mayonnaise
Small loaf each of French bread and party rye, sliced and toasted

Mix butter, green chilies, and garlic. In another bowl mix cheese and mayonnaise. Spread toast rounds with green chili mixture, then with cheese mixture. Broil until bubbly. Serve hot.
Serves 12.
Mrs. William F. Turman (Sally Williams)

Spinach Dip

1   package frozen, chopped spinach, well drained
½   c. fresh, finely chopped parsley
1   t. salt

1   t. pepper
½   c. finely chopped onions
2   c. mayonnaise

Mix all ingredients in blender; chill.
Yields 3 cups/Keeps several weeks in refrigerator.
Mrs. C. Dean Davis (Mollie Villeret)

Stuffed Mushrooms

8 large mushrooms	1 T. fresh, chopped parsley
¼ c. butter	2 T. sour cream, or enough
2 T. chopped green onion	to moisten
¼ c. toasted bread crumbs	Salt and pepper to taste
2 T. finely chopped, cooked	Dash cayenne
veal, chicken, or ham	Grated mild cheese

Wipe mushrooms. Chop stems, reserving the whole caps. Sauté stems in 2 tablespoons of the butter 2 to 3 minutes. Add onion, 2 tablespoons of the bread crumbs, meat, and parsley. Add sour cream. Season to taste with salt, pepper, and cayenne. Stuff mixture into mushroom caps. Sprinkle with remaining bread crumbs and then with cheese. Pour remaining butter over top. Bake at 375° for 15 to 20 minutes. Mushrooms may be prepared and stuffed a day ahead and baked when served. For a quick variation, deviled ham and onion salt may be substituted for the meat and onions.
Mrs. Jack Roche (Josephine Klotz)

Crabmeat Epicurean

¼ c. minced onion	1 t. salt
1½ c. sliced mushrooms	¼ t. pepper
½ c. butter, melted	2 c. light cream
1 lb. lump crabmeat	2 egg yolks, slightly beaten
1 c. bread crumbs	¾ c. buttered bread crumbs
½ t. thyme	Paprika

Sauté onion and mushrooms in butter; simmer over low heat for 5 to 7 minutes. Add crabmeat, bread crumbs, and seasonings. Combine cream with egg yolks; mix with crabmeat. Place in a buttered, 2 quart casserole or ramekins or crab shells; top with buttered crumbs and paprika. Bake at 375° for 20 to 25 minutes or until hot.
Serves 8 to 10.
Mrs. Roy P. Ward (Anna Marie Schulz)

Empanadas

1	small onion, finely chopped	2	T. sweet pickle relish
1	small bell pepper, finely chopped	½	t. sugar
3	T. butter	½	t. salt
½	lb. ground pork	20 to 22	unbaked pastry rounds, 3 to 4 inches in diameter (made from enough dough for 3 standard pie shells)
1	T. finely chopped parsley		
2	T. chopped ripe or green olives		
3	T. currants		

Sauté onion and pepper in butter. Brown pork, draining excess fat, and combine with onion and pepper. Stir in remaining ingredients, except pastry, and mix well. Place approximately 1½ tablespoons of pork mixture on each pastry circle; fold over and press edges together with a fork. Bake on a cookie sheet at 425° for approximately 12 minutes or until brown.

A spicy Mexican fried pie.
Yields 20 to 22.
Mrs. Sam Fason (Maydelle Foster)

Camille's Mantequilla de Pobre

4	tomatoes, finely diced	2	T. fresh, minced cilantro, if available
4	avocados, peeled and finely diced	2	T. vegetable oil
2	bunches green onions, thinly sliced	⅓	c. red wine vinegar
1½	t. salt		Tostados

Mix chopped ingredients together; add salt. Add cilantro, oil, and vinegar. Use as a dip with tostados. Best made about 1 hour ahead of time.

Newer than guacamole.
Serves 10 to 12.
Mrs. Benjamin McPherson, Jr. (Marie Lois Leopold)

Spicy Picadillo

2 large onions, finely chopped
2 T. bacon drippings or butter
2 lb. ground beef
2 cloves garlic, minced
2 t. ground cloves
2 t. cinnamon
2 10 oz. cans Ro-Tel brand
  tomatoes and green chilies

2 t. sugar
1 c. raisins
2 t. ground cumin
1¼ c. slivered almonds, toasted
Salt to taste
Corn chips or tostados

Brown onion in bacon drippings or butter in a large pan. Add beef and brown, stirring to break up. Drain excess drippings. Add garlic, cloves, cinnamon, tomatoes, and sugar. Simmer, covered, approximately 1 hour. Add raisins and cumin; simmer, covered, 20 minutes. Add almonds; simmer, covered, 10 minutes. Salt to taste. Serve hot in a chafing dish with corn chips or tostados.
Try also as an empanada filling.
Yields 2 quarts/Freezes.
Mrs. Frank N. Ikard, Jr. (Carol Foster)

Hot Crabmeat Dip

2 T. chopped onion
1 garlic clove, minced
2 T. butter
3 T. flour
¾ c. heavy cream
¼ c. dry sherry
¼ c. chili sauce

1 t. Worcestershire sauce
Dash Tabasco
1 t. monosodium glutamate
Salt to taste
½ lb. fresh lump crabmeat
  or 1 16½ oz. can crabmeat
Melba rounds

Brown onions and garlic in butter; stir in flour. Add cream, sherry, chili sauce, Worcestershire sauce, Tabasco, monosodium glutamate, and salt. Blend well and cook slowly until thick. Stir in crabmeat. Serve hot in a chafing dish with melba rounds.
Serves 6 to 8.
Mrs. Laurens B. Fish, Jr. (Julia Corley)

Liptauer Cheese

¼ c. gin
2 c. creamed cottage cheese
8 anchovy fillets
2 8 oz. packages cream cheese,
   at room temperature
1 c. butter, at room temperature
2 t. dry mustard

¼ c. caraway seeds
¼ c. paprika
1 t. white pepper
1 t. salt
6 T. capers, drained
Crackers, raw vegetables, or
   party rye bread

Combine in blender, gin, cottage cheese, and anchovy fillets. Combine in mixer, cream cheese and butter. Add cottage cheese mixture, mustard, caraway seeds, paprika, pepper, and salt. Blend well. Stir in capers by hand so they remain whole. Allow to ripen, in the refrigerator, covered, for 1 week. Serve with crackers, raw vegetables, or party rye bread.
A basic Czechoslovakian dish.
Yields 5 cups/Keeps indefinitely in refrigerator/Freezes.
Mrs. Larry Temple (Louann Atkins)

Texas Picadillo

1 lb. ground beef
1 lb. ground pork
2 t. salt
½ t. pepper
8 tomatoes, peeled and diced
6 green onions, finely chopped
6 medium potatoes, peeled
   and finely diced
1½ c. chopped pimientos

1½ c. toasted, slivered
   almonds
6 garlic cloves, minced
2 6 oz. cans tomato paste
4 jalapeño peppers, chopped
1½ c. seedless raisins
½ t. oregano
Corn chips or tostados

Cover meat with water in deep pot. Add salt and pepper; simmer 30 minutes. Add rest of ingredients; simmer, covered, until potatoes are done. Drain off excess liquid. Serve hot with corn chips or tostados.
Unique in its use of potatoes.
Serves approximately 30/Freezes.
Mrs. C. Dean Davis (Mollie Villeret)

Chutney Cream Cheese Spread

2   8 oz. packages cream cheese,
    at room temperature
½   c. chopped chutney
1   t. curry powder

¾   c. coarsely chopped maca-
    damia nuts or almonds
Crackers or toast rounds

Mix all ingredients; refrigerate several hours. Spread on crackers or toast rounds.
Mrs. Sam Fason (Maydelle Foster)

Kinser Cheeseball

10 oz. sharp Cheddar cheese
2   8 oz. packages cream cheese,
    at room temperature
1   4 oz. jar chopped pimiento,
    drained

½   c. finely chopped bell pepper
2   T. dried onion soup mix
Finely chopped pecans
Paprika

Combine cheeses, pimiento, bell pepper, and soup mix and blend well. Roll into a ball, then roll in pecans and sprinkle with paprika. Chill.
Keeps well several weeks in refrigerator.
Mrs. Ronald S. Driver (Susan Page)

Cheese Dip for Vegetables

1   8 oz. package cream cheese,
    at room temperature
¼   onion, grated
3   T. catsup
1½ t. salt

½   t. dry mustard
¼   t. cayenne
Dash Worcestershire sauce
2 to 4 T. cream

Combine all ingredients in the mixer (not the blender). Prepare the day before and refrigerate. Serve with raw vegetables.
Yields approximately 1 cup.
Mrs. Sam Fason (Maydelle Foster)

Vegetable Dip

1 c. sour cream	1 t. dried dill weed
¾ c. mayonnaise	1 green onion, minced
1 t. Beau Monde seasoning	Raw vegetables or chips

Mix and let set 2 to 3 hours in refrigerator. Serve with raw vegetables or chips. Keeps very well in refrigerator and flavor improves with age.
Yields 1 cup.
Mrs. Jerry Prestridge (Joyce Michels)

Chili Dip

1 lb. regular bulk sausage
1 lb. grated Velveeta brand
process cheese
1 24 oz. can chili without beans
Corn chips or tostados

Brown sausage; pour off excess drippings. Add cheese and chili. Simmer over low heat in a double boiler to let flavors meld. Serve hot from chafing dish with corn chips or tostados.
Yields 1½ quarts/Freezes.
Mrs. Beverly Sheffield (Lois Crow)

Sombrero Dip

½ lb. ground beef	1 8 oz. can red kidney beans
½ c. chopped onion	½ c. grated sharp cheese
¼ c. chili sauce	¼ c. chopped stuffed olives
1½ t. chili powder	Tostados or corn chips
½ t. salt	

Brown meat and ¼ cup of the onion in skillet. Stir in catsup, chili powder, and salt. Mash in beans with liquid; heat and stir in cheese. Top with olives and remaining onions. Serve with tostados or corn chips.
Yields 1½ cups/Freezes.
Mrs. David Davenport (Diane Wilder)

Deviled Spinach Eggs

1	10 oz. package frozen chopped spinach, cooked and drained	1	T. butter, at room temperature
1	t. salt	4	oz. cream cheese, at room temperature
	Pepper to taste	6	hard-cooked eggs, halved
1	t. tarragon		Mayonnaise

Squeeze all liquid out of spinach; season with salt, pepper, and tarragon. Mix in butter and cream cheese and blend well. Mash egg yolks with mayonnaise. Stuff egg whites with spinach mixture and place a dab of deviled yolk on top of each. Arrange on a platter and chill.
Luxurious picnic fare.
Serves 6 to 8.
Mrs. Ed Auler (Susan Teeple)

Black-eyed Pea Dip

4	c. black-eyed peas, cooked and drained	1	4 oz. can chopped, green chilies
5	small or 3 large jalapeños, optional	1	clove garlic, minced
1	T. jalapeño pepper liquid, optional	½	lb. Old English process chesse, grated
½	medium onion, chopped	1	c. butter
			Corn chips

Combine black-eyed peas, peppers and liquid, onion, green chilies, and garlic in mixer or blender. Melt cheese and butter in double boiler; stir in black-eyed pea mixture. Serve in a chafing dish with large corn chips.
Omit jalapeños for a milder flavor.
Freezes.
Mrs. John C. Oliver (Mary Ellen Dooley)

Mushroom Caviar

1   medium onion, minced
2   T. butter
½   lb. fresh mushrooms, finely
     chopped
2   T. lemon juice
1   t. Worcestershire sauce

Salt, garlic salt, and
     pepper to taste
1½ T. mayonnaise
Toast rounds or wheat thins
Fresh parsley

Sauté onion in butter until golden. Add mushrooms; sauté 5 minutes. Add lemon juice and Worcestershire sauce; remove from heat and cool. Add salt, garlic salt, pepper, and mayonnaise. Mound on serving plate; chill well. Garnish with parsley; serve with toast rounds or wheat thins.
Serves 6 to 8.
Mrs. Glenn Foster (Marcia Ungren)

Eggplant Caviar

2   large eggplant
1   c. finely chopped onion
3   medium tomatoes, peeled
     and chopped
1   bell pepper, finely chopped
¼   c. chopped parsley
½   c. olive oil
1   T. dry vermouth

1   T. lime juice
3   cloves garlic, crushed, or
     ½ t. garlic powder
1   t. oregano
2   t. salt
1   t. cracked black pepper
Melba toast, thin rye bread,
     or unleavened Armenian bread

Bake the eggplant whole in a 350° oven for 1 hour or until soft. After baking, slit the eggplant so the steam will escape; peel and chop very finely. Add onion, tomatoes, bell pepper, parsley, olive oil, lime juice, vermouth, and seasonings; mix well. Make at least 1 day ahead and store, covered, in refrigerator until serving. Serve with melba toast, thin rye bread, or unleavened Armenian bread.
So named because the eggplant seeds resemble caviar.
Yields 2 quarts/Keeps approximately 2 weeks in refrigerator.
Mrs. Charles E. Bates (Linda Steinhauser)

Marinated Carrots

8	small carrots, peeled and	1	small clove garlic, crushed
	cut into 3 inch sticks	¾	t. seasoned salt
3	T. vinegar	¼	t. salt
3	T. salad oil		Minced parsley

Place carrot sticks into shallow dish. Combine remaining ingredients, except parsley; pour over carrots, coating all well. Cover tightly; refrigerate overnight. Drain marinade; sprinkle carrots with parsley and serve.

Serves 6 to 8.

Mrs. Rox Covert (Elizabeth Rogers)

Party Pâté

½	c. butter	½	t. salt
2	onions, chopped	½	t. pepper
1	clove garlic, minced	2	hard-cooked eggs, coarsely
1	lb. chicken livers		chopped
2	T. Cognac		Parsley
¼	c. chopped parsley		Toast rounds

Melt butter in heavy skillet. Sauté onion and garlic until tender. Increase heat; add chicken livers and saute quickly, turning them to brown on all sides. Put butter, onions, garlic, and livers into blender; add Cognac, ¼ cup parsley, salt, and pepper. Blend well on high speed. Add eggs; blend again. Pour into crock or serving dish. Cover with plastic wrap; chill at least 12 hours. Garnish with parsley; serve with toast rounds.

Hard-cooked eggs add an interesting texture contrast to the pâté.

Yields approximately 2 cups/Freezes; stir well after thawing.

Mrs. James H. Albright (Mary Margaret Carlson)

Goose Liver Roll

1 lb. goose liver	Dash Tabasco
1 c. chopped pistachio nuts	1 3 oz. package cream cheese,
3 T. lemon juice	at room temperature
1 t. prepared mustard	1 T. mayonnaise
1 t. Worcestershire sauce	Parsley
1½ T. Cognac, optional	Crackers

Combine liver, nuts, 2 tablespoons of the lemon juice, mustard, Worcestershire sauce, Cognac, and Tabasco. Form into roll. Combine cream cheese with the remaining 1 tablespoon of lemon juice. Ice goose liver roll with cream cheese mixture and chill. Garnish with parsley and serve with crackers.

Mrs. Jack Corley (Frances Barton)

Chicken Curry Balls

1 8 oz. package cream cheese	3 T. chopped chutney
¼ c. mayonnaise	1 t. salt
2 c. cooked, chopped chicken	2 t. curry powder
1½ c. chopped almonds	Grated coconut

Cream thoroughly cream cheese and mayonnaise. Stir in chicken, almonds, chutney, salt, and curry powder. Chill. Shape into bite-size balls. Roll each ball in grated coconut. Chill, covered, until ready to serve.

Beautiful piled high in a crystal bowl lined with leaf lettuce. Especially nice for brunch.

Yields approximately 8 dozen/Freezes.

Mrs. Larry Temple (Louann Atkins)

Cucumber Sandwiches

2 cucumbers, peeled
1 12 oz. package cream cheese,
   at room temperature
¼ c. mayonnaise
Salt and pepper to taste

Dash cayenne
¼ c. chopped parsley
1 T. lemon juice
White or whole wheat bread,
   crusts removed

Grate cucumbers or put through a food grinder and twist into a ball in the corner of a tea towel to extract as much liquid as possible. Beat cream cheese and mayonnaise in mixer until smooth. Add drained cucumbers, spices, parsley, and lemon juice. If mixture is too thick, add additional mayonnaise. Spread on white or whole wheat bread and cut into thirds for finger sandwiches.
A special version of a party favorite.
Yields 60 finger sandwiches.
Mrs. Charles E. Bates (Linda Steinhauser)

Braunschweiger Loaf

1 8 oz. package braunschweiger
   sausage
2 T. dried onion soup mix
Dash Tabasco
Dash Worcestershire sauce
1 3 oz. package cream cheese

Mayonnaise
Milk
Caviar or green, stuffed olives
Parsley
Crackers or toast rounds

Mix sausage and onion soup mix together; season with Tabasco and Worcestershire sauces. Shape into loaf. (Can freeze at this point. Thaw before proceeding.) Mix cream cheese with enough mayonnaise to make a spreadable consistency, using a small amount of milk to thin, if necessary. Flavor with dash of Tabasco and Worcestershire sauces. Coat the loaf with this mixture. Decorate with a strip of caviar or sliced olives down the center of the loaf. Chill until time to serve. Surround with parsley and serve with crackers or toast rounds.
Serves 12.
Mrs. Terrence Watt (Mary Avery)

Mediterranean Loaf

1 unsliced loaf French or Italian bread, baked until brown	½ c. chopped stuffed green olives
8 slices bread, crumbled	2 T. chopped parsley
1 14½ oz. can Italian tomatoes, drained and chopped	2 T. grated Cheddar cheese
½ c. chopped onion	½ t. thyme
½ c. chopped ripe olives	2 T. olive oil
	Juice of 1 lemon
	Salt and pepper to taste

Slice off ends and scoop out center of bread. Combine bread crumbs from loaf with crumbs from bread slices; add all remaining ingredients. Mix well, with hands, and pack firmly into loaf shell. Refrigerate overnight. Serve in slices.
Serves 12 to 16/Freezes.
Mrs. Ray Hall (Jan Cooper)

Smoked Oyster Loaf

1 T. mayonnaise	Garlic powder or salt to taste
1 8 oz. package cream cheese, at room temperature	2 3½ oz. cans smoked oysters, drained and chopped
2 t. Worcestershire sauce	Parsley
¼ small onion, pressed	Sesame crackers or toast rounds
Pinch salt	

Cream mayonnaise with cream cheese. Add Worcestershire sauce, onion, salt, and garlic salt. Press into rectangular shape ½ inch thick on wax paper. Evenly cover with oysters; press into and roll. May be easier to roll if chilled first. After rolling, chill 12 to 24 hours. Garnish with fresh parsley; serve with small sesame crackers or toast rounds.
Mrs. Terrell James (Dianne Hill)

Ham Salad Baked in Rolls

1	c. chopped cooked ham	2	c. grated Cheddar cheese
¼	c. chopped sweet pickle		Salt and pepper to taste
1	T. grated onion		16 to 20 finger rolls
1	t. Worcestershire sauce		Butter, at room temperature
6	T. mayonnaise		

Combine all ingredients, except rolls and butter. Split rolls in half lengthwise; scoop out centers and spread with butter. Fill with ham mixture and replace top. May be covered with foil and refrigerated or frozen at this point. Bake at 325° until filling is hot and melted.
Yields 16 to 20/Freezes.
Mrs. Duke Matthews Covert (Lynne Carole Shapiro)

Shrimp Spread

For 150:

6	8 oz. packages cream cheese, at room temperature	5	c. diced celery
6	4½ oz. cans shrimp, drained and chopped	½	cup plus 1 T. mayonnaise
		1	small onion, grated
			Ritz crackers or toast rounds

For 25:

1	8 oz. package cream cheese, at room temperature	1	c. diced celery
1	4½ oz. can shrimp, drained and chopped	1½	T. mayonnaise
		2	T. grated onion
			Ritz crackers or toast rounds

Mix all ingredients with an electric beater early in day or day before. Chill. Serve in a mound with crackers or toast rounds.
Mrs. Robert Morrison (Verna Mae Hardy)

Shrimp Roll

2   8 oz packages cream cheese,   ½   c. salted peanuts, chopped
    at room temperature   1   t. curry powder
1   onion, finely chopped   2   hard-cooked eggs, chopped
1   bell pepper, finely chopped   Salt to taste
3   to 4 ribs celery, finely chopped Chopped chutney
1½ c. shrimp, cooked and chopped   Crackers

Combine cream cheese, onion, pepper, celery, shrimp, peanuts, curry powder, eggs and salt. Roll in shape of log and chill. Serve with crackers and chutney.
Serves 12 to 16.
Mrs. R. Kinnan Golemon (Jackie Burst)

George Covert's Marinated Shrimp

3   lb. shrimp, peeled and deveined   1½ c. white wine vinegar
1   c. water   1   garlic clove, crushed
¼   t. McCormick brand Italian   1   c. vegetable oil
    Seasoning   ½   t. cayenne pepper
1   bay leaf   ½   t. Reese's "Bit-O-Pepper"
1   t. Spice Islands brand   Sauce (Jamaican sauce)
    Pickling Mix   1   6 oz. can pitted ripe olives,
1   t. salt   drained
¼   t. paprika   1   16 oz. can whole mushrooms,
½   t. oregano   drained
¼   t. summer savory   1   12 oz. can whole jalapeño
¼   c. tarragon wine vinegar   peppers, drained (reserve juice)

Boil shrimp (do not overcook); drain. Combine all ingredients. Marinate in the refrigerator at least 48 hours. Taste and add reserved jalapeño juice, if desired.
Yields 3 quarts/Will keep in refrigerator several days.
Mrs. George Covert (Helen Cook)

Del Rio Steak Tartare

1	lb. ground sirloin	2	tomatoes
1	lb. ground, cooked ham	1 to 5	jalapeño peppers
1	onion	1	large sour pickle
1	lemon, unpeeled	½	lb. sharp cheese
1	apple, unpeeled and cored		Salt and pepper to taste
1	bell pepper, seeded		Crackers
1	rib celery		

Grind all ingredients, except crackers, together using medium blade of grinder; drain excess liquid. Pack into 2-quart mold; chill several hours or overnight. Serve with crackers.
Serves 30.
Mrs. Walter Reifslager, Jr. (Janet Sadler)

Caviar Pie

6	hard-cooked eggs	1½ t. grated onion
Salt		1 2 oz. jar caviar
White pepper		Parsley
1½ T. mayonnaise		Toast rounds
1 c. sour cream		

Press the eggs through a sieve or finely grate. Add salt and pepper to taste. Add mayonnaise; press mixture firmly into an 8 inch pyrex pie plate or a 9 x 5 loaf pan that has been lined with plastic wrap. Refrigerate until set (approximately 1 to 2 hours). Turn out onto serving plate. Frost with sour cream seasoned with onion. Spread caviar across top. Garnish with fresh parsley. Serve with toast rounds.
Perfect for cocktail hour birthday celebrations with a candle in it.
Serves 10 to 15.
Mrs. Sam Fason (Maydelle Foster)

Caviar Dip

1   8 oz. package cream cheese,
   at room temperature
2   c. sour cream
1   T. chopped green onion

Dash Worcestershire sauce
1   2 oz. jar black or red caviar
Small toast rounds

Whip cream cheese and mix with sour cream. Add onion and Worcestershire sauce. Carefully stir in caviar and mix well; chill. Serve with small toast rounds.
Serves 8 to 10.
Mrs. Paul Vescovo (Susan Kay Kuper)

Soups

Texas Chili Tradition

Chili recipes have developed according to specific preferences from family to family representing a wide variety of tastes and styles. Fortunately, part of the tradition is sharing; the following are three of the best.

Pedernales River Chili

4	lb. coarsely ground chili meat (round steak or chuck)	2	T. chili powder, more if desired
1	large onion, chopped	1½	c. canned whole tomatoes, drained
2	cloves garlic		2 to 6 dashes Tabasco
1	t. oregano		Salt to taste
1	t. cumin	2	c. hot water

Sauté meat, onions, and garlic in large, heavy frying pan or Dutch oven. Add oregano, cumin seed, chili powder, tomatoes, Tabasco, salt, and hot water. Bring to a boil; lower heat and simmer for approximately 1 hour. Skim off fat during cooking.
Serves 8/Freezes.
Mrs. Patrick J. Nugent (Luci Johnson)

Gregg Chili

1	lb. dried pinto beans	2	T. salt
2	t. salt	6	cloves garlic, minced
2	slices salt pork	½	c. chili powder
6	T. vegetable oil	4	t. cilantro
6	lb. coarsely ground beef or game	2	t. sugar
9	onions, chopped	2	t. Tabasco
		6	jalapeño peppers, chopped
4	14½ oz. cans tomatoes	2	t. cinnamon

Simmer beans in water with salt and salt pork until cooked. In a 12 quart pot, heat oil and slowly brown meat and onions. Add all remaining ingredients and simmer 1 hour. Stir in beans and simmer 30 minutes, stirring occasionally.
Yields 9 to 10 quarts/Freezes.
Mrs. Frank Gregg (Beverly Lamb)

Drake Chili

1	piece suet	1	T. chili powder
2	lb. cubed round steak	1	tomato can of hot water
	(beef or venison)	1	onion, quartered
3	dried red chilies	2 or 3 garlic cloves	
1	1 lb. can tomatoes	Cheesecloth	
1	T. salt		

Render suet for 1 hour in a large pot. Remove suet and cook meat until pink color is gone. Boil chilies for ½ hour or until soft. Drain and mash through a sieve until only the seeds are left. Discard seeds. Heat tomatoes and mash, undrained, through sieve. Discard remainder in sieve. Add sieved chilies and tomatoes to pot. Add salt, chili powder and hot water. Tie onion and garlic into a piece of cheesecloth and drop into pot. Simmer for 2½ hours. Squeeze juices from cheesecloth and remove.

Serves 4 to 6/Freezes.
Mrs. William S. Drake, Jr. (Eleanor Critchlow)

Portuguese Soup

2 to 2½ lb. beef brisket or stew meat, cut into 1 inch cubes		2	t. salt
		¼	t. pepper
¼	c. vegetable oil	½	t. crushed coriander
1	large onion, chopped	1	bay leaf
3	cloves garlic, pressed	2	large potatoes, peeled and cut into 1 inch cubes
1	qt. water		
2	15 oz. cans tomato sauce with tomato bits	1	c. port or red wine
		1	bunch Swiss chard, collards, spinach, or kale, chopped
¼	c. chopped parsley		

In a kettle or Dutch oven, brown meat in oil. Add onion, garlic, water, tomato sauce, parsley, salt, pepper, coriander, and bay leaf. Simmer, covered, for 3 hours. Stir in potatoes and wine and simmer, covered, for 30 minutes. Add greens and simmer, uncovered, for 10 minutes. Remove bay leaf.

During hunting season, substitute venison for beef.
Serves 6 to 8/Freezes.
Mrs. Joan White (Joan Elise Taylor)

Greek Lemon Soup

8	c. chicken with rice soup	3	egg yolks
½	c. butter		Juice of 2 lemons
1	T. instant chicken stock granules		Thin lemon slices
½	c. sauterne		Chopped parsley

To the soup add butter, powdered chicken stock, and sauterne; simmer gently for 20 to 30 minutes. Beat egg yolks and lemon juice until frothy. Just before serving, stir 1 cup of the hot soup into the egg-lemon mixture slowly so that eggs do not curdle. Pour this into the soup and stir. Serve immediately garnished with lemon slices and parsley.
Adding more rice, as the Greeks do, makes a fine one-course meal.
Serves 8.
Mrs. L. Allen Searight (Charleen Smith)

Russian Borsch

2	lb. chuck roast or round steak, trimmed and cubed		Salt and pepper to taste
2	T. butter	1	small head cabbage, shredded
2	large onions, minced	1	16 oz. can whole beets, drained and sliced
2	large carrots, peeled and chopped	2	8 oz. cans tomato sauce
3	medium potatoes, peeled and diced	2	T. vinegar
1	bell pepper, chopped	1	c. sour cream
1	T. sugar	6	slices bacon, fried and crumbled

Brown meat in butter; add onions and enough water to cover. Simmer slowly for 30 minutes. Add carrots, potatoes, bell pepper, sugar, salt, and pepper; simmer until tender. During the last 15 minutes, stir in cabbage, beets, and tomato sauce. May add water as needed, if soup becomes too thick. Just before serving, mix in vinegar. Serve topped with a dollop of sour cream and crumbled bacon.
Serves 8 to 10.
Mrs. Sam Fason (Maydelle Foster)

Ranch Soup

1 lb. dried pinto beans	1 t. garlic salt
1 lb. ground venison	2 8 oz. cans tomato sauce
1 large onion, chopped	2 T. Worcestershire sauce
1 bell pepper, chopped	2 T. brown sugar
2 T. chili powder	Salt and pepper to taste
¼ c. vegetable oil	

Cover beans with water and boil for 20 minutes, then simmer, covered, for 1 hour. May add additional water as needed. Sauté venison, onion, and bell pepper in vegetable oil. Add to beans along with chili powder, garlic salt, tomato sauce, Worcestershire, brown sugar, salt and pepper. Cover and barely simmer for 4 to 6 additional hours.
Serves 8/Freezes.
Mrs. Joe Thorne Gilbert (Ailine Burch)

Mexican Black Bean Soup

3¼ c. dried black beans	½ t. sugar
8 c. water	½ c. dry red wine
1 T. salt	1½ t. salt, or to taste
½ t. pepper	12 drops Tabasco
2 small ham hocks or 2 pieces salt pork or ham	1 T. Worcestershire sauce
¼ t. minced garlic	1 t. monosodium glutamate
2 onions, chopped	Freshly ground pepper to taste
3 carrots, peeled and sliced	Squeeze of lime
5 ribs celery with leaves, chopped	Onion, thinly sliced, or finely chopped green onion
2 T. butter, omit if meat is fatty	Lime slices
½ t. thyme	Croutons
Dash cayenne	½ t. dry sherry for each serving, optional

Wash beans thoroughly; cover with water and soak overnight. Drain and place in large kettle. Add fresh water, salt, pepper, and meat. Cook over slow to medium heat until tender. If needed, add 1 more cup of water as beans cook. Remove all bones in meat; add garlic, onions, carrots, celery, butter, thyme, cayenne, sugar, and wine. Cook until vegetables are tender. Add salt. Put about 3 cups at a time in blender and purée. Return to kettle; add Tabasco sauce, Worcestershire sauce, monosodium glutamate, pepper, and lime. To serve, top each serving with onion, slice of lime, croutons, and sherry, if desired.

Developed by the Greggs, both cooks, after a trip to Mexico where they enjoyed a similar soup.

Serves 8/Yields approximately 15 cups/Freezes.
Mrs. Frank Gregg (Beverly Lamb)

Tortilla Soup

6 green onions, chopped	Vegetable oil
3 medium tomatoes, peeled and diced	4½ c. chicken broth
	1 bay leaf, crushed
3 ribs celery, chopped	½ t. coriander
1 T. chopped green chilies	Salt and pepper to taste
½ bell pepper, chopped	Cheddar cheese, grated
2 T. vegetable oil	
6 corn tortillas, halved and sliced in ¼ inch strips	

Sauté onions, tomatoes, celery, green chilies, and bell pepper in the 2 tablespoons of vegetable oil until soft. Remove with a slotted spoon and set aside. Fry tortilla strips in more vegetable oil until crisp. Drain on paper towel. Bring chicken broth to boil and add vegetables, tortilla strips, bay leaf, and coriander. Simmer, covered, 30 minutes. Add salt and pepper to taste. Serve with grated cheese.

Taste the elixir of tortillas.

Serves 6/Freezes.
Mrs. Benjamin McPherson, Jr. (Marie Leopold)

Gumbo

¾ lb. ham, cubed	3 qt. water
¾ c. bacon drippings	2 T. Worcestershire sauce
1 c. vegetable oil	6 drops Tabasco
1½ c. flour	2 bay leaves, crushed
¼ c. olive oil	¼ t. marjoram
3 c. coarsely chopped celery	⅛ t. rosemary
3 large onions, chopped	¼ t. thyme
2 bell peppers, chopped	Salt and pepper to taste
2 cloves garlic, minced	1 qt. oysters, optional
½ c. chopped parsley	1 lb. crabmeat
1 lb. okra, sliced	2 lb. shrimp, peeled
2 28 oz. cans tomatoes	2½ T. gumbo filé, optional
1 10 oz. can tomatoes with green chilies	Cooked rice

In a large pot, sauté ham in ¼ cup of the bacon drippings. Blend remaining bacon drippings and ¾ cup of the vegetable oil with flour in a skillet. Cook over low heat 30 to 40 minutes, stirring constantly, until flour is a rich, dark brown. In another large skillet, heat olive oil and remaining vegetable oil. Add celery, onions, bell peppers, garlic, parsley, and okra. Cook until soft. In the large pot with the ham, add tomatoes, water, Worcestershire sauce, Tabasco, bay leaves, marjoram, rosemary, thyme, salt, and pepper. Bring to a simmer. Add vegetables and roux. Cook slowly for at least 2 hours. Add seafood 10 minutes before serving. Remove from heat and stir in gumbo filé. Serve in soup bowls over rice.

This recipe may be made with shrimp only, using 3 pounds.
Serves 10/Freezes.
Mrs. Robert G. Umstattd (Jeanne Smith)

"Real Texas" New England Clam Chowder

2 c. peeled, quartered potatoes	3 c. milk
4 slices bacon	1 c. light cream
2 c. chopped onions	Salt and pepper to taste
2 c. clams	½ pat butter per serving

Boil potatoes until almost done; drain and dice. Fry bacon until crisp (reserve bacon drippings); crumble bacon. Cook onions in drippings until clear.

To prepare clams: if frozen or canned, thaw and chop; if fresh and in shell, place in pot with *no* water and heat until clams open. Drain, clean, and chop. In large pan heat potatoes, bacon, onions, clams, milk, cream, salt, and pepper. Do not boil. Float butter on each serving.

This recipe is the result of the husbands' experiments in the kitchen during family summers together sailing in Maine.

Serves 4 to 6.

Mrs. Victor Szebehely (Jo Betsy Lewallen)
Mrs. Conrad P. Werkenthin (Clare Coates)

Cream of Split Pea Soup

2 c. dried split peas	1 t. sugar
Ham bone	Dash cayenne
2 c. diced ham	¼ t. thyme
1 c. chopped onions	Dash Tabasco
1½ c. chopped celery with leaves	1 t. Worcestershire sauce
1 c. chopped carrots	2 T. butter or soup fat
1 clove garlic	2 T. flour
1 bay leaf	2 c. heavy cream

Soak peas in water overnight; drain and reserve the liquid. Add enough water to the liquid to make 10 cups; add peas, ham bone, and ham. Simmer, covered, over medium heat 2½ to 3 hours. Add onions, celery, and carrots; simmer 30 minutes. Add garlic, bay leaf, sugar, cayenne, thyme, Tabasco, and Worcestershire sauce; simmer 30 minutes to 1 hour. Remove bones; put soup through a sieve. Chill; remove soup fat. If thickening is desired, melt 2 tablespoons of the soup fat or butter in a saucepan; stir in flour and cook until bubbly. Slowly add about ¼ cup of soup mixture at a time and cook, stirring, until bubbly. Repeat until 2½ cups of soup mixture have been added. Stir this into reheated soup; blend well. Add 1 cup of the cream; blend well. Whip the remaining 1 cup cream; serve a dollop of whipped cream on each steaming bowl of soup.

Serves 16 to 18/Freezes.

Mrs. Richard T. Weber, Jr. (Susan Blyth Donoghue)

Cream of Chicken Soup

⅓ c. butter
¾ c. flour
5 c. chicken stock
1 c. milk

1 c. heavy cream
1½ to 2 c. diced chicken
Salt and pepper to taste
Paprika, parsley, or chives

Melt butter over low heat, blend in flour and cook for 1 minute. Slowly add 2 cups of the chicken broth, the milk and cream. Cook slowly, stirring occasionally, for 20 to 30 minutes or until thick. Add remaining stock and chicken; heat to boiling point. Season with salt and pepper. Sprinkle with paprika and parsley or chives.
A perfect version of a soup tradition.
Serves 6/Freezes.
Mrs. Duke Matthews Covert (Lynn Carole Shapiro)

Cream of Cucumber Soup

½ c. minced green onions
3 T. butter
1½ lb. cucumbers, peeled and
   cut into ½ inch pieces
6 c. chicken broth
1½ t. wine vinegar
¾ t. dill weed or tarragon

¼ c. quick-cooking farina
   (Cream of Wheat)
Salt and white pepper to taste
½ to 1 c. sour cream
Chopped parsley
Thin slices of cucumber

Sauté green onions in butter for several minutes; add cucumbers, broth, vinegar, and dill or tarragon. Bring to boil; add farina. Simmer, partially covered, for 20 to 25 minutes. Pour a small amount of the soup at a time into blender and purée. Return to pot and season with salt and pepper.
To serve hot: bring to simmer and beat in ½ cup sour cream. Garnish each serving with parsley.
To serve cold: beat in ½ to 1 cup sour cream and stir several times while cooling. Serve in chilled mugs topped with thin slices of cucumber.
This soup is delicious hot or cold.
Yields 6 to 7 cups.
Mrs. Thomas E. Nelson, Jr. (Carol Corley)

Sour Cream Soup

1	medium onion, chopped	Salt and pepper to taste	
1	long green chili, chopped	¼ lb. Monterey Jack cheese,	
1	T. butter	cubed	
1	qt. sour cream	Paprika or chopped parsley	
¼	c. milk		

Cook onions and chili in butter until tender. Add sour cream, milk, salt, and pepper. Heat thoroughly. Add cheese just before serving; heat until melted. Do not boil. Garnish with paprika or parsley.
Serves 4/Freezes.
Mrs. H.Y. Cartwright, Jr. (Nancy Jo Casey)

Lentil Soup

1	lb. dried lentils	1½	c. chopped tomato	
8	slices bacon, cut into	6	T. butter	
	small pieces	6	T. flour	
2	c. chopped leeks or	1	10½ oz. can condensed	
	green onion		beef bouillon, undiluted	
1	c. chopped onion	4	t. salt	
1	c. chopped carrot	¼	c. vinegar	
1½	c. chopped bell pepper			

In a large kettle, cover lentils with 5 cups water. Simmer, covered, for 1 hour. In a skillet, crisply fry bacon; add vegetables and sauté 5 to 10 minutes; stir into lentils. Melt butter in a skillet. Add flour, stirring until smooth. Gradually stir in bouillon, salt, and vinegar. Bring to a boil, stirring, and pour into lentil mixture. Simmer over low heat, stirring frequently, for 30 minutes.
Serves 8/Freezes.
Mrs. McNay Crossland (Sara McNay)

Pinto Bean Soup

½ c. chopped onions
3 T. butter
3 c. cooked pinto beans
2 c. homemade chicken stock
½ c. pinto bean broth

Garlic salt to taste
Salt and pepper to taste
½ c. tomato juice
1 c. heavy cream, whipped

Sauté onions lightly in butter. Combine with beans, chicken stock, bean broth, garlic salt, salt, and pepper. Purée in blender, a small amount at a time. Transfer to saucepan; simmer 10 to 15 minutes. Add tomato juice, heat, and serve. Float a dollop of whipped cream in each cup of soup.
Serves 6/Freezes.
Mrs. Richard T. Weber, Jr. (Susan Blyth Donoghue)

The Best Vegetable Soup

2 or 3 meaty soup bones
1 onion, chopped
Salt and pepper to taste
½ c. dried split peas; 1 c.,
   if thicker soup desired
3 carrots, peeled and chopped
2 ribs celery, chopped

1 15 oz. can tomatoes
1 8 oz. can tomato sauce
1 potato, peeled and chopped
1 16 oz. can corn or 1 c.
   frozen corn
1 16 oz. can peas or 1 c.
   frozen peas

Cover bones with cold water in large pan; skim froth as it rises until it disappears; add onion, salt, pepper, and split peas. Simmer several hours, covered, stirring occasionally. Remove meat from bones; discard bones and return meat to soup. Add carrots, celery, tomatoes, and tomato sauce; simmer 20 minutes. Add potato; simmer 20 to 30 minutes. Add corn and peas for last 5 minutes of cooking. Best if made the day before serving. If freezing, substitute ½ cup rice or barley for potato. For variety add yellow squash or cabbage.
Serves 8/Freezes.
Mrs. John C. Donovan (Anne Peterson)

Mexican Spinach Soup

¼	c. chopped onion	1	c. cooked chopped spinach
1	large tomato, peeled and chopped	2	qt. beef stock
			Salt and pepper to taste
1	t. chopped parsley		Dash Tabasco
3	T. butter		Grated Romano cheese

Sauté onion, tomato, and parsley in butter for 3 to 5 minutes. Add spinach, stock, salt, pepper, and Tabasco; bring to a boil. Serve hot with a sprinkling of Romano cheese.
Serves 8/Freezes.
Mrs. Thomas Irvin Lowry (Katherine Sangster)

Broccoli Bisque

2	10 oz. packages frozen, chopped broccoli or 1 to 1½ lb. fresh broccoli, chopped	1	t. salt
		1	t. curry powder
			Dash pepper
3	cups chicken broth	2	T. lime juice
1	medium onion, quartered	½	c. sour cream
2	T. butter	1	T. fresh, chopped chives

In a large saucepan bring broccoli and broth to a boil; add onion, butter, salt, curry powder, and pepper. Reduce heat; simmer 10 to 12 minutes. Place ½ of this mixture in blender and blend at low speed until smooth; repeat with remaining mixture. Stir in lime juice. Refrigerate at least 4 hours. Serve in chilled bowls with a dollop of sour cream and sprinkling of chives on top.
Serves 6 to 8/Freezes.
Mrs. John Peterson (Frankie Gist)

Brown Corn Soup

1	c. corn	3	c. beef bouillon
1	c. boiling water	1	t. salt
1	t. grated onion	½	t. pepper
2	T. butter		Chives or parsley
2	T. flour		

Place corn, water, and onion in blender on low speed for 5 seconds; then simmer for 15 minutes. In another pan, make a roux of the butter and flour. Add bouillon, salt, and pepper and simmer for 5 minutes; add corn mixture and simmer for 5 minutes. Serve hot garnished with chives or parsley.

Serves 6/Freezes.
Mrs. Glenn Foster (Marcia Ungren)

Jones Corn Soup

6	slices bacon	¼	t. white pepper
1	c. chopped onion	1	scant T. salt
2	1 lb. 1 oz. cans cream-style corn	1	qt. milk
1	12 oz. can whole kernel corn, drained	2	c. light cream
			Paprika or chopped parsley

Fry bacon and crumble. Sauté onion in bacon drippings; add corn, pepper, salt, milk, and cream. Simmer, but do not boil, for 15 minutes. Add bacon and serve hot, garnished with paprika or parsley. Best if made early in the day and reheated.

A thick cream soup.
Serves 8/Freezes.
Mrs. Albert P. Jones (Annette Lewis)

Clear Tomato Soup

3	c. canned tomatoes, undrained	1	bay leaf
2	c. water	3	cloves
1	onion, sliced	2	T. butter
1 to 2	ribs celery or ¾ t. celery seed	1	T. flour

Combine all ingredients, except butter and flour, and simmer for 20 minutes; sieve mixture. Brown butter slightly and stir in flour to form a smooth paste. Stir in sieved mixture. Simmer over low heat for 10 to 15 minutes, until soup coats a wooden spoon.
Yields 6 cups/Freezes.
Mrs. James A. Williams (Priscilla Nichols)

Green Summer Soup

1	medium onion, peeled and sliced	2	cans water, with 2 T. flour mixed with enough of the water to form a thin, smooth paste
2	T. butter, melted	1	10 oz. package frozen peas
1	head lettuce, washed and chopped		Salt and pepper to taste
2	10¾ oz. cans condensed chicken broth, undiluted	½	c. heavy cream

Sauté onions in butter in a saucepan for 2 minutes. Add lettuce, chicken broth, water, flour mixture, frozen peas, salt, and pepper. Bring to a boil; simmer 5 minutes. Remove from heat and cool; purée a small amount at a time in a blender. Return purée to saucepan; add cream. Return just to boil; serve hot.
Serves 8/Freezes.
Mrs. Milner S. Thorne (Polly Perry)

Summer Fresh Tomato and Avocado Soup

12 medium tomatoes, peeled and chopped	2 cloves garlic, sliced in half
12 green onions, chopped	12 peppercorns
2 t. salt	2 bay leaves
2 t. sugar	2 avocados, diced
6 c. beef consommé	1 c. sour cream
	Lemon wedges

Combine tomatoes, onions, salt, and sugar; stir into consommé. Tie garlic, peppercorns, and bay leaves in cheesecloth and add. Chill thoroughly. Remove cheesecloth bag; spoon soup into bowls and add avocado. Top with a dollop of sour cream sprinkled sparingly with salt. Serve with lemon wedge.
A Tarry House specialty under Judy Rutledge's management.
Serves 10.
Mrs. Robert Ewell Jenkins (Carlene Johnson)

Cool, Cool Asparagus Soup

15 to 20 fresh asparagus spears, 2 14½ oz. cans asparagus drained, or 2 10 oz. packages frozen asparagus	¼ c. water
	2 c. chicken broth
	Salt and white pepper to taste
4 to 6 green onions, sliced with tops	¼ t. nutmeg
	1 c. heavy or light cream

Remove the ends of asparagus. Reserve the tips for garnish. Slice the remaining stalks in ½ inch pieces. Simmer with green onions in water until very tender. (If using canned asparagus, simmer only the onions in water.) Place asparagus-onion mixture, broth, and seasonings in blender; blend until smooth. Stir in cream. Chill. Serve very cold and garnished with 3 to 4 asparagus tips.
Serves 6/Freezes.
Mrs. Charles E. Bates (Linda Steinhauser)

Artichoke Soup

3	artichokes	1	bay leaf
3	T. chopped green onion	¼	t. thyme
3	T. chopped celery	1	T. lemon juice
¼	c. butter		Salt and white pepper to taste
3	T. flour	1	c. heavy cream
3	c. chicken broth		

Boil artichokes until tender, approximately 50 minutes; drain and cool. Scrape the meat from the leaves with a spoon; mash the artichoke bottoms. Sauté onions and celery in butter until soft. Add flour and cook over low heat until flour browns, stirring often (approximately 15 to 20 minutes). Gradually stir in chicken broth; add bay leaf, thyme, artichoke meat, lemon juice, salt, and pepper. Bring to a boil and simmer until slightly thickened. May be made to this point and frozen. Add cream, heating just to boiling; do not boil.
Most unusual.
Yields 1 quart/Freezes.
Mrs. Stephen Clark (Kate Eustis)

Chilled Cucumber Soup

1	c. condensed chicken broth		Dash garlic powder
2	T. lemon juice plus 1 t.	1	c. sour cream
	grated lemon rind	1	c. yogurt
¼	c. finely chopped onion	2	c. peeled, seeded, chopped
1	t. salt		cucumber
½	t. dill weed		Cucumber and lemon slices

In blender combine broth, lemon juice, lemon rind, onion, salt, dill, and garlic. Blend, covered, until smooth, 1 to 2 minutes. Add sour cream and yogurt. Blend, covered, 15 to 20 seconds. Add chopped cucumber. Serve very cold, floating cucumber and lemon slices on top.
Serves 8.
Mrs. Roger Barton Tyler, Jr. (Doris Taylor)

Chilled Avocado Soup

2 ripe avocados, peeled and diced
1/8 t. onion juice
1 c. chicken broth
1/2 c. sour cream

1/2 c. light cream
1/4 t. salt
Freshly ground pepper
Chopped green onions or paprika

Combine ingredients in blender and purée, or mash avocados and beat in other ingredients until smooth. Chill at least 3 hours. Garnish with chopped green onions or paprika.
Serves 4.
Mrs. Gray B. Jolink (Kingslea Thomas)

Oven-Baked Minestrone

1 1/2 lb. lean, beef stew meat, cut into 1 inch cubes
1 c. coarsely chopped onion
1 t. minced garlic
1 t. salt
1/4 t. pepper
2 T. olive oil
3 10 1/2 oz. cans condensed beef broth
2 cans water
1 1/2 t. Italian herb seasoning

1 16 oz. can tomatoes, undrained
1 15 oz. can kidney beans, undrained
1 6 oz. can pitted, ripe olives, undrained
1 1/2 c. peeled, thinly sliced carrots
1 c. small, seashell macaroni, uncooked
2 c. sliced zucchini
Grated Parmesan cheese

Combine beef, onion, garlic, salt, and pepper in a Dutch oven or heavy saucepan. Add olive oil; stir to coat meat evenly. Brown, uncovered, at 400°, approximately 40 minutes, stirring once or twice. Reduce heat to 325°. Add broth, water, and Italian seasoning. Cover and bake 1 hour until meat is almost tender. Remove from oven; stir in tomatoes, beans, olives, carrots, and macaroni. Spread zucchini on top. Cover and return to oven to bake 40 to 45 minutes longer until macaroni is tender. Serve with Parmesan cheese.
A robust meal with salad and thickly sliced, toasted French bread.
Serves 10 to 12/Freezes.
Mrs. James Eckhardt (Louise Adams)

Vichysquash

1 medium onion, sliced	½ c. chicken broth
2 T. butter	Salt and pepper to taste
6 medium yellow squash, sliced	1 c. light cream or milk
	Chopped chives

Sauté onion in butter until wilted, but not brown. Add squash and broth; cover and cook briskly until squash is tender, approximately 15 minutes. Cool. Purée mixture in blender or put through a food mill. Season with salt and pepper. Chill; stir in cream or milk. Serve sprinkled with chives.
Yields 2 cups/Freezes.
Mrs. Robert M. Kinnan (Betty Ann Carrier)

Senegalese Soup

1 small onion, coarsely chopped	1 t. whole cloves
1 carrot, coarsely chopped	5 c. strong chicken broth
1 rib celery, coarsely chopped	1 T. tomato paste
5 T. butter	3 T. almond paste
1½ t. curry powder	1 T. currant jelly
4 small cinnamon sticks	3 t. flour
2 bay leaves	Salt and white pepper to taste
	2 c. heavy cream
	Shredded coconut, toasted

Sauté onion, carrot, and celery in 2 tablespoons of the butter. Add curry powder, cinnamon sticks, bay leaves, cloves, broth, tomato paste, almond paste, and jelly. Mix well and bring to a boil; simmer, partially covered for 1 hour. Knead remaining butter with flour and gradually add to soup. Simmer 5 minutes, until soup has thickened slightly. Strain, taste for seasoning, and chill. Stir in cream just before serving and sprinkle with coconut.
Many adjectives for this soup—subtle, mysterious, smooth, exotic.
Serves 6 to 8/Freezes.
Mrs. Stephen S. Clark (Kate Eustis)

Gazpacho

1	c. finely chopped, peeled tomato	1	small clove garlic, mashed
½	c. finely chopped bell pepper	3	T. wine vinegar
½	c. finely chopped celery	2	T. vegetable oil
½	c. finely chopped cucumber	1	t. salt
½	c. finely chopped onion	¼	t. pepper
2	t. chopped parsley	½	t. Worcestershire sauce
1	t. chopped chives or green onion tops	2	c. tomato juice
			Seasoned croutons

Combine all ingredients except croutons. Cover and chill for at least 4 hours. Serve in chilled cups topped with seasoned croutons. Keeps well for several days in refrigerator.
Chop, don't blend, for best results.
Serves 6.
Mrs. James H. Albright (Mary Margaret Carlson)

Potage Paul

1	T. butter	1	T. curry powder
2	T. vegetable oil	3	T. flour
1	onion, finely chopped	2	c. clear chicken broth
1	clove garlic	¾ to 1	c. light cream
1	10 oz. package frozen peas or 2 cups shelled, fresh peas	¼	c. finely shredded, cooked chicken
Salt and pepper to taste			

Heat butter and oil in a saucepan; add onion and garlic. Sauté over low heat for 3 minutes. Add peas, salt, and pepper; cook until peas are very soft. Stir in curry powder; cook 1 minute. Remove from heat; stir in flour. Gradually add chicken broth, blending well. Stir soup over medium heat until it comes to a boil. Pour through a fine strainer or food mill. Add cream and chicken; reheat, but do not boil. This soup is good cold, but may need to be thinned with milk.
A fancy pea soup with curry.
Yields 2 quarts/Freezes.
Mrs. Homer Scace (Betty Gatch)

Celestial Potato Soup

2 medium potatoes, peeled
   and diced
2 carrots, grated
1 rib celery, finely chopped
1 turnip, peeled and diced
3 T. minced onion
1 T. dried vegetable flakes
1 t. monosodium glutamate

Salt and pepper to taste
3 T. butter
2 T. flour
1½ c. milk
1½ c. sour cream
3 slices bacon, fried and
   crumbled

Combine potatoes, carrots, celery, turnip, onion, vegetable flakes, monosodium glutamate, salt, and pepper; cover with water and simmer 30 minutes. In another saucepan, melt butter and stir in flour; add a small amount of liquid from potato mixture to form a paste. Cool and stir in milk and sour cream. When vegetables are cooked, mash or purée them and add flour and milk mixture. Do not boil. Serve sprinkled with bacon.
Also serve cold.
Serves 6/Freezes.
Mrs. Winston Harwood (Puddin Hopkins)

Salads

Jordan Parsley Dressing

1	egg	1	t. Worcestershire sauce
1	green onion, chopped		Dash Tabasco
1	clove garlic	1	c. parsley
1	t. sugar	3	T. vinegar
1	t. salt	¾	c. vegetable oil

Blend egg, green onion, garlic, sugar, salt, Worcestershire sauce, Tabasco, and vinegar in blender until smooth. Add half the oil and blend; add parsley and blend; add remaining oil and blend until smooth. Delicious as salad dressing or sandwich spread. For Green Eggs, put halves of deviled eggs together and cover with Parsley Dressing.
Yields approximately 1 cup.
Mrs. George O. Slaughter (Hallie Groos)

Green Goddess Salad Dressing

1	very ripe avocado	2	cans (approximately 5 T.) anchovy fillets, well-rinsed, drained and chopped
1	c. mayonnaise		
½	c. sour cream		
¼	c. tarragon vinegar	2	T. finely chopped green onions
¼	c. wine vinegar	1	small garlic clove, minced
1	T. lemon juice		Salt and pepper to taste

Whirl all ingredients in blender. Chill for 24 hours.
Yields 2 cups.
Mrs. Vernon L. Elledge, Jr. (Sharon Prentice)

Italian Salad Dressing

¼	c. olive oil	1	clove garlic, pressed
2	T. lemon juice	1	T. fresh, grated Romano cheese
1	t. grated lemon rind		
¼	t. salt	½	t. freshly ground pepper
½	t. thyme		

Mix all ingredients well. Chill before serving.
Yields ½ cup.
Mrs. Russell Painton (Ann "Aggie" Mullins)

Tart Garlic Dressing

1 c. olive oil (do not substitute)	1 t. pepper
1 c. vinegar	2 T. crushed, chopped garlic
½ t. salt	

Mix ingredients and shake vigorously.
Marinates meat as well as salad.
Yields 2 cups.
Mrs. Conrad P. Werkinthin (Clare Coates)

Blue Cheese Dressing

4 oz. blue cheese	1 c. sour cream
¾ c. vegetable oil	½ t. garlic salt
1 t. grated lemon rind	1 t. salt
¼ c. lemon juice	½ t. monosodium glutamate

Blend blue cheese and oil; beat until smooth. Stir in all remaining ingredients; mix well. Cover and chill for several hours. Bring to room temperature before serving.
Lemon—a fresh twist to a popular recipe.
Yields 2 cups/Keeps well in refrigerator for several weeks.
Mrs. Vernon L. Elledge, Jr. (Sharon Prentice)

Piquant Salad Dressing

1 medium onion, diced	3 T. sugar
3 medium cloves garlic, minced	2 c. vegetable oil
1 T. salt	¾ c. apple cider vinegar
¼ t. dry mustard	¼ c. water
¼ t. paprika	1 t. dried parsley
⅛ t. pepper	

Blend all ingredients in blender. Chill 24 hours.
A dressing with an affinity for tomato aspic, avocados and grapefruit, or avocados and tomatoes.
Yields approximately 1 quart.
Mrs. Richard T. Weber, Jr. (Susan Blyth Donoghue)

Argyle Salad Dressing

4   egg yolks, beaten
¼   c. tarragon vinegar
1   T. sugar
1   T. butter
1   t. salt

1   t. dry mustard
1   t. water
Dash cayenne
2   cups heavy cream, whipped

Combine all ingredients except cream in a double boiler. Cook, stirring constantly, until thick. Cool. Fold in whipped cream just before serving.
Yields 3 cups.
Mrs. W. R. Long, III (Carol Tyler)

Poppy Seed Dressing

¾   c. sugar
1   c. vegetable oil
1   t. dry mustard
1   t. salt

⅓   c. vinegar
1½ T. minced onion
2   T. poppy seeds

Combine all ingredients and mix in a blender. Serve over fruit or green salads.
The crunch of poppy seeds and the piquancy of sugar and onion combined.
Yields 2 cups/Lasts indefinitely in refrigerator.
Mrs. Jack Gray (Margaret Bellmont)

Red French Dressing

1   c. vegetable oil
½   c. sugar
¼   c. vinegar
½   c. catsup
3   drops Tabasco

2   t. paprika
Juice of 1 lemon
1   small onion, grated
Dash garlic salt or 1 clove
    garlic

Combine all ingredients in jar; refrigerate. Shake well before serving. Good with fruit or vegetable salads, but especially with grapefruit and avocado.
Yields approximately 1½ pints.
Mrs. W. R. Long, Jr. (Elizabeth Baker)

Avocado Bowl

2	large tomatoes, cut in small wedges		Italian dressing (page 43.)
1	c. pitted ripe olives, slivered	1	clove garlic, pressed
1	10 oz. package frozen artichoke hearts, thawed and drained	¼	c. tarragon vinegar
		2 or 3	large avocados, sliced
			Lettuce

Place tomatoes, olives, and artichoke hearts in shallow bowl; cover with mixture of Italian dressing, garlic, and vinegar. Cover and refrigerate overnight. To serve, line a large salad bowl with lettuce leaves, cover with avocados, then with drained vegetables.
Serves 6.
Mrs. J. T. Bowman (Gladys Greenlee)

Gazpacho Salad with Avocado Mayonnaise

2	T. unflavored gelatin	2	tomatoes, peeled and diced
1	18 oz. can V-8 juice	1	large cucumber, peeled and diced
2	T. wine vinegar	1	bell pepper, diced
2	T. lemon juice	¼	c. finely chopped green onion
1	t. salt		
Dash Tabasco			

Avocado Mayonnaise
1   ripe avocado, peeled
½   c. mayonnaise

Sprinkle gelatin over ½ cup of V-8 juice. Add vinegar, lemon juice, salt, Tabasco, and remaining V-8 juice and dissolve over low heat. Chill to the consistency of an egg white. Fold in tomatoes, cucumber, pepper, and onion. Pour into an oiled 1½ quart mold and refrigerate until congealed.

Avocado Mayonnaise   In blender, purée avocado and mayonnaise until smooth; chill. Serve over gazpacho salad.
Serves 8.
Mrs. Charles E. Bates (Linda Steinhauser)

Elegant Avocado Aspic

2   10½ oz. cans condensed
    consommé
1   T. unflavored gelatin
2   T. water
2   T. lemon juice
1   t. dry mustard
¼   t. seasoned salt

½   c. mayonnaise
2   avocados, peeled and cubed
4   hard-cooked eggs, chopped
¾   c. pitted ripe olives,
    sliced
Leaf lettuce

Heat consommé to boiling. Soften gelatin in water and dissolve in hot consommé. Add lemon juice, mustard, and seasoned salt. Chill until mixture starts to thicken. Fold in mayonnaise, avocados, eggs, and olives. Pour into an oiled 1½ quart ring mold. Chill thoroughly. Unmold on leaf lettuce.
Serve with mayonnaise in the center, surrounded by cherry tomatoes, artichoke hearts, hearts of palm, and radishes.
Serves 8 to 10.
Mrs. J. Chrys Dougherty (Mary Ireland Graves)

Guacamole Mousse

3   c. mashed, ripe avocado
2   T. lemon juice
2   T. finely chopped green onion,
    tops and bottoms
2   t. picante sauce
1   t. Worcestershire sauce
Salt to taste

2   T. unflavored gelatin
½   c. cold water
½   c. heavy cream, whipped
½   c. mayonnaise
Leaf lettuce
Cherry tomatoes
Melba toast or tostados

Combine avocado, lemon juice, green onion, picante sauce, Worcestershire sauce, and salt in mixer and blend. Sprinkle gelatin over water and place over low heat, stirring constantly until dissolved. Cool. Combine whipped cream and mayonnaise; add gelatin. Combine avocado and cream mixtures. Pour into an oiled 1½ quart ring mold. Chill until firm. Unmold on platter covered with leaf lettuce; fill center and surround mold with cherry tomatoes. Serve with melba toast or tostados.
Serves 8.
Mrs. Charles E. Bates (Linda Steinhauser)

Mexican Congealed Salad

1	T. unflavored gelatin	¼	c. minced onion
½	c. cold water	1	avocado
1	10½ oz. can condensed	1	T. lemon juice
	tomato soup	½	t. ground cumin
1	T. vinegar	½	t. chili powder
	Tabasco	½	c. mayonnaise
1	tomato, peeled and chopped		Lettuce
½	c. finely chopped bell pepper		

Soften gelatin in water; blend in soup, vinegar, and 2 dashes Tabasco. Heat and stir until gelatin dissolves. Chill until almost set; fold in tomato, bell pepper, and onion. Pour into a 3 cup ring mold and chill until firm. Mash avocado; add lemon juice, cumin, chili powder, and 2 dashes Tabasco. Blend and correct seasonings. If serving immediately, stir in mayonnaise. Otherwise, spread mayonnaise over avocado mixture, cover and refrigerate. Unmold salad on lettuce and fill with avocado mixture.
Serves 4 to 6.
Mrs. Charles Crites (Mildred "Milly" Holmes)

Fire and Ice Tomatoes

6	large tomatoes, peeled and quartered	⅛	t. mustard seed
		½	t. salt
1	large bell pepper, sliced into strips	⅛	t. cayenne
		⅛	t. pepper
1	large red onion, thinly sliced	¼	c. cold water
¾	c. vinegar	1	large cucumber, pared and thinly sliced
1½	t. celery salt		
4½	t. sugar		

Arrange tomatoes, bell pepper, and onion on a large glass platter. Combine all other ingredients, except cucumber, and boil rapidly for 1 minute. Pour sauce over vegetables and chill. Just before serving, arrange cucumber with other vegetables.
Serves 6.
Mrs. Howard Rose, Jr. (Patsy Patteson)

Mushroom Tossed Salad

¼ lb. mushrooms, thinly sliced
¼ c. chopped bell pepper
¼ c. thinly slice onion rings
½ c. sliced celery

2 heads Boston lettuce, torn
into bite-size pieces
Grated Parmesan cheese

Dressing

1 package Parmesan salad
dressing mix
¼ c. red wine vinegar
⅔ c. vegetable oil

2 T. lemon juice
2 t. Worcestershire sauce
1 T. capers
2 T. water

In a salad bowl, combine mushrooms, bell pepper, onions, and celery. Add ½ cup of salad dressing and toss lightly. Chill for 2 hours. Just before serving add lettuce and toss. Sprinkle with Parmesan cheese.

Dressing Combine all ingredients and mix well.
Serves 6 to 8.
Mrs. E. R. L. Wroe, Jr. (Ammon Neyland)

Sarah's Marinated Mushroom-Cauliflower Salad

1 lb. mushrooms
1 c. vegetable oil
⅓ c. wine vinegar
2 T. minced onion
1½ t. salt
1 t. sugar
½ t. pepper

¼ t. dry mustard
½ medium cauliflower, broken
into flowerets and thinly
sliced
1 c. sliced celery
1 bell pepper, cut into strips
8 cherry tomatoes, halved

Thinly slice mushrooms. In large bowl combine oil, vinegar, onion, salt, sugar, pepper, and mustard. Add mushrooms and toss. Add cauliflower, celery, and green pepper. Let marinate 1 hour, stirring occasionally. Just before serving, stir in tomatoes.
Yields 1½ quarts/Serves 8.
Mrs. H. Phillip Whitworth (Nancy Scott Denton)

Mushroom, Ham, and Artichoke Salad

2   T. lemon juice
½   lb. fresh mushrooms, thinly sliced
2   slices boiled ham, cut into thin strips
1   14 oz. can artichoke hearts, drained and coarsely chopped

2   T. minced onion
½   c. olive oil
¼   c. wine vinegar
1   t. salt
Pepper and savory to taste

Sprinkle lemon juice over mushrooms. Arrange mushrooms, ham, and artichokes on a serving platter. Mix onion, olive oil, vinegar, salt, pepper, and savory; pour over salad. Chill.
Serves 4 to 6.
Mrs. Benjamin McPherson, Jr. (Marie Lois Leopold)

September Salad with Sweet French Dressing

1   head lettuce, broken into pieces
1   head escarole or endive, broken into pieces

2   oranges, peeled and sectioned
½   red onion, thinly sliced
½   bell pepper, thinly sliced

Sweet French Dressing

¼   c. brown sugar
½   t. dry mustard
¼   t. pepper
¼   t. celery salt
½   t. salt

½   t. Worcestershire sauce
½   c. catsup
¾   c. vegetable oil
¼   c. vinegar
2   T. chopped onion

Mix salad greens, oranges, onion, and bell pepper; chill. Combine dressing ingredients; mix well and chill. Pour desired amount of dressing over chilled salad and toss.
Nice variations: the addition of a sliced avocado or a change to poppy seed dressing.
Serves 8 to 10.
Mrs. Albert M. Tate (Patricia Loessin)

Sweet and Sour Tomato Salad

2 tomatoes, peeled and sliced
1 onion, thinly sliced
1 bell pepper, sliced in rings

Sweet and Sour Dressing

½ c. cider vinegar
¼ c. vegetable oil (not olive oil)
¾ t. salt
¼ t. pepper

1 T. Worcestershire sauce
1 T. A-1 sauce
5 T. sugar
Dash Tabasco

Layer tomatoes, onion, and bell pepper in a shallow container. Combine dressing ingredients; shake well to dissolve sugar. Pour desired amount of dressing over all and marinate overnight. Remove from dressing and arrange in a shallow bowl or platter.
Serves 4.
Mrs. Richard T. Weber (Violetta Van Devanter)

Snow Pea Salad

1 lb. fresh snow peas
1 head cauliflower, broken into small flowerets
⅓ c. milk
1 5 oz. can sliced water chestnuts, drained
2 T. chopped pimiento

2 T. sesame seeds, toasted
⅓ c. vegetable oil
1 T. lemon juice
1 T. vinegar
1 T. sugar
1 small clove garlic, minced
¾ t. salt

Chill snow peas in cold water 2 hours. Cook in boiling salted water for 1 minute. Drain and dry. Simmer cauliflower for 5 minutes in salted water, to which milk has been added. Drain. Combine peas, cauliflower, water chestnuts, and pimiento; chill. Mix remaining ingredients. Shortly before serving, dress salad lightly.
Delicate alone; for robust appetites, offer a bowl of a creamy dressing on the side.
Serves 8 to 10.
Mrs. Fred L. Sharp (Margaret Howie)

Green Bean Salad

3 9 oz. packages frozen green
  beans, cooked and drained
2 large tomatoes, peeled and
  cut into chunks
½ c. vegetable oil

½ c. tarragon vinegar
½ t. salt
⅛ t. pepper
1 teaspoon finely grated onion
⅛ t. tarragon

Mix green beans with tomatoes in large bowl. Combine remaining ingredients; pour over beans and tomatoes and toss. Refrigerate for 24 hours.
Serves 8/Keeps in refrigerator 1 week.
Mrs. James A. Williams (Priscilla Nichols)

Red, White and Green Salad

5 c. broccoli flowerets
  (2 bunches)
2½ c. cauliflower flowerets
  (1 head)
1 onion, chopped
2 c. cherry tomatoes, halved

1 c. mayonnaise
½ c. sour cream
1 T. vinegar
2 T. sugar
Salt and pepper to taste

Combine broccoli, cauliflower, onion, and tomatoes. Stir together mayonnaise, sour cream, vinegar, and sugar; pour over vegetables and toss. Sprinkle with salt and pepper. Chill 3 to 4 hours. Salad will keep for several days.
Serves 6 to 8.
Mrs. Ashley Bracken (Susan Fry)

Layered Picnic Salad

1 head lettuce, shredded
  with knife
1 large red onion, grated
3 carrots, peeled and grated
4 ribs celery, chopped

1 17 oz. can green peas
Homemade mayonnaise
3 heaping t. sugar
4 slices bacon, crisply fried
  and crumbled

Layer lettuce, onion, carrots, celery, and peas in a salad bowl. Top with small dabs of mayonnaise; sprinkle with a heaping teaspoon of sugar. Repeat until there are at least 3 layers. Over the top layer, sprinkle bacon. Cover with a damp tea towel; refrigerate until chilled. Do not toss before serving.
The secret's in the melding of mayonnaise, sugar and onion.
Serves 4 to 6.
Mrs. Larry Temple (Louann Atkins)

Sesame Salad

1 head lettuce, torn into pieces	3 dashes soy sauce
4 avocados, peeled and sliced	½ c. sesame oil
3 tomatoes, quartered	½ c. red wine vinegar
1 red onion, sliced into rings	Sesame seeds, toasted

Combine lettuce, avocados, tomatoes, and red onion in a serving bowl. For dressing, combine soy sauce, sesame oil, and vinegar. Toss salad with desired amount of dressing and sprinkle generously with sesame seeds.
The distinctive taste of sesame oil and sesame seed.
Serves 4 to 6.
Mrs. Frank N. Ikard, Jr. (Carol Foster)

Sweet Pickled Asparagus

⅔ c. vinegar	½ c. water
½ c. sugar	2 15 oz. cans asparagus, drained,
½ t. salt	or 2 10 oz. packages frozen
3 sticks cinnamon	asparagus, cooked and drained
1 t. whole cloves	Grated hard-cooked egg
1 T. celery seed	

Combine vinegar, sugar, salt, and spices in saucepan with water; bring to a boil. Place asparagus in shallow baking dish; cover with boiling liquid. Cover and refrigerate for at least 24 hours. To serve, drain and sprinkle with grated, hard-cooked egg.
Serves 6.
Mrs. Glenn Foster (Marcia Ungren)

Copper Carrots

1	lb. fresh carrots, scraped, sliced in rounds and cooked, or 3 16 oz. cans sliced carrots, drained	½	c. vegetable oil
		¾	c. vinegar
		1	c. sugar
1	purple onion, chopped	1	t. prepared mustard
1	bell pepper, chopped	1	t. Worcestershire sauce
1	10½ oz. can condensed tomato soup	1	t. salt
		1	t. pepper

Combine all ingredients and place in a jar. Marinate in refrigerator 2 or 3 days. Drain and serve cold or at room temperature as a salad or relish. *The rare recipe in which a canned vegetable can be used as successfully as its fresh counterpart.*
Serves 12 as a salad/24 as a relish.
Mrs. Don Rylander (Joan Loffland)

Vegetable Platter with Crab Dressing

1	15 oz. can white asparagus, drained	1	14 oz. can artichoke hearts, drained
1	16 oz. can small whole carrots, drained, or fresh cooked strips	4	hard-cooked eggs, quartered
1	16 oz. can beet slices, drained	1	16 oz. can Blue Lake green beans, drained, or fresh cooked
4	tomatoes, cut into wedges		Leaf lettuce
3	avocados, peeled, sliced, and sprinkled with lemon juice		

Arrange vegetables and eggs over lettuce on a platter.

Crab dressing

2	c. mayonnaise		Salt and pepper to taste
1	c. heavy cream		Tabasco to taste
½	c. dill pickle relish	2	hard-cooked eggs, chopped
	Juice of 1 lemon	½	lb. lump crabmeat

Combine dressing ingredients; chill. Serve dressing with vegetables.
Serves 8.
Mrs. James A. Williams (Priscilla Nichols)

German Potato Salad

3   large new potatoes, boiled,
     peeled, and sliced
½   c. chopped bell pepper
3   ribs celery, chopped
6   green onions, chopped
¼   c. chopped parsley
8   slices bacon, fried and
     crumbled, with drippings
     reserved

2   T. vinegar
3   hard-cooked eggs, sliced
Salt and pepper to taste
Parsley

Layer potatoes and chopped vegetables in a bowl. Heat bacon drippings and combine with vinegar; pour over salad and toss. Add bacon, eggs, salt, and pepper; toss. Garnish with additional parsley. Serve hot or cold.
Serves 6.
Mrs. Thomas F. Reese (Mary Lynn Roth)

Overnight Salad

1   10 oz. package spinach, torn
     into bite-size pieces
1   head lettuce, torn into
     bite-size pieces
1   lb. bacon, crisply fried
     and crumbled
1   10 oz. package frozen green
     peas, thawed

4   green onions, sliced (white
     part only)
10   hard-cooked eggs, sliced
1   c. mayonnaise
1   c. Miracle Whip salad dressing
½   lb. Swiss cheese, grated

In a glass bowl, layer ingredients, except dressings and cheese, in the order listed, pressing spinach and lettuce firmly into the bowl. Arrange several of the egg slices against the side of the bowl for decoration. Frost with combined mayonnaise and Miracle Whip; sprinkle with cheese. Cover tightly and refrigerate overnight.
Rich shades of green.
Serves 10 to 12.
Mrs. Travis Eckert (Carol Foust)

Cucumber Salad Mold

2	c. peeled and diced cucumbers	2	t. salt
2	c. sour cream		Dash white pepper
1/4	c. vinegar	2	T. unflavored gelatin,
1/4	c. minced chives		softened in 1/2 c. cold water

Mix cucumbers, sour cream, vinegar, chives, salt and pepper. Refrigerate 1 hour. Dissolve gelatin and water over low heat; cool and stir into cucumber mixture. Mix well and pour into an oiled 1½ quart mold. Chill.
Serves 6 to 8.
Mrs. Shannon Ratliff (Gay Kokernot)

Cucumber Salad

2	large cucumbers, sliced	1/2	c. vinegar
1½	t. salt	2	T. sugar
1	bell pepper, sliced into rings	2	T. vegetable oil
1	medium onion, sliced and	1/2	t. dill weed
	separated into rings		Leaf lettuce
1	T. chopped parsley		

Slice cucumbers into bowl; sprinkle with 1 teaspoon of the salt and let stand 1 hour. Drain off liquid; rinse and drain well. Add bell pepper and onion; sprinkle with parsley. Combine remaining ingredients; add remaining 1/2 teaspoon salt. Pour over vegetables; cover and chill overnight. Serve on leaf lettuce.
Sour cream added to the leftovers—a new salad.
Serves 4 to 6.
Mrs. Grant W. Simpson (Mary Ellen Reese)

Bacon Slaw

6	slices bacon	¼	t. pepper
1	T. vinegar	2	c. shredded cabbage
⅓	c. mayonnaise	1	T. minced onion
½	t. salt	¼	c. minced bell pepper

Fry bacon until crisp; crumble and reserve 2 tablespoons drippings. Combine drippings with vinegar, mayonnaise, salt, and pepper. Toss cabbage with onion, bell pepper, and dressing; mix well. Add bacon just before serving.
You'll never want "plain" slaw again.
Serves 6.
Mrs. Jack Steinhauser (Cissy Wheat)

Korean Salad

2	10 oz. bags fresh spinach, stemmed	1	16 oz. can bean sprouts, drained
1	8½ oz. can water chestnuts, sliced and drained	8	slices bacon, fried and crumbled
3 to 4	green onions and tops, chopped	4	hard-cooked eggs, chopped

Vinegar Dressing

1	c. vegetable oil	2	t. salt
⅔	c. sugar	½	c. catsup
½	c. vinegar		

Toss salad ingredients together. Mix dressing well and pour desired amount over salad.
Serves 8.
Mrs. Maury Hughes, Jr. (Phoebe Foster)

Tabooli Salad

1 c. cracked wheat
1 bunch green onions, finely chopped
½ bunch mint, finely chopped or 3 T. dried mint flakes

4 large tomatoes, finely chopped
Juice of 4 lemons
½ c. olive oil
Salt and pepper to taste
Lettuce leaves

Soak wheat in water until soft, approximately 25 minutes. Drain in fine strainer until dry. Mix together the onions, mint, and tomatoes; add wheat and remaining ingredients and mix well. Serve on lettuce leaves.
A Lebanese dish compatible with American tastes.
Serves 6 to 8/Keeps well in refrigerator.
Mrs. Edward Clark (Ann Metcalf)

Spinach Salad

1 lb. fresh spinach
1 bunch watercress
¼ t. garlic salt
½ t. salt
½ t. grated lemon rind
¼ t. paprika

¼ t. freshly ground pepper
2 T. tarragon vinegar
½ c. vegetable oil
2 T. sour cream
6 slices bacon, fried and crumbled

Rinse and dry spinach and watercress. Remove large stems and veins from spinach and tear into bite-size pieces. Chill both. Combine all remaining ingredients, except bacon, beating in oil and sour cream. Just before serving, pour dressing over greens and toss well. Sprinkle with bacon.
The bite of watercress and the tang of lemon.
Serves 4 to 6.
Mrs. Richard T. Doyle (Grace Odem)

Spinach and Mushroom Salad with Mustard Dressing

½ c. red or white wine vinegar
½ c. Dijon mustard
2 t. salt
¼ t. white pepper

1 t. sugar
1 c. olive oil
Leaf spinach
Fresh mushrooms

Combine vinegar, mustard, salt, pepper, and sugar; beat well. Slowly add oil, beating with wire whisk. Serve dressing over salad of leaf spinach and fresh mushrooms.
Yields 2 cups.
Mrs. George E. Heyer (Hallie Dewar)

Joy's Molded Spinach Salad

2 10 oz. packages frozen, chopped spinach
¼ c. sour cream
3 T. chopped celery
2 T. chopped onion

1 T. vinegar
Salt and pepper to taste
Marinated whole mushrooms
Cherry tomatoes

Cook spinach according to package directions. Drain well; cool. Mix with remaining ingredients. Pack into oiled mold; chill at least 2 hours. Serve on lettuce leaf garnished with marinated, whole mushrooms and cherry tomatoes.
Serves 6.
Miss Harriet Hahn

Sauerkraut Slaw

1⅓ c. sugar
⅔ c. vegetable oil
½ c. vinegar
⅓ c. water
1 1 lb., 11 oz. can sauerkraut, drained

1 c. chopped onion
1 c. chopped celery
1 2 oz. jar chopped pimiento, drained
1 bell pepper, chopped
Salt and pepper to taste

Combine sugar, oil, vinegar, and water and bring to a boil; cool. Combine sauerkraut with remaining ingredients. Pour liquid mixture over sauerkraut mixture; refrigerate overnight.
Serves 12.
Mrs. Joe R. Greenhill (Martha Shuford)

Wild Rice Salad or Appetizer

1 6 oz. package long grain and wild rice	1 T. chopped parsley
	⅓ c. mayonnaise
1 c. finely diced, cooked chicken or ham	1 T. lemon juice
	Salt to taste
½ c. finely chopped celery	Cherry tomatoes or medium tomatoes
2 T. chopped green onion	

Cook rice as directed; cool. Add meat, celery, onion, parsley, mayonnaise, lemon juice, and salt to taste. Mix well and chill. Scoop out tomatoes and fill with rice mixture. Use cherry tomatoes for appetizers and larger tomatoes for salad.
Unusual as an hors d'oeuvres.
Yields approximately 100 cherry tomatoes.
Mrs. H. Phillip Whitworth (Nancy Scott Denton)

Rice Salad

1½ c. uncooked rice	2 t. prepared mustard
3 c. chicken stock	¼ c. chopped green onions
¼ c. vegetable oil	1 c. chopped ripe olives
2 T. vinegar	2 hard-cooked eggs, chopped
1½ t. salt	1½ c. chopped celery
⅛ t. pepper	¼ c. chopped dill pickle
⅛ t. cayenne	1 small onion, chopped
½ to ¾ c. mayonnaise, or enough to bind	Parsley

Cook rice in chicken stock; cool. Mix oil, vinegar, salt, pepper, and cayenne; pour over rice. Add remaining ingredients, except parsley. Mix well; pour into 2 quart mold, that has been well-oiled with mayonnaise. Chill. Serve garnished with parsley.
Serves 8.
Mrs. Benjamin McPherson, Jr. (Marie Lois Leopold)

Rice Ring

2 T. unflavored gelatin	1 c. heavy cream, whipped
½ c. cold water	2½ c. cooked rice, cooled
1 13¾ oz. can chicken broth	¾ c. chopped celery
¾ c. mayonnaise	¼ c. chopped green onion
2 T. lemon juice	Chopped parsley

Soften gelatin in cold water. Bring chicken broth to a boil; add gelatin and dissolve. Beat in mayonnaise and lemon juice. Chill until partially set. Whip until light and fluffy. Fold in whipped cream, rice, celery, and green onion. Turn into a greased 1½ quart ring mold. Chill for at least 6 hours. Unmold and fill ring with cold shrimp, cherry tomatoes, or any cold vegetable. Sprinkle with chopped parsley.
Serves 8 to 10.
Mrs. Mary Jo Ramsey (Mary Jo Peterson)

Chicken-Wild Rice Salad

1 6 oz. package long grain and wild rice mix	½ c. mayonnaise
2 c. cooked, cubed chicken	2 T. Russian salad dressing
¼ c. chopped bell pepper	1 T. lemon juice
2 T. chopped pimiento	¼ t. salt
½ c. chopped water chestnuts	2 avocados, sliced

Cook rice and cool. Add chicken, bell pepper, pimiento, and water chestnuts. Combine mayonnaise, salad dressing, lemon juice, and salt. Toss dressing into rice mixture. Chill. To serve, spoon chicken mixture over avocado slices.
Serves 4 to 6.
Mrs. Robert Ewell Jenkins (Carlene Johnson)

German Cabbage Salad

1   head cabbage, shredded
1   bell pepper, chopped
1   large onion, shredded
1   c. sugar
1   c. vinegar

¾ c. vegetable oil
1   t. mustard seed
1   t. celery seed
1   T. salt

Combine cabbage, bell pepper, and onion in large bowl; sprinkle with sugar. Bring to a boil the remaining ingredients; pour over cabbage. Cover and refrigerate overnight.

Mrs. Howell M. Finch (Diane Hierholzer)

Orange Salad

1   head romaine lettuce, broken
    into pieces
1   11 oz. can mandarin
    oranges, drained

1   4 oz. package salted peanuts
Poppy seed dressing, page 45.

Combine lettuce, oranges, and peanuts. Toss with desired amount of poppy seed dressing.

Serves 4.

Mrs. Frank N. Ikard, Jr. (Carol Foster)

Frozen Cranberry Salad

1   16 oz. can whole cranberry
    sauce
1   8 oz. can crushed pineapple
2   T. sugar

2   T. mayonnaise
2   3 oz. packages cream cheese,
    at room temperture
2   c. heavy cream, whipped

Combine all ingredients. Freeze in 2 quart mold or dish.

Also good as a luncheon dessert.

Serves 12 to 16.

Mrs. Robert L. Buford (Nancy Peoples)

Mint Julepeach Salad

1   6 oz. package lemon-
    flavored gelatin
1½ c. hot water
½   c. frozen lemonade concentrate
1   7 oz. bottle ginger ale, chilled

⅛   t. peppermint extract
2   c. fresh peach balls
1   c. honeydew melon balls
1   c. seedless green grapes

Dissolve gelatin in water. Add lemonade concentrate, ginger ale, and peppermint extract. Chill until partially set. Add fruit and spoon into a 2 quart mold. Chill until set.
Serves 8.
Mrs. Maury Hughes, Jr. (Phoebe Foster)

Citrus Salad with Mint Dressing

2   grapefruit, sectioned
3   oranges, peeled and thinly
    sliced
Leaf lettuce
Fresh mint

Dressing
6   T. mint jelly or apple-mint jelly
2   T. honey
Grated peel and juice of 2 limes
Juice of 2 lemons

Arrange grapefruit and oranges on a bed of lettuce. Whirl dressing ingredients in blender. Pour dressing over salad and garnish with mint leaves.
Try this dressing over avocados and mangos.
Serves 4.
Mrs. Larry Temple (Louann Atkins)

Frozen Fruit Salad

1 c. mayonnaise
2 c. heavy cream, whipped
1 16 oz. can pears, cut into small pieces, drained
1 17 oz. can Queen Anne cherries, drained
1 8½ oz. can pineapple chunks, drained

1 c. fresh strawberries, sliced
2 bananas, diced and dipped in lemon juice
1 c. chopped pecans
1 c. chopped dates

Fold mayonnaise into whipped cream. Stir in fruit, pecans, and dates. Pour into a 3 quart mold or 20 individual molds and freeze. Remove from freezer 10 minutes before serving.
Serves 20.
Mrs. Norman M. Barker (Mary Brownlee)

Raspberry Salad

1 3 oz. package raspberry-flavored gelatin
1¼ c. boiling water
1 10 oz. package frozen raspberries, partially thawed

1 8¼ oz. can crushed pineapple
1 large banana, peeled and sliced
½ c. chopped pecans or walnuts

Dressing
1 c. sour cream
1½ c. miniature marshmallows
1 T. sugar
3 T. lemon juice

Add boiling water to gelatin; stir until gelatin dissolves. Add raspberries; stir until thawed. Chill until mixture begins to thicken. Add remaining ingredients; pour into oiled, 1 quart mold and chill until congealed.

Dressing Combine all ingredients; chill overnight.
Serves 8.
Mrs. Thomas E. Nelson, Jr. (Carol Corley)

Bing Cherry Salad

1 16 oz. can pitted, dark, sweet cherries	2 T. unflavored gelatin
½ c. sherry	⅓ c. chopped pecans
1⅓ c. orange juice	1 3 oz. package cream cheese,
Juice of ¼ lemon	at room temperature
⅔ c. sugar	Lettuce leaves

Drain cherries, reserving juice. Combine and bring to boil cherry juice, sherry, 1 cup of the orange juice, lemon juice, and sugar. Dissolve gelatin in remaining ⅓ cup of the orange juice; add to hot mixture. Chill until mixture begins to thicken. Add cherries stuffed with pecans and cream cheese. Pour into ring mold or individual molds and chill until firm. Serve on lettuce leaves.
Serves 8.
Mrs. Vernon L. Elledge, Jr. (Sharon Prentice)

Spicy Orange Salad

1 c. water	1 T. lemon juice
1 stick cinnamon	1 11 oz. can mandarin
8 whole cloves	oranges, drained
1 3 oz. package orange-flavored gelatin	Sour cream
1 6 oz. can frozen orange juice concentrate, thawed and undiluted	

In saucepan combine water, cinnamon, and cloves; bring to boil; reduce heat and simmer 10 minutes. Remove spices; add dry gelatin, stirring until dissolved. Add orange juice concentrate and lemon juice; mix well. Chill approximately 1 hour until slightly thickened; fold in oranges. Pour into oiled, 3 cup mold and chill until firm. Top with sour cream.
Serves 4 to 6.
Mrs. David Gaffey Ford (Laura Lee Hill)

Beaumont Inn Grapefruit Salad

2   T. unflavored gelatin
1   17 oz jar pitted, light
    sweet cherries, drained with
    juice reserved
1   15¼ oz. can crushed or chunk
    pineapple, drained with juice
    reserved

1   c. sugar
Pinch Salt
2   c. water
½   c. vinegar
4   grapefruit, peeled and
    sectioned

Sprinkle gelatin over ½ cup of juices reserved from cherries and pineapple. Boil sugar, salt, and water until sugar dissolves. Remove liquid from heat and add vinegar; add softened gelatin and fruits. Pour into 12 oiled, individual molds or a 3 quart mold. Chill until firm.
Serves 12.
Mrs. George O. Slaughter (Hallie Groos)

Mango Salad

3   3 oz. packages lemon-flavored
    gelatin
3   c. boiling water
1   8 oz. package cream cheese,
    at room temperature

1   16 oz. can mangos, drained
    and juice reserved
1   c. mango juice (if needed,
    add water to make 1 c.)
1   c. sour cream
1 to 2 T. honey

Dissolve gelatin in boiling water. In blender, combine cream cheese, mangos, and mango juice; stir in gelatin. Pour into 2½ quart mold and chill to jell. Serve with dressing made of sour cream sweetened with honey.
Serves 12 to 15.
Mrs. Howard Rose, Jr. (Patsy Patteson)

Cranberry Salad

2 c. fresh cranberries	Juice of 1 lemon
1 c. sugar	1 c. diced apple
1 c. water	1 c. finely chopped celery
1½ T. unflavored gelatin	1 c. chopped pecans
Juice of 1 orange	Leaf lettuce

Cook cranberries slowly with sugar and water until berries burst. Sprinkle gelatin over orange and lemon juices to soften; add to cooked cranberries; cool. Add apple, celery, and pecans; pour into 2 quart mold; chill. Serve on leaf lettuce.
Serves 10.
Mrs. George O. Slaughter (Hallie Groos)

Green Gage Plum Salad

1 c. plum juice, heated	2 3 oz. packages cream cheese, at room temperature
1 6 oz. package lime-flavored gelatin	½ c. mayonnaise
1 c. mashed green gage plums	½ c. chopped pecans

Add hot juice to gelatin and cool. Add plums. Cream the cheese and mayonnaise; add to the plum mixture. Stir in the nuts and pour into an 8 x 8 glass dish or individual molds. Chill.
Serves 8.
Mrs. Shannon Ratliff (Gay Kokernot)

Salade Niçoise

3	c. green beans, cooked and chilled	1	c. tuna, drained and broken into chunks
4	tomatoes, peeled and quartered	½	c. ripe olives
3	c. boiled potatoes, peeled, diced and chilled	3	hard-cooked eggs, quartered
1½	c. olive oil and vinegar dressing	6 to 12	anchovy fillets
2	large heads Boston or Bibb lettuce	1	t. chopped parsley
		1	t. chives
		1	t. basil

In separate bowls, toss green beans, tomatoes, and potatoes with enough dressing to coat. Toss lettuce in dressing and arrange around sides of large salad bowl. Place potatoes in center of bowl; arrange green beans, tomatoes, tuna, ripe olives, eggs, and anchovies in the salad bowl. Pour remaining dresing over salad. Sprinkle with herbs. *Nothing else needed.*
Serves 8 as a first course/4 as an entrée.
Mrs. Stephen S. Clark (Kate Eustis)

Taco Salad

1	onion, chopped	1	large avocado, diced
4	tomatoes, peeled and chopped	1	lb. ground beef, well-browned, drained and cooled
1	head lettuce		
4	oz. Cheddar cheese, grated	1	8 oz. can ranch style beans, drained
1	c. Thousand Island dressing		
1	6¼ oz. package tortilla chips, crushed		

Combine all ingredients and arrange on serving platter.
Serves 4 to 6.
Mrs. R. Kinnan Golemon (Jackie Burst)

Pickled Shrimp Salad

2   lb. raw shrimp, peeled and
    veined
2   medium onions, sliced
1   14 oz. can artichoke hearts,
    drained
1   5 oz. jar pimiento stuffed
    olives, drained
1½ c. salad oil

1   c. white wine vinegar
3   T. sugar
2   t. salt
1½ t. celery seed
1   garlic clove, crushed
¼   c. capers, with liquid
1   head lettuce, torn into
    bite-size pieces

Boil shrimp 3 minutes or until pink. Drain and chill. Combine shrimp,
onions, artichokes, and olives. Mix oil, vinegar, sugar, salt, celery seed,
garlic and capers; pour over shrimp mixture. Cover and refrigerate 6
hours or overnight, stirring occasionally. Toss with lettuce.
Serves 8 to 10.
Mrs. Penny Baker (Susan Bleakney)

For Tender, Flavorful Shrimp

Do not overcook.

Add shrimp to rapidly boiling, well salted water, return to boil, and
cook from 1 to 5 minutes, depending on size. Shrimp are done when
they become opaque. Drain immediately.

When deveining shrimp, don't run water over them; just dip them in
their stock.

When freezing shrimp, leave their heads on, if possible, place in plastic
containers, and fill containers with water.

Shrimp Mousse

4 T. unflavored gelatin
1 13 oz. can red Madrilene
  consommé
Juice of 1 lemon
½ t. Worcestershire sauce
Dash Tabasco
2 3 oz. packages cream cheese,
  at room temperature
½ c. sour cream
½ c. mayonnaise
¾ c. catsup

½ c. finely chopped green
  onions
½ c. finely chopped celery
¼ c. chopped parsley
1 T. chopped chives
1 lb. boiled shrimp, peeled
  and finely chopped
½ t. salt
¼ t. cayenne
Sliced, hard-cooked eggs
Parsley

Vinaigrette Dressing

1 c. olive oil
⅓ c. wine vinegar
1 t. pepper
1 t. salt
1 t. prepared Creole mustard

2 T. chopped parsley
1 T. chopped pimiento
1 T. capers
1 hard-cooked egg, chopped

Soften 2 tablespoons gelatin in ⅓ cup cool water. Combine consommé, lemon juice, Worcestershire, and Tabasco; heat to boiling. Stir in softened gelatin until dissolved. Pour enough consommé mixture into an oiled, 6 cup mold to line bottom. Refrigerate until set. Soften the two remaining tablespoons of gelatin in ⅓ cup cool water; dissolve in the remaining consommé mixture. Beat cream cheese, mayonnaise, and sour cream with mixer until smooth. Add remaining ingredients; mix well. Stir in remaining consommé mixture. Pour into the prepared mold; chill overnight. Serve the mousse with the dressing and garnish with sliced hard-cooked eggs and parsley.

Vinaigrette Dressing Combine in blender olive oil, wine vinegar, pepper, salt, mustard, and parsley. Stir in pimiento, capers, and egg. Cover and chill.
Serves 12.
Mrs. Jerry P. Bordelon (Joyce Graves)

Summer Salmon Mousse

3   T. unflavored gelatin
½ c. cold water
2   beef bouillon cubes
1   c. boiling water
¼ c. lemon juice
1   t. salt
1   c. mayonnaise
1   c. heavy cream, whipped

2   16 oz. cans salmon, drained
    and flaked
½ c. grated onion
Dash cayenne
1   t. Worcestershire sauce
Lettuce
12 large boiled shrimp, split

Soften gelatin in cold water. Dissolve bouillon cubes in boiling water; add gelatin, lemon juice, and salt. Chill until slightly thickened. Mix mayonnaise with cream; fold into chilled mixture. Add remaining ingredients; pour into an oiled, 2 quart ring mold. Chill until set. Unmold on lettuce leaves. Garnish with shrimp. Serve with Avocado Cream or Cucumber Sauce.
Serves 10 to 12 for main dish/20 as appetizer

Avocado Cream
2   large avocados
½ t. salt
½ c. sour cream
Dash Tabasco
1   T. lime or lemon juice

Combine all ingredients in blender and blend until smooth.
Yields 1½ cups

Cucumber Sauce
½ cucumber, peeled, grated,
    and drained
1   c. sour cream
½ t. salt

½ t. coarsely ground pepper
Fresh dill or dried dill weed
    to taste
1   t. lemon juice

Combine all ingredients in mixer.
Yields 1½ cups
Mrs. Charles E. Bates (Linda Steinhauser)

Red Ceviche Acapulco

2	lb. raw fresh fish fillets (red, flounder, or any firm white fish)	1	c. V-8 juice
	Juice of 9 limes	¾	c. chili sauce
1	large onion, minced	2	T. olive oil
16	stuffed olives, chopped	1	t. oregano
2	T. olive juice	½	t. cayenne
3	medium tomatoes, peeled and finely minced		Tabasco to taste
		1	clove garlic, crushed
		2	t. salt

Cut fish into bite-size pieces and cover with lime juice; all of the fish must be covered. Refrigerate overnight. Rinse in cold water and drain. Combine other ingredients and pour over fish; chill.
Be brave—the lime does cook the fish.
Serves 12 to 16
Mrs. Winston Harwood (Puddin Hopkins)

Crab Salad

1	T. unflavored gelatin		Dash cayenne
⅔	c. sour cream	1	c. diced celery
2	c. crab meat, flaked	2	T. chopped bell pepper
2	T. chili sauce	¼	c. sliced stuffed green olives
1½	T. lemon juice		
1	t. salt	2	T. grated onion

Sprinkle gelatin over ¼ cup cold water; dissolve over low heat. When cool, mix in sour cream. Stir in remaining ingredients. Pour into a 1½ quart pyrex dish and chill until firm.
Serves 6.
Mrs. James Swearingen (Jonilu Sellers)

Confetti Chicken Mold

4 c. diced, cooked chicken	2 hard-cooked eggs, chopped
1 T. finely minced green onion, including tops	1 2-oz. jar chopped pimientos, drained
1 c. finely chopped celery	½ c. mayonnaise
1 t. salt	1½ T. unflavored gelatin
1 t. pepper	¼ c. cold water
Dash cayenne	½ c. hot chicken broth
2 T. lemon juice	

Combine chicken, green onion, celery, salt, pepper, cayenne, lemon juice, eggs, pimientos, and mayonnaise. Sprinkle gelatin over cold water and soak for 10 minutes. Dissolve gelatin in hot chicken broth. Combine broth with chicken mixture; mix well. Pack in a 1 quart ice cream carton which has been dipped in cold water or a 1 quart mold. Chill until firm. Unmold and serve with caper sauce.
Serves 8.
Mrs. Maury Hughes, Jr. (Phoebe Foster)

Caper Sauce

1 c. mayonnaise
2 T. Dijon mustard
2 t. capers
1 T. lemon juice

Combine all ingredients and chill.
Yields approximately 1 cup.
Mrs. W.R. Long, III (Carol Tyler)

Entrées

Huevos Rancheros

2 yellow onions, chopped	½ t. salt
2 bell peppers, chopped	½ t. pepper
3 tomatoes, chopped	1 t. Tabasco
Jalapeño peppers, optional	⅛ t. garlic powder
6 T. bacon drippings	Scrambled or fried eggs

Sauté onions, peppers, tomatoes and jalapeños in drippings. Add salt, pepper, Tabasco, and garlic powder. Simmer, covered, for 10 minutes over medium heat. Add ¼ cup water. Simmer slowly, covered, for 30 minutes, stirring occasionally. May add additional water if mixture becomes too thick. Serve over eggs.
Serve with soft tortillas for brunch.
Yields approximately 1½ cups.
Mrs. Charles E. Bates (Linda Steinhauser)

Eggs Olé

12 hard-cooked eggs, peeled and halved	1 4½ oz. can deviled ham
Durkee's sauce	1 T. chili powder
Mayonnaise	1 t. Worcestershire sauce
Salt and pepper to taste	1 clove garlic, pressed
1 10½ oz. can condensed tomato soup	1 T finely chopped onion
1 10½ oz. can condensed cream of mushroom soup	1 T. finely chopped onion
	1 c. grated Cheddar cheese

Mash egg yolks with Durkee's, mayonnaise, salt and pepper. Fill egg whites and press halves together to make a whole egg. Arrange in a shallow 9 x 13 pyrex casserole. Mix soups, deviled ham, chili powder, Worcestershire sauce, garlic, onion, salt and pepper; pour sauce over eggs and sprinkle with cheese. (May be prepared in advance and refrigerated.) Bake at 350° in a warm water bath for approximately 30 minutes.
Serves 8 to 10.
Mrs. Charles E. Bates (Linda Steinhauser)

Egg and Cheese Strata

8 slices bread, decrusted and diced into ½ inch cubes	6 eggs, beaten
½ lb. American cheese, grated	3 c. milk
½ lb. sharp Cheddar cheese, grated	¾ t. dry mustard
	Dash salt
	Dash cayenne

Alternate layers of bread and cheese in a 2 quart, buttered soufflé dish or casserole. Mix eggs, milk, mustard, salt, and cayenne; pour over bread and cheese. Leave in refrigerator overnight. Bake at 350° for 1 hour.
Serves 4 to 6.
Mrs. Dudley McCalla (Maline Gilbert)

Savory Eggs

2 c. grated American cheese	¼ t. pepper
¼ c. butter	1 t. dry mustard
1 c. light cream	12 eggs, slightly beaten
½ t. salt	

Spread cheese in buttered 9 x 13 baking dish. Dot with butter. Combine cream, salt, pepper, and mustard. Pour half the mixture over cheese. Pour eggs into baking dish. Add remaining cream mixture. Bake at 325° for approximately 40 minutes or until set. Serve hot.
Serves 8.
Mrs. Thomas F. Sedberry (Ellen Warren)

Creole Eggs

1 large onion, finely chopped	12 hard-cooked eggs
1 c. finely chopped bell pepper	Dash cayenne
2 T. butter	Salt and pepper to taste
1 T. flour	Dash Tabasco
1 16 oz. can tomatoes, drained	Dash Worcestershire sauce
1 c. finely chopped celery	1 c. medium white sauce
1 8 oz. can mushrooms, drained	Toast

Sauté onion and peppers in butter with flour until tender but not brown. Add tomatoes, celery, mushrooms, and finely chopped egg whites. Season with cayenne, salt, pepper, Tabasco, and Worcestershire sauce. Bring to a boil, stirring constantly. Add white sauce and mashed egg yolks; mix well. Serve on toast.
Serves 10.
Mrs. Charles F. Herring (Doris Wallace)

Migas

2 T. butter	2 T. finely chopped bell pepper
Dash Tabasco	¼ c. grated Cheddar cheese
4 eggs, lightly beaten	Tostados, crumbled
2 T. finely chopped onion	

Melt butter in a large skillet; allow to cool slightly. Stir Tabasco into eggs and pour into skillet; return to heat. As soon as eggs begin to cook, add onion and bell pepper; stir. When eggs are almost cooked, add cheese and turn heat to lowest setting. Stir in crumbled tostados. Serve hot.
Serves 2.
Mrs. Charles Crites (Mildred "Milly" Holmes)

Russian Eggs

9 eggs, at room temperature	½ t. salt
5½ oz. Camembert cheese, cubed	½ c. white wine
¼ to ½ t. tarragon	½ t. curry powder
½ t. cracked pepper	

Combine all ingredients and stir. Melt butter in a skillet; pour egg mixture in and scramble. Serve immediately.
Serves 6 to 8.
Mrs. George K. Meriwether (Sara May McCampbell)

Swiss Fondue

1 clove garlic	1 scant T. Kirsch
2 T. butter	Lightly toasted, large, bite-
3 c. white wine	size pieces French bread
2 lb. cheese, chopped (Gruyère	1 egg
and/or Swiss)	

In a heavy pot, sauté garlic in butter for 2 to 3 minutes. Discard garlic and add wine; heat to boiling. Pour into fondue pot. Over heat, add cheese and stir with wire whisk until melted. Just before serving, stir in Kirsch. To serve, let each person spear French bread with a fondue fork and dip it into cheese. When you reach the bottom of the pot, stir egg and a few pieces of French bread into pot. Cook several minutes. Fondue pot should be kept over low heat during serving.
Serves 4.
Mrs. W.T. Archer (Dorothy Newton)

Beer Cheese

1 lb. sharp Cheddar cheese	1 t. salt
1 lb. mild Cheddar cheese	1 t. dry mustard
3 garlic cloves	Dash cayenne
3 T. Worcestershire sauce	¾ bottle of beer

Grind together cheeses and garlic. Stir in Worcestershire, salt, mustard, and cayenne. Using electric mixer, add enough beer to make a smooth paste.
Handy to keep on hand for several uses: a sandwich spread, a dip, or heated for a rarebit.
Yields approximately 1 quart.
Mrs. Lindsey A. Williams, Jr. (Penelope Lord)

California Cheese Casserole

2 4 oz. cans chopped green chilies, drained	2 eggs, slightly beaten
1 lb. Monterey Jack cheese, sliced	1 t. salt
½ c. flour	1 16 oz. can stewed tomatoes
2 c. milk	1 t. oregano
	1 T. minced onion

Cover bottom of a buttered, 11 x 7 (2 quart) casserole with green chilies; top with cheese. Combine flour, milk, eggs, and salt; pour over chilies and cheese. Bake at 350° for 40 minutes. Simmer tomatoes, oregano, and onion for 20 to 30 minutes; pour over hot chilies and cheese; serve.
Serves 6 to 8.
Mrs. William S. Drake, Jr. (Eleanor Critchlow)

Brunch Casserole

12 hard-cooked eggs, cut in halves	¾ c. butter, melted
½ lb. ham, diced or ground	1 lb. Velveeta brand process cheese, grated
1 t. vinegar	Approximately 2 cups medium white sauce
¾ t. dry mustard	1 lb. bacon, fried and crumbled
Salt and pepper to taste	
Dash cayenne	

Remove egg yolks and mash; add ham, vinegar, mustard, salt, pepper, cayenne, and butter. Stuff egg whites with yolk mixture and place in greased casserole. Add cheese to white sauce and pour over eggs. Top with bacon and bake at 350° for 10 minutes.
Serves 10 to 12.
Mrs. H. Philip Whitworth (Nancy Scott Denton)

Tomato-Cheese Tart

2	tomatoes, peeled	½	c. grated Provolone cheese
¼	c. flour	¾	c. grated Cheddar cheese
½	t. salt	2	eggs, slightly beaten
⅛	t. pepper	1	c. heavy cream
2	T. butter	½	t. salt
¼	c. ripe olives, sliced	⅛	t. pepper
1	c. minced green onions,	⅛	t. nutmeg
	including tops		Dash cayenne
1	9 inch pie shell, baked		Paprika

Slice tomatoes ¼ to ½ inch thick; dredge in flour seasoned with salt and pepper. Quickly sauté tomatoes in melted butter; drain. Place olives and green onions in pie shell; add tomatoes. Mix cheeses together; sprinkle over tomatoes. Combine eggs, cream, and seasonings; pour over tomatoes and cheeses. Sprinkle with paprika. Bake at 375° for 40 to 45 minutes or until set. Cool for 5 to 10 minutes before cutting. The tart may be assembled, partially baked, and refrigerated until ready to brown just before serving.
Mrs. Charles E. Bates (Linda Steinhauser)

Leek and Mushroom Quiche

¼	c. butter	1	9 inch pie shell, baked for
1	c. thinly sliced leeks,		5 minutes
	white part only	1½	c. light cream
½	lb. fresh mushrooms, sliced	3	eggs
1	c. grated Swiss or Gruyère	½	t. salt
	cheese		

In 2 tablespoons of the butter, sauté leeks until soft. Remove from pan and sauté mushrooms in remaining butter until lightly brown. Sprinkle half of the cheese over pie shell. Cover with leeks, mushrooms, and remaining cheese. Mix cream, eggs, and salt and pour into pie shell. Bake at 325° for 35 minutes.
You'll love the subtle taste of leeks.
Mrs. Jack McKay (Tinka Reilly)

Mike and Charlie's Quiche

12 slices bacon	1 t. salt
2 onions, sliced	½ t. coarsely ground black
2 c. coarsely-chopped ham	pepper
2 c. grated Cheddar cheese	½ t. dry mustard
2 c. grated Swiss cheese	⅛ t. cayenne
1 T. flour	½ t. nutmeg
2 10 inch pie shells, baked	Nutmeg, paprika, and dried
6 eggs, beaten	parsley flakes
2 c. light cream, heated	

Fry bacon until crisp and crumble, reserving drippings. Sauté onion in bacon drippings until soft; set aside. Sauté ham in the drippings for approximately 5 minutes. Combine cheeses and toss with flour. Sprinkle bacon, then onion over bottom of pie crusts. Layer half of the ham and half of the cheeses. Add the remaining ham and top with the cheeses. Beat the eggs with the warm cream, salt, pepper, dry mustard, cayenne, and nutmeg. Pour egg mixture over the filled pie shells; let stand 10 minutes. Sprinkle lightly with nutmeg, paprika, and dried parsley. Bake at 350° for 30 to 40 minutes or until custard is set. To freeze, bake pie at 350° for 20 minutes. Cool; wrap with foil and freeze. To serve, bake frozen pie for 20 minutes.
Yields 2 pies/Freezes.
Mrs. Charles E. Bates (Linda Steinhauser)

Onion Pie

4 c. sliced onions	1½ c. grated sharp Cheddar
3 eggs, slightly beaten	cheese
½ c. light cream	Paprika
½ t. salt	1 9 inch pie shell, unbaked

Parboil onions and set aside to drain. Combine all other ingredients. Stir in onions and pour into pie shell. Bake at 425° for 15 minutes; reduce heat to 350° for 20 minutes. Let pie cool several minutes before slicing.
Serve hot or cold with barbequed ribs and cole slaw.
Mrs. John Thomas (Martha Helen Hall)

Green Tomato Pie

6   green tomatoes, thinly
    sliced
2   onions, thinly sliced
1   c. grated Mozzarella cheese
1¼ c. mayonnaise

1   garlic clove, pressed
Salt and pepper to taste
1   9 inch pie shell, baked for
    5 minutes

Combine tomatoes, onions, ½ cup of the cheese, mayonnaise, garlic, salt and pepper. Pour into pie shell. Top with remaining cheese. Bake at 300° for 35 to 40 minutes.
Trust us regarding cooked mayonnaise.
Freezes.
Mrs. Robert H. Bowman (Mary Ann Lewis)

Chilaquiles

2   large white onions,
    coarsely chopped
3   cloves garlic, chopped
½   c. olive oil
2   10 oz. cans Ro-tel brand
    tomatoes and green chilies,
    undrained
1   16 oz. can tomatoes,
    undrained

1   T. coriander
Salt to taste
24 tortillas
2   lb. Monterey Jack cheese,
    grated
2   c. sour cream

Sauté onion and garlic in olive oil until tender. Add both cans of tomatoes, coriander, and salt; simmer, uncovered, approximately 10 minutes. In a separate skillet heat shortening; dip tortillas, one at a time, into hot shortening just until softened. Stack tortillas on paper towels and cut into fourths. In a 9 x 13 casserole layer tortillas, sauce, and cheese. This may be refrigerated or frozen. When ready to serve, bake at 350° for 20 to 30 minutes or until hot. Serve with sour cream.
Mexican cheese casserole.
Serves 8 to 10.
Mrs. Jean Gilbert (Jean Summers)

Fettucini

6 T. butter	1 c. grated Parmesan cheese
1½ c. heavy cream	Salt and freshly ground pepper
1 12 oz. package fine egg	to taste
noodles, cooked and drained	Dash nutmeg

Lightly brown butter in a frying pan. Add ½ cup of the cream and boil until shiny clear bubbles appear. Fold in noodles. Alternately add cheese and remaining cream in three parts. Add salt, pepper and nutmeg. Serve at once.

A godsend for the gourmet in a hurry.

Serves 8.

Mrs. Duke Matthews Covert (Lynne Carole Shapiro)

Chalupas

1 lb. dried pinto beans	3 tomatoes, chopped
1 T. salt	1 onion, chopped, optional
2 T. bacon drippings or lard	1 c. Italian dressing
1 10 oz. can Ro-tel brand	5 avocados
tomatoes and green chilies	Salt and pepper to taste
16 tortillas	3 T. lemon juice
1 head lettuce, shredded	½ lb. sharp cheese, grated

Rinse pinto beans. Cover with water, add salt, and simmer for 3 hours or until soft. Remove from heat, drain, and mash. Stir in bacon drippings and tomatoes with chilies. Keep warm in top of double boiler over low heat. Fry tortillas in hot oil until crisp; drain and salt. Marinate lettuce, tomatoes, and onion in approximately ¾ cup Italian dressing, or enough to cover. Peel and seed avocados. Mash together with salt, pepper, lemon juice, and 3 tablespoons of the Italian dressing. On each crisp tortilla spread the beans, sprinkle with cheese, and cover with lettuce and tomato mixture. Top with a tablespoon of avocado mixture.

The Mexican Dagwood—a stacked meal.

Yields 16 chalupas.

Mrs. Bryan Spires (Wesie Brenner)

Spaghetti Armando

4	tomatoes, peeled, seeded, and chopped	2	cloves garlic, crushed
1	lb. Mozzarella cheese, grated	1/3	c. olive oil
1/4	c. minced fresh basil		Salt and pepper to taste
		1	lb. hot cooked spaghetti

Combine tomatoes, cheese, basil, and garlic. Stir with olive oil, salt, and pepper; let stand 30 minutes. Toss with spaghetti and serve immediately.
Serves 4.
Mrs. Sam Fason (Maydelle Foster)

Substitute for Fresh Basil

If you must use dried basil in Pasta al Pesto or Spaghetti Armando, substitute 1½ tablespoons dried basil for each ¼ cup fresh basil and add to the recipe a handful of fresh, minced parsley and several fresh minced spinach leaves.

Pasta al Pesto

1 c. chopped fresh basil leaves	Pepper to taste
2 T. pine nuts or walnuts	¼ c. grated Parmesan cheese
1 clove garlic	¼ c. grated Romano cheese
½ t. salt	1 c. olive oil
	12 oz. spaghetti, cooked

Place basil, nuts, garlic, salt, and pepper in blender and purée. Add cheeses and oil; blend for 1 minute. Serve warm over hot spaghetti. *For those who know their gastronomy.*
Serves 4/Sauce freezes.
Mrs. Sam Fason (Maydelle Foster)

Carbonara

8 slices bacon	4 to 5 eggs, beaten
1 medium onion, chopped	8 oz. thin spaghetti, cooked and drained
½ c. grated Parmesan cheese	Salt to taste
4 oz. Swiss cheese, grated	

Fry bacon and crumble. In bacon drippings, sauté onion. Combine the cheeses, bacon, onion, and eggs. Toss mixture with spaghetti. Sprinkle with salt. Serve immediately.
Serves 4.
Mrs. Thomas F. Reese (Mary Lynn Roth)

Crêpes Florentine

Basic Crêpes

3 eggs, separated	½ t. salt
1 c. milk	½ c. flour
1 T. vegetable oil	½ t. cream of tartar
1 t. sugar	

In blender, beat egg yolks slightly. Add ½ cup of the milk, oil, sugar, salt, and flour; beat until smooth and add remaining milk. Beat egg whites, adding cream of tartar, until stiff and fold into batter. Refrigerate several hours or overnight. Heat crêpe pan over moderately high heat and brush lightly with butter or cooking oil. Spoon a scant ¼ cup of batter into the middle of pan. Quickly tilt pan in all directions so that batter covers pan with a thin film. Cook approximately 1 minute; turn crêpe and cook approximately 30 seconds. Slide crêpe onto a plate and continue with remaining batter, greasing pan lightly when necessary. Crêpes can be stacked, separated by wax paper.
Yields 8 crêpes.

Florentine filling

1 medium onion, chopped	2 c. grated Monterey Jack cheese
7 T. butter	
6 T. flour	½ lb. mushrooms, sliced
3 c. milk	2 10 oz. packages fresh spinach, cooked and drained
1 t. salt	
⅛ t. Tabasco	¼ c. heavy cream, whipped

Sauté onion in 4 tablespoons of the butter; add flour and milk, stirring constantly until mixture thickens. Remove from heat and stir in salt, Tabasco, and cheese. Set aside ½ cup of the sauce for topping. Sauté mushrooms in remaining butter and stir into cheese sauce along with spinach. Spread ¼ cup of the filling on each crêpe, roll, and arrange in a buttered 2½ quart baking dish. Fold whipped cream into reserved cheese sauce and spoon over crêpes. Heat at 425° for 15 to 20 minutes until hot and cheese topping has browned lightly.
Serves 8/Freezes.
Mrs. David Davenport (Diane Wilder)

Beef Tenderloin

1   beef tenderloin, approximately
    4 lb., at room temperature
Worcestershire sauce
3   cloves garlic, slivered
Bacon slices

Sprinkle tenderloin generously with Worcestershire sauce. Arrange garlic slivers and bacon slices over meat. Place, uncovered, in a roasting pan. Roast at 400° approximately 40 minutes for rare.
Serves 8.
Mrs. George O. Slaughter (Hallie Groos)

Beef Tenderloin Stuffed with Mushrooms

4 lb. beef tenderloin	1/8 t. pepper
1/4 c. butter	1/8 t. sage
1 lb. mushrooms, chopped	1/8 t. thyme
1/2 c. chopped celery	2 T. flour
1/2 c. chopped onion	Salt and pepper to taste
1/4 c. chopped bell pepper	Sliced mushrooms
1 t. salt	Parsley

Have butcher cut a pocket in beef, or, using a long knife, start at the widest end and slit the tenderloin down the middle, being careful not to cut through the sides. Melt butter in a skillet; add mushrooms and brown. Add celery, onion, bell pepper, salt, pepper, sage, and thyme. Sauté until the vegetables are tender. Blend in flour; cook for 1 minute. Stuff mixture into pocket of beef. Fasten opening with skewers; lace with string. Season with additional salt and pepper. May be refrigerated until ready to bake; 1 hour before roasting, remove from refrigerator and let meat reach room temperature. Roast in a 325° oven for 20 minutes per pound for medium rare. Serve garnished with mushrooms and parsley.
Serves 12.
Mrs. Homer Scace (Betty Gatch)

Pineapple Beef Teriyaki

¼	c. packed brown sugar	1	minced garlic clove
¼	c. soy sauce	2	lb. sirloin or tenderloin,
2	T. lemon juice		cut in 1 inch pieces
1	T. vegetable oil	1	pineapple, cut in 1 inch
¼	t. ginger		chunks

Mix all ingredients except pineapple; marinate, covered, in refrigerator for at least 1½ hours. Skewer meat and pineapple; broil.
Oriental kabobs.
Serves 4 to 6.
Mrs. Benjamin McPherson, Jr. (Marie Lois Leopold)

Tuscan Roast

1	5-lb. top or bottom round roast	2	cloves garlic, minced
Salt		¾	c. butter
2	T. vegetable oil	2	tomatoes, chopped
1	c. red wine	2	c. pitted ripe olives, chopped
1	c. water	1	t. salt
2	bell peppers, chopped	2	T. wine vinegar
1	bunch green onions, chopped		

Sprinkle roast with salt and brown in oil. Simmer in wine and water for 2½ to 3 hours. Sauté peppers, green onions, and garlic in ¼ cup of the butter. Stir in tomatoes, olives, salt, and vinegar. Slice roast vertically, almost to the bottom. Baste with remaining butter and pack vegetable mixture between slices. Wrap tightly in aluminum foil and let stand 1 to 2 hours. Serve at room temperature.
Serves 8.
Mrs. John Philip Ferguson (Mitzi Ann Riddle)

Brisket and Sauerkraut

3	lb. beef brisket	2	c. water
1	onion, chopped		Salt and pepper to taste
3	T. bacon drippings	1	T. caraway seed
1	27 oz. can sauerkraut	1	c. dry white wine

Tie brisket into a compact shape. Sauté onions in bacon drippings. Add brisket and brown thoroughly on all sides. Pour sauerkraut over meat. Add water and simmer, covered, for 3 hours, or until tender. Add salt, pepper, caraway seed, and wine during last 30 minutes of cooking.
Serves 6 to 8/Freezes.
Mrs. Warren Freund, Jr. (Karen Thatcher)

Beef à la Deutsch

1	lb. ground beef	1	5 oz. package thin egg noodles, cooked and drained
1	8 oz. can tomato sauce		
1	clove garlic, crushed	1	c. sour cream
2	t. salt	1	3 oz. package cream cheese, at room temperature
	Pepper to taste		
2	t. sugar	6	green onions, chopped
1	16 oz. can tomatoes, undrained	1½	c. grated Cheddar cheese

Brown meat; drain excess drippings and add tomato sauce, garlic, salt, pepper, sugar, and tomatoes. Simmer, covered, over low heat for 45 minutes. Combine hot noodles with cubed cream cheese and stir to melt cheese; add sour cream and green onions. Layer meat, noodle mixture, and Cheddar cheese alternately in an oiled, 3 quart casserole. Bake, uncovered, at 350° for 35 minutes. Flavor improves when reheated.
Serves 4 to 6/Freezes.
Mrs. John C. Donovan (Anne Peterson)

Lemon Barbequed Steak

1 2 lb. steak, 1½ inches thick	1½ t. salt
1 t. grated lemon peel	⅛ t. pepper
⅔ c. lemon juice	1 t. Worcestershire sauce
⅓ c. vegetable oil	1 t. prepared mustard
	2 green onion tops, sliced

Score fat edges of meat and place in a shallow dish. Combine remaining ingredients and pour over steak. Let stand 3 hours at room temperature or 6 hours in refrigerator, turning several times. Remove from marinade and blot to remove excess moisture. Grill over hot coals, brushing occasionally with marinade.
Lemon juice tenderizes an economical cut of meat.
Serves 4.
Mrs. John Philip Ferguson (Mitzi Ann Riddle)

Pepper Steak Caballero

1½ lb. sirloin steak, cut into ⅛ inch strips	2 large tomatoes, peeled and diced
1 T. paprika	1 c. beef broth
Salt and pepper to taste	¼ c. water
2 cloves garlic, crushed	2 T. cornstarch
2 T. butter	2 T. soy sauce
1 c. sliced green onions, with tops	3 c. hot cooked rice
2 bell peppers, cut into strips	

Sprinkle steak with paprika, salt, and pepper. Stir fry steak with garlic in butter until meat is browned. Add onions and bell peppers, cooking until vegetables wilt. Stir in tomatoes and broth; cover and simmer 15 minutes. Blend water with cornstarch and soy sauce; stir into steak and boil rapidly until thick. Serve over rice.
Serves 6/Freezes.
Mrs. Don Flournoy (Mary Faulkner Marsh)

Anacuchos

1¼ c. wine vinegar		4	chili serranos or jalapeño peppers, finely chopped
1 c. water		1	t. oregano
2 t. salt		3	lb. boneless sirloin steak, cut into 1½-inch squares
½ t. pepper			
2 garlic cloves, crushed			

Combine all ingredients, except meat, in blender and whirl until thoroughly puréed. Pour over meat and marinate in a glass container 8 to 10 hours or overnight. Turn occasionally if meat is not covered by liquid. Remove from marinade and arrange 4 or 5 pieces on each skewer. Broil, brushing frequently with marinade.
Skewered beef.
Serves 6.
Mrs. George O. Slaughter (Hallie Groos)

Pot Roast

1	3 to 4 lb. beef chuck or boneless sirloin roast	1	carrot cut into strips
1	t. salt	¾	c. dry red wine
¼	t. pepper	¾	c. sour cream, at room temperature
2	T. vegetable oil	½	c. water
1	clove garlic, minced	2 to 3	T. flour
½	t. Beau Monde	1	T. lemon juice
1	onion, sliced		

Rub meat with salt and pepper. Brown meat in oil over medium heat in Dutch oven. Add garlic, Beau Monde, onion and carrot. Sauté for 3 minutes or until the onions are golden. Reduce heat; stir in wine and sour cream. Cover and slowly simmer for 2 to 2½ hours or until meat is tender. Remove meat; skim fat from pan juices. Make a paste of flour and water. Add to pan juices, stirring until thickened. Add more water if gravy is too thick. Stir in lemon juice.
Serves 6 to 8/Freezes.
Mrs. Charles Michael Smith (Sally Thomas)

French Beef

1	6 to 7 lb. chuck roast, rolled or boned	1	T. savory
1	bay leaf	1	T. garlic powder
1	T. cracked pepper	1	beef bouillon cube
1	T. salt		Salt and pepper to taste
1	T. oregano		Pumpernickel or onion rolls
1	T. rosemary		Hot mustard

Place roast in large pan. Cover halfway with water. Add all remaining ingredients except bread and mustard and bring to a boil. Reduce heat and barely simmer, covered, 8 to 9 hours. Check every hour or two, sprinkling with salt and pepper each time. Do not add water. Just before serving, shred meat with 2 forks. Serve on pumpernickel or onion rolls with hot mustard.
Serves 16.
Mrs. James A. Williams (Priscilla Nichols)

Hot Mustard

1 c. dry mustard
1 c. cider vinegar
1 c. packed brown sugar
1 egg, beaten

Mix mustard and vinegar and allow to stand for 2 hours. Stir in brown sugar and egg. Cook in double boiler until thick. Refrigerate.
Served with Chinese food, meats, vegetables, and sandwiches.
Yields 2 cups.
Mrs. Thomas F. Reese (Mary Lynn Roth)

Cold Pepper Roast

4 to 5 lb. rolled eye of round roast	Salt and coarsely ground pepper to taste
Unseasoned meat tenderizer	1 T. rosemary
Garlic salt to taste	Hot mustard

Sprinkle meat thoroughly with tenderizer; let stand several hours or overnight. Sprinkle with garlic salt, salt, pepper, and rosemary, pressing as much into meat as possible. Insert meat thermometer into thickest part of meat; roast at 350° until thermometer reaches 130° (approximately 1½ to 2½ hours). It must be rare to be tender. Chill thoroughly. Slice very thinly and serve with hot mustard.

A natural for cocktail parties and summertime entrées.
Serves 8 to 10.
Mrs. Wayland Rivers (Ann Staacke)

Carne Asada

1½ lb. round steak
Worcestershire Sauce
Garlic salt
Pepper

Trim excess fat and gristle from meat. Tenderize by pounding with mallet. Cut into long strips 1½ inches wide. Marinate strips in Worcestershire sauce, garlic salt, and pepper overnight. Grill over charcoal, 5 minutes on each side.

A perfect accompaniment to Green Tomato Enchiladas, page 135.
Serves 6 to 8.
Mrs. James H. Albright (Mary Margaret Carlson)

Corned Beef Blackburn

7 qt. water	20 peppercorns
Approximately 3 c. rock salt	1 bay leaf
1 raw egg in shell	1 t. thyme
1 6 to 9 lb. beef brisket	1½ t. saltpeter (at drug
3 cloves garlic	store)
20 whole cloves	

Pour water into a large earthenware crock, or an enamel or stainless steel bowl. Add salt, stirring to dissolve. Test salt content by placing egg in crock. If egg floats, brine is ready. If not, continue to add salt in small amounts until egg floats. Remove egg and add brisket, garlic, cloves, peppercorns, bay leaf, thyme, and saltpeter; stir well. Place a heavy weight on meat so it remains covered by brine. Cover crock and refrigerate 8 to 12 days. Turn brisket occasionally, but keep it covered with weight. To cook corned beef, remove from brine and rinse well.

To Cook Corned Beef

1 6 to 9 lb. corned beef	1 clove garlic, sliced
1 bay leaf	1 carrot, cut into 3 inch
1 onion, sliced	lengths
1 t. thyme	2 ribs celery, cut into
16 peppercorns	3 inch lengths

Place ingrediets in a large kettle. Add water to 1 inch over top of beef. Bring to a boil and simmer for 2½ to 3 hours.
Homemade is best.
Serves 12 to 14.
Mrs. Frank N. Ikard, Jr. (Carol Foster)

Meat Loaf

4 lb. ground beef	4 t. salt
1 lb. salt pork, ground	4 t. lemon juice
8 egg yolks	1 small onion, chopped
1⅓ c. bread crumbs	6 T. milk
⅓ c. chopped parsley	1 lemon, seeded and finely
1 t. pepper	chopped, rind included

Combine all ingredients and blend well. Pack into 3 greased 9 x 5 x 3 loaf pans. Add 3 tablespoons of water to each pan. Dot with butter. Bake at 350° for 1 hour. Serve hot or cold.
Beef and lemon belong together.
Serves 4 to 6 per loaf/Freezes.
Mrs. Edward Robinson, Jr. (Mercedes Jensen)

Stew in a Pumpkin

2	c. chopped onion	2	c. beef broth
2	c. chopped bell pepper	2	c. sliced yellow squash
2	T. olive oil	2	c. cut fresh green beans
2	T. butter	2	c. carrots, cut into
3	lb. stew meat		½ inch rounds
2	t. salt	1	16 oz. can tomatoes,
Pepper to taste			drained
1	bay leaf	1	10½ oz. package frozen
½	t. thyme		or 1 12-oz. can corn
1	T. tomato paste	1	pumpkin
2	cloves garlic, minced	½	c. milk
½	c. dry red wine	Salt and pepper	

Slightly brown onion and pepper in olive oil and butter. Remove to a large oven-proof casserole. Brown meat, adding more olive oil, if necessary, and mix with onions. Stir in seasonings, tomato paste, garlic, and wine. Simmer, covered, for 5 minutes. Add broth and bring to a simmer. Cover and bake at 325° for 1½ hours. Stir in vegetables and return to oven for 20 to 30 minutes. Slice off top of pumpkin and scoop out inside. Rinse with milk and sprinkle with salt and pepper. Replace top and bake on a cookie sheet at 350° for 45 minutes to 1 hour. Ladle hot stew into pumpkin for serving. Scoop a little pumpkin out with each serving.
When the frost is on the pumpkin and the stew is in it, you have a winner.
Serves 6 to 8/Stew freezes.
Mrs. John Morehead (Susan Kline)

Beef Jerky

1 to 2 lb. flank steak
Garlic salt
Freshly ground pepper

Soy sauce
Worcestershire sauce

Trim all fat from meat and slice *with* the grain into thin strips. Place in a shallow glass pan and sprinkle well with remaining ingredients; toss to coat. Cover tightly and refrigerate 6 to 12 hours, stirring occasionally. Arrange strips on a wire rack above a cookie sheet. Bake at 150° for 8 to 10 hours. Store in an air-tight jar.
Mrs. Tom McCrummen, Jr. (Marian Marley)

Flank Steak with Onions

1   flank steak, approximately
    1½ lb.
⅓   c. vinegar
⅓   c. vegetable oil

3   T. brown sugar
3   T. soy sauce
2   medium onions, sliced
½   t. coarsely ground pepper

Place steak in shallow pyrex dish. Combine remaining ingredients; pour over steak. Cover and refrigerate 8 hours or overnight, turning occasionally. Remove steak and onions from marinade; sauté onions in additional vegetable oil until just tender. Broil or grill steak; slice thinly across the grain and serve topped with sautéed onions.
Serves 4.
Mrs. Jack A. Collins (Nancy Chapman)

Oriental Beef

1   lb. flank or round steak,
    thinly sliced into bite-
    size pieces
3   T. soy sauce
3   T. corn starch
½   c. peanut oil
½   lb. spinach, rinsed and
    finely chopped

1   5 oz. can water chestnuts,
    thinly sliced
6   T. soy sauce
½   t. monosodium glutamate
3   c. hot, cooked rice

Marinate beef in soy sauce and corn starch for 5 minutes. Over high heat, sauté beef in oil for approximately 2 minutes, until brown. Stir in remaining ingredients and toss until spinach begins to wilt. Serve over hot rice.
Distinctively different.
Serves 6.
Mrs. James Chrisman Phillips (Meg Phillips)

Broiled Flank Steak

4 T. vegetable oil	1 t. pepper
2 T. wine vinegar	½ t. basil
1 onion, chopped	½ t. rosemary
2 cloves garlic, crushed	1½ to 2 lb. flank steak
2 t. salt	Mushrooms, optional

Combine oil, vinegar, onion, garlic, salt, pepper, basil, and rosemary in a shallow glass pan. Coat both sides of meat with mixture and marinate for 2 hours or more. Broil meat 3 to 6 inches from heat for approximately 5 to 7 minutes. Turn, brush with marinade, and broil for another 4 to 6 minutes. Slice meat diagonally across the grain as thinly as possible. If desired, add mushrooms to the marinade, then pour marinade over meat. This may be made ahead of time, then wrapped in foil and kept warm in 175° oven.
Serves 4 to 6.
Mrs. William Green (Jeanie Mullins)

Chipped Beef Deluxe

¼ lb. mushrooms, sliced	1 c. milk
2 T. butter	1 c. sour cream
¼ lb. chipped beef	1 c. grated Cheddar cheese
2 T. minced onion	2 T. chopped parsley
½ c. butter	Toast points or toasted
3 T. flour	English muffins

Sauté mushrooms in 2 tablespoons butter. In a heavy skillet sauté beef and onion in ½ cup butter until onion is translucent. Blend in flour and milk; simmer, stirring, until thick and smooth. Remove from heat; add mushrooms, sour cream, and cheese. Stir until well blended and cheese is melted. Garnish with parsley. Serve over toast points or toasted English muffins.
Serves 4.
Mrs. James M. Dunnam (Anne Jeffers)

Stefado with Wild Rice

½ c. butter	2 cloves garlic, crushed
3 lb. beef round steak, cut into bite-size pieces	1 bay leaf
	1 cinnamon stick
2½ lb. small onions, peeled	¼ t. cumin
1 6 oz. can tomato paste	½ t. whole cloves
⅓ c. dry red wine	4 c. cooked wild rice or
2 T. red wine vinegar	long grain and wild rice
1 T. brown sugar	combination

Melt butter in a large skillet and set aside. When butter has cooled, place meat in skillet and coat with butter; top with onions. Combine tomato paste, red wine, vinegar, brown sugar, and garlic; pour over meat and onions. Add bay leaf, cinnamon stick, cumin, and cloves. Cover and simmer for 3 hours; do not remove cover while cooking. Remove cinnamon stick and cloves. Serve with wild rice.
Spicy Greek stew.
Serves 8.
Mrs. Philip F. Patman (Katherine Ashley Sellers)

Meat Pie Robertson

½ lb. ground beef
½ c. mayonnaise
½ c. milk
2 eggs
1 T. cornstarch

¾ c. grated Cheddar cheese
¾ c. grated Swiss cheese
⅓ c. sliced green onions
Salt and pepper to taste
1 9 inch pie shell, unbaked

Brown meat; drain and set aside. Blend mayonnaise, milk, eggs, and cornstarch until smooth. Stir in meat, cheeses, onion, salt, and pepper. Turn into pastry shell. Bake at 350° for 35 to 40 minutes.
Serves 4 to 6/Freezes.
Mrs. Pat H. Robertson (Carol Worthen)

Rouläden

10 ¼ inch thick slices sirloin
    tip or round steak. Meat
    should be 8 to 10 inches
    long and 3 to 4 inches
    wide
Dusseldorf mustard
1 large onion, thinly sliced

Sweet pickle relish
Salt and pepper
10 slices bacon
Olive oil
1 T. flour
Pinch sugar

Trim meat of all fat and gristle; lay on a flat surface. Liberally spread mustard on each slice. Arrange onion slices on large end of meat; add relish toward the middle. Sprinkle with salt and pepper. Lay bacon lengthwise on meat. Roll each piece, starting with wide end. Tie securely with thread. Brown meat rolls in olive oil, turning once. Add enough hot water to cover meat halfway. Simmer, covered, for approximately 1 hour. When tender, remove meat rolls from liquid and arrange on a warm serving platter. Remove thread. Mix flour with 4 teaspoons cold water and sugar; stir into sauce and simmer until slightly thickened. Pour sauce over meat rolls.
Serves 4/Freezes.
Mrs. Norman M. Barker (Mary Brownlee)

Herbed Beef Stew with Almond-Poppy Seed Noodles

¼	c. butter	½	t. savory
4	lb. beef chuck, cut into 1½ inch cubes	2	bay leaves, crushed
1	lb. mushrooms, sliced	¼	t. pepper
6	yellow onions, coarsely chopped	1	10½ oz. can condensed beef consommé
2	cloves garlic, crushed	2	28 oz. cans tomatoes
1	T. salt	1	bunch carrots, peeled and cut into 2 inch pieces
1	t. dried dill weed	6	T. flour
¾	t. basil	½	c. cold water
½	t. thyme		Parsley or green peas

Almond-Poppy Seed Noodles

1	c. butter	½	c. poppy seeds
1½	c. slivered almonds, chopped	¾ to 1	t. salt
		2	8 oz. packages noodles

Melt butter in large kettle or Dutch oven; brown meat, a few pieces at a time. Add mushrooms, onions, garlic, salt, dill, basil, thyme, savory, bay leaves, and pepper; sauté slowly, stirring occaionally until onions and mushrooms are tender. Add consommé and tomatoes; simmer 1½ hours or until meat is tender. Add carrots and simmer, covered, until carrots are tender. Mix flour with cold water until smooth; add gradually to stew, stirring constantly. Continue to stir and heat until gravy is thickened. Garnish with parsley or green peas and serve with Almond-Poppy Seed Noodles.

Noodles   Melt butter slowly so that it does not brown; add almonds, poppy seeds, and salt and sauté gently until almonds are a light brown. Cook noodles in salted water; drain and turn into serving dish. Pour butter mixture over and toss lightly.

Serves 20/Stew freezes.
Mrs. Charles E. Bates (Linda Steinhauser)

Cornish Pasties

Pie dough for double crust pie
1   lb. sirloin steak or tips,
    cut in small cubes
3   potatoes, peeled and cut
    in small cubes

3   green onions, finely
    chopped
Salt and pepper to taste

Roll pie dough ⅛ inch thick; cut into 6 circles that are 6 inches in diameter. Mix remaining ingredients; place ⅙ of mixture in the center of each circle. Moisten edge of each pastie; press halves together and seal with a fork. Make a slit in each. Bake at 425° for 15 minutes. Reduce oven to 300° and continue baking until browned. May be served hot or cold.
Pack in a picnic basket.
Yields 6 pasties/Freezes.
Mrs. C. Dale Parker (Marilyn Burns)

Cabbage Rolls

1   cabbage, approximately
    2½ lb.
1   lb. ground beef
½   c. uncooked rice
1   egg
¼   c. diced onion
1   t. pepper

2   t. salt
1   c. beef broth or bouillon
1   16 oz. can tomatoes,
    undrained
2   T. flour
1½ T. sugar

Core cabbage and place in a deep pan. Pour boiling water to cover and set pan over low heat. As leaves become pliable, remove them. Combine meat, rice, egg, onion, pepper, and 1 teaspoon of the salt. Place approximately 1 tablespoon of the meat mixture on each cabbage leaf; roll leaves, tucking ends underneath. Arrange rolls in layers in a Dutch oven and pour broth over them. Simmer, covered, over low heat for 1 hour. Pour tomatoes over cabbage rolls and cook 1 hour. Make a sauce of the flour, sugar, remaining 1 teaspoon of salt, and enough water to make a thin paste. Add to cabbage rolls and cook 30 minutes.
A small wrapped gift.
Serves 4/Freezes.
Mrs. James A. Williams (Priscilla Nichols)

Savory Meat Balls

1 lb. ground meat (venison, antelope, beef)
⅓ lb. ground pork
½ c. applesauce
¾ c. bread crumbs
1 egg, slightly beaten

1 medium size onion, chopped
Salt and pepper
Flour
3 T. bacon drippings
⅔ c. catsup
½ c. water

Combine meats, applesauce, bread crumbs, egg, onion, salt and pepper. Shape into small balls for appetizers, larger balls for an entrée. Roll in flour and brown in bacon drippings. Transfer to a shallow casserole. Mix catsup and water and pour over meat balls. Bake, covered, at 375° 35 to 40 minutes.
Serves 4 to 6/Freezes.
Mrs. James M. Dunnam (Anne Jeffers)

Lasagne Napoli

1 medium onion, finely chopped
1 clove garlic, crushed
2 T. olive oil
1 lb. ground beef
10 mushrooms, sliced
1 8 oz. can tomato sauce
1 6 oz. can tomato paste
2 t. salt
1 t. oregano
¾ c. water

2 eggs
1 10 oz. package frozen spinach
1 c. cream-style cottage cheese
¾ c. grated Parmesan cheese
1 12 oz. package lasagne, cooked and drained
16 oz. Mozzarella cheese, grated

Sauté onion and garlic in 1 tablespoon of the olive oil. Add ground beef and brown. Blend in mushrooms, tomato sauce, tomato paste, 1 teaspoon of the salt, oregano, and water. Simmer 15 minutes. Combine one of the eggs, spinach, cottage cheese, Parmesan, 1 tablespoon of the olive oil and 1 teaspoon of the salt. Beat the other egg slightly and toss with the cooked lasagne. Pour half the meat mixture into a 9 x 13 baking pan. Cover with a layer of half the lasagne. Sprinkle with half of the

Mozzarella cheese, then cover with all the spinach mixture. Complete the layers with remaining meat and lasagne. Cover and bake at 350° for 45 minutes. Arrange the remaining Mozzarella cheese on top, cover and bake 15 minutes.
Spinach is the difference.
Serves 8 to 10/Freezes.
Mrs. Leon Bronson Dorsey, Jr. (Cathryn Seymour)

Lasagne

1   lb. ground beef
1   lb. bulk sausage, hot or regular
2   onions, chopped
2   15 oz. cans tomato sauce
1   12 oz. can tomato paste
1   16 oz. can stewed tomatoes undrained
1 to 2 packages spaghetti sauce mix

Salt and pepper to taste
Dash basil
Pinch sugar
16 oz. lasagne noodles
4   eggs beaten with 2 16-oz. cartons cream-style cottage cheese
2   c. grated Parmesan cheese
6   oz. Mozzarella cheese

Brown beef, sausage, and onions, pouring off excess liquid. Stir in tomato sauce, tomato paste, tomatoes, and spaghetti sauce mix, salt, pepper, basil, and sugar; simmer 30 minutes. Boil noodles in water for 15 minutes, adding a few drops of olive oil. Drain. While noodles cook, mix eggs with cottage cheese. In 2 buttered 9 x 13 casseroles, layer noodles, meat sauce, salt, pepper, eggs, cheese, and Parmesan cheese. Repeat layers. Bake at 350° for 30 minutes; add Mozzarella cheese and return to oven for 5 to 10 minutes.
Serves16/Freezes.
Mrs. John H. Coates (Ann Cox)

Spaghetti with Beef and Wine Sauce

2	T. olive oil	1	lb. beef chuck, ground twice
2	T. butter	1½	t. salt
2	garlic cloves, minced		Freshly ground pepper to taste
3	T. minced Canadian bacon or prosciutto	2	c. beef bouillon
		½	c. dry Marsala
8	mushrooms, chopped	8	oz. spaghetti, cooked

Heat oil and butter and gently brown garlic; add mushrooms, bacon or prosciutto, and sauté 3 to 4 minutes. Add beef, salt, and pepper; brown meat, stirring to break it up, for 15 minutes. Mix in bouillon and wine; simmer uncovered for 10 minutes. Correct seasoning. Spoon over spaghetti and serve at once.

Spaghetti sauce sans tomato.
Serves 4 to 6/Freezes.
Mrs. William A. Penn (Lou Boyd)

Chilies Rellenos

8	chilies poblanos	½	c. raisins, plumped in boiling water
1	T. vegetable oil		
1	c. finely chopped onion	4	eggs, separated
1	lb. ground beef		Flour
1	lb. ground pork	½	lb. grated Cheddar cheese, optional
1	T. whole cumin seed		
1¾	t. salt	1	c. sour cream
¾	t. pepper		

Sauce

1	c. finely chopped onion	½	t. salt
2	T. vegetable oil	3	medium tomatoes, finely chopped
2	fresh jalapeños, finely chopped		

Drop chilies into boiling water just long enough to heat through. Put each chili on a long fork and hold it over a flame, turning constantly so it won't burn, until the skin pops and blisters all over. Immediately wrap in a damp towel for an hour; remove skin, then veins and seeds through a lengthwise slit in the side. Sauté onion in the oil; add meat to brown. Add cumin seed, 1½ teaspoons of the salt, pepper, and raisins. Stuff the chilies with meat mixture and secure with toothpicks. Stiffly beat the egg whites. Add the yolks, slightly beaten, and ¼ teaspoon of the salt. Roll the stuffed chilies in flour, dip in the egg and fry in 1½ inches of moderately hot oil until golden. May serve immediately or place in casserole, sprinkle cheese on top, and warm until cheese melts. Serve with bowls of sour cream, sauce, and any left-over meat.

Sauce Sauté onion in oil, then add remaining ingredients. Simmer 10 minutes.
Mexico's haute cuisine.
Serves 4 to 6/Freezes.
Mrs. John H. Tyler, Jr. (Patricia Robinson)

Liver Teriyaki

1	lb. calf's liver	¼	t. dry mustard
¼	c. soy sauce	¼	t. onion powder
¼	c. vinegar	⅛	t. garlic powder
2	T. honey or sugar	¼	c. vegetable oil
½	t. ginger	2	c. cooked rice or noodles

Place liver in shallow pan. Combine soy sauce, vinegar and seasonings, and pour over liver; marinate 20 minutes. Remove liver from marinade and slice into very thin strips. Heat oil in a skillet and stir-fry liver until light pink in center, 3 to 4 minutes. Do not overcook. Serve over rice or noodles.
Serves 4.
Mrs. Victor Szebehely (Jo Betsy Lewallen)

Sautéed Liver with Herbs

1	lb. calf's liver, thinly sliced (slice while partially frozen)	⅛	t. pepper
		3	T. butter
		¼	t. chopped parsley
2	T. flour	¼	t. thyme
1	t. Mei Yen seasoning	½	c. dry sherry or dry vermouth
½	t. salt		

Dip liver in combined flour, Mei Yen seasoning, salt, and pepper. Quickly sauté liver in butter over medium high heat, turning only once. Remove to a heated platter. Add parsley, thyme, and wine to pan drippings. Bring to a boil and simmer 2 to 3 minutes, scraping pan well. Pour sauce over liver and serve at once.
Serves 4.
Mrs. James Chrisman Phillips (Meg Phillips)

German Cheese Schnitzel

1½	lb. cube steak or veal cutlets	½	c. fine bread crumbs
2	T. lemon juice	⅓	c. grated Parmesan cheese
Pepper		⅓	c. flour
2	eggs	6	T. butter
2	T. cold water	Paprika	
2	T. vegetable oil	Lemon slices	

Sprinkle both sides of meat with lemon juice. Let stand at room temperature for 30 minutes. Sprinkle both sides with pepper. Blend eggs, water, and oil in a bowl. Combine bread crumbs and cheese in another bowl. Coat meat with flour, then dip in egg mixture. Let excess roll off, then coat with cheese mixture. Let stand 15 minutes. Melt butter in a large skillet and sauté meat. Sprinkle with Parmesan cheese and paprika and garnish with lemon slices.
Serves 4.
Mrs. Charles Crites (Mildred "Milly" Holmes)

Veal Scaloppine alla Vanessa

1½ lb. sliced veal, cut into
    2 inch squares and pounded
    until thin
Flour
2 T. olive oil
1 T. butter
2 medium green onions, finely
    chopped

1 clove garlic, minced
½ lb. mushroom caps, sliced
Salt and pepper to taste
Pinch rosemary
½ c. dry Marsala
1 t. minced parsley

Dredge veal in flour; sauté quickly on both sides in olive oil and butter. Remove to warm platter. Stir in onions, garlic, mushrooms, salt, pepper, and rosemary. Simmer for 2 minutes. Stir in Marsala and parsley and simmer for 5 minutes. Pour sauce over veal.
Serves 6/Freezes.
Mrs. Robert L. Buford, Jr. (Nancy Peoples)

Fresh Tomato Veal Cutlets

¼ c. vegetable oil
2 lb. veal cutlets
½ c. water
6 tomatoes, peeled
¼ c. chopped green onions

2 T. sugar
2 t. salt
2 t. basil
2 T. cornstarch

In large skillet over medium-high heat, in hot oil, sauté the veal, several pieces at a time, approximately 10 minutes. Remove to a heated platter and keep warm. Reduce heat to medium; add to skillet ¼ cup of the water, 3 of the tomatoes, chopped, onions, sugar, salt, and basil. In a small bowl blend cornstarch and the remaining ¼ cup cold water until smooth. Gradually stir into the tomato mixture, stirring constantly until thickened. Slice the remaining 3 tomatoes and add. Cook until hot and spoon over meat. Serve immediately.
Serves 6 to 8.
Mrs. Charles Crites (Mildred "Milly" Holmes)

Oven Barbecued Beef Brisket

4 to 5 lb. boneless beef
    brisket
Salt and pepper to taste

Garlic powder to taste
1 c. barbecue sauce
1 c. water

Sprinkle both sides of the brisket with salt, pepper, and garlic powder. Cook covered with no water at 325°, allowing 1 hour per pound. Before last hour of cooking, remove brisket and slice. Return to pan and add barbecue sauce mixed with water. Almost cover meat with sauce; cook 1 hour longer, covered.
Serves 8 to 10.
Mrs. William Milstead (Jacqueline Wheeler)

Barbeque Sauce

1 14 oz. bottle catsup
1 5 oz. bottle Worcestershire
    Sauce
1 c. vinegar
½ c. brown sugar
2 T. dry mustard

2 T. prepared horseradish
2 T. Tabasco
1 can beer
2 T. butter
Juice of 1 lemon
Salt to taste

Stir all together in a pot and simmer, uncovered, until sauce is thick, approximately 3 to 5 hours.
Yields 1 quart.
Mrs. John Coates (Ann Cox)

Glazed Pork Ribs

3 to 4 pounds pork ribs
Approximately ½ c. apricot
  preserves
Approximately ¼ c. soy sauce

Arrange pork ribs in 9 x 13 casserole. Pour apricot preserves and soy sauce over ribs. Cover and bake at 300° for 3 hours, removing cover for the last 30 minutes to allow ribs to brown. If browning too much, additional soy sauce and water may be added.
Serves 4.
Mrs. James Kreisle (Natalie Atwell)

Roast Pork with Apricot Glaze

1 loin, rib, or shoulder
   pork roast
Salt and pepper
Whole cloves

1 c. dried apricots
2 c. water
½ c. brown sugar
1 T. cornstarch

Score roast. Rub with salt and pepper; stick with cloves. Place on rack in open roasting pan, fat side up. Roast at 350° for 35 minutes per lb. Simmer apricots in water until tender. Pour off juice and save 1 cup of liquid. Set apricots aside. Combine brown sugar, cornstarch, and apricot juice. During last 30 minutes of roasting time, spoon over meat, basting often with mixture and drippings until pork has golden glaze. Put roast on platter; circle with cooked apricots.
As visually appealing as it is tasty.
Mrs. Thomas P. Francis (Nelda Cummins)

Roast Leg of Pork

1 leg of pork (fresh ham)	1½ t. savory
1 clove of garlic per lb. of ham	1½ t. salt
1½ t. thyme	

Pierce surface of meat in a number of places and insert a sliver of garlic in each gash. Crush thyme, savory, and salt together in a mortar with pestle; press mixture into meat. Roast at 325° for approximately 25 minutes per pound until meat thermometer registers 185°.
An elegant way to serve a large number.
Serves 15 to 20.
Mrs. Frank N. Ikard, Jr. (Carol Foster)

Tourtière (French-Canadian Christmas Pie)

3 lb. ground pork	¼ t. ground cloves
¾ to 1 c. boiling water	1 bay leaf, crushed
⅓ to ½ c. finely chopped onion	1 small clove garlic, crushed
1 rib celery, chopped, or	½ t. dry mustard
¾ t. celery salt	½ t. thyme
1½ to 2 t. salt	½ t. sage
⅛ t. pepper	Pastry for 3, 8 inch double-crust
⅛ to ¼ t. poultry seasoning	pies

Simmer pork in water 5 minutes; add remaining ingredients and simmer until pork is white, approximately 45 minutes. Skim off fat as it simmers. Turn meat mixture into 3 pastry-lined pans and cover each with a top crust. Crimp edges and cut steam vents. Bake at 425° for 30 minutes or until brown.
A special for breakfast: individual pies made in muffin tins and served with scrambled eggs and baked fruit.
Freezes.
Mrs. James A. Williams (Priscilla Nichols)

Pork Scallopini

3   lb. pork tenderloin, sliced
    into ½ inch pieces
½   c. flour
2   T. vegetable oil
2   T. butter
½   c. dry vermouth or sherry
¼   c. water
1   6 oz. can sliced mush-
    rooms, drained

1   onion, chopped
1   garlic clove, minced
¼   t. thyme
¼   t. rosemary
¼   t. oregano
Salt and pepper to taste
Hot cooked rice

Dredge pork in flour and brown quickly in oil and butter. Stir in all other ingredients except rice. Cover and simmer over low heat 45 minutes to 1 hour. Serve over rice.
Serves 6/Freezes.
Mrs. Paul Vescovo (Susan Kay Kuper)

Louisiana Red Beans and Sausage

1½ c. chopped green onions
2   c. chopped onions
1   c. chopped celery
1   clove garlic, minced
¼   c. bacon drippings
1   lb. dried, red kidney beans,
    rinsed and drained
Ham bone
1   lb. smoked sausage, cut in
    ½ inch slices

10 c. water
2   bay leaves
½   t. salt
2   t. pepper
1   t. Worcestershire sauce
¼   t. Tabasco
⅓   c. chopped parsley
Cooked rice

Sauté onions, celery, and garlic in bacon drippings in Dutch oven until tender; add beans, ham bone, sausage, water, bay leaves, and all seasonings except parsley. Simmer, partially covered, over low heat for 3 to 4 hours. Remove bay leaves; add parsley before serving. Serve over hot, fluffy rice.
A traditional entrée from the South.
Serves 6/Freezes.
Mrs. Stephen Clark (Kate Eustis)

Marinated Baked Ham

2	cans beer	¾	t. ground cloves
½	c. packed brown sugar	1	t. lemon-pepper
1	c. water	½	t. celery seed
½	c. red wine vinegar	1	14 to 16 lb. ham, scored
1	t. mustard seed		

Combine all ingredients, except ham, and bring to a boil. Place ham in glass baking dish and pour marinade over. Refrigerate for 12 hours. Bake at 325° for 4 to 4½ hours, basting frequently with marinade. Continue to baste after ham is removed from oven until it is carved. Serve sauce separately.
Serves 30.
Mrs. Jack A. Collins (Nancy Chapman)

Ham Rolls Continental

6	very thin slices ham	2	T. flour
6	slices Swiss cheese	½	t. salt
1	10 oz. package frozen broccoli spears, defrosted	¼	t. basil
1	c. thinly sliced onions	Dash pepper	
2	T. butter	1	c. milk

Top ham slices with cheese. Place broccoli spear on each slice and roll. Secure with toothpicks. Place in shallow baking dish. Sauté onions in butter until tender, but not brown. Blend in flour, salt, basil, and pepper. Add milk and stir until thickened. Pour over ham. Bake at 350° for 25 minutes.
Serves 6.
Mrs. James. M. Dunnam (Anne Jeffers)

Knackwurst and Sauerkraut

2	large onions, sliced	1	t. celery seed
3	T. olive oil	12	knackwurst or bratwurst
3	16 oz. cans sauerkraut		sausages
Approximately ½ lb. Irish		1	apple, peeled and grated
	potatoes (1½ c. when grated)		

Lightly sauté onions in olive oil. Stir in sauerkraut and simmer over low heat for 8 to 10 minutes. Grate potatoes and add with celery seed. Cover with boiling water and simmer, uncovered, over low heat 30 minutes. Meanwhile, cover sausages with cold water, bring to a boil and simmer over low heat for 10 minutes; drain. Add sausages and apple to sauerkraut, cover, and simmer 30 minutes.
Substantial and satisfying.
Serves 6 to 8.
Mrs. James N. Ludlum (Dorothy Standifer)

Sausage and Lentils

1	c. dried lentils	2	Polish sausages, casings
2	medium onions, chopped		removed
3	cloves garlic, chopped	1	t. sugar
2	T. vegetable oil	½	t. pepper
1	16 oz. can tomatoes, drained	1	bay leaf
	and chopped	Salt to taste	

Soak lentils in water overnight. Drain. Cover with lightly salted water and simmer 20 minutes. Drain and reserve liquid. Sauté onions and garlic in oil until tender. Stir in tomatoes and simmer until liquid is absorbed. Cut sausage into ½ inch pieces and add to onions and tomatoes. Mix in lentils, sugar, pepper, bay leaf, and salt. Stir in lentil liquid and bake in a 1½ quart baking dish at 350° for 30 minutes. Add more water, if necessary, during cooking.
For a cold winter night.
Serves 6/Freezes.
Mrs. Robert H. McIntyre (Danya Nicholson)

Duke of Windsor Sandwich

Butter
1 slice black bread, lightly toasted
Thinly sliced ham or turkey

Sliced pineapple, optional
Grated Cheddar cheese
Chutney

Butter bread and arrange on it ham or turkey and pineapple. Top with grated cheese and chutney. Broil until cheese melts and serve immediately.
Variation of a Neiman-Marcus specialty.
Serves 1.
Mrs. Sam Fason (Maydelle Foster)

Posole

3 lb. pork loin, cubed
12 c. water
1 medium size onion, chopped
6 bay leaves
3 15 oz. cans hominy
¼ c. chopped parsley
Salt and pepper to taste
8 t. seasoned salt

2 garlic cloves
4 ribs celery, chopped
2 T. chili powder
Shredded lettuce
Sliced green onion
Oregano
Sliced radishes
Lime wedges

Combine all ingredients except chili powder and simmer 3 to 4 hours or until meat is tender. Remove bay leaves and garlic and add chili powder. Simmer 20 minutes. Serve in bowls. Accompany with separate bowls of shredded lettuce, green onions, oregano, radishes, and lime; let each guest top the stew with his choice of condiments. Flavor is richest if stew is made a day ahead and reheated.
Pork stew well known in New Mexico—a unique experience.
Serves 8.
Mrs. Charles Sikes (Carole McIntosh)

Breaded Breakfast Bacon

1 egg	1 t. vinegar
½ t. dry mustard	4 slices bacon, thick sliced
Dash cayenne	¾ c. corn flake crumbs

Beat egg slightly; add mustard, cayenne, and vinegar. Dip slices of bacon in egg mixture and roll in corn flake crumbs. Place on wire rack in baking pan; bake at 350° until brown and crisp, approximately 20 to 25 minutes.
Serves 4.
Mrs. Maury Hughes, Jr. (Phoebe Foster)

Ham Loaf with Horseradish Sauce

1 c. milk	¼ c. water
1 c. dry bread crumbs	¼ c. vinegar
2 eggs, beaten	2 t. dry mustard
2 lb. ground smoked ham	Parsley
1½ lb. lean ground pork	Spiced apples
¾ c. brown sugar	

Horseradish Sauce

¼ c. prepared horseradish	¼ t. Worcestershire sauce
1½ T. vinegar	Dash cayenne
1 T. prepared mustard	Dash paprika
½ t. salt	½ c. heavy cream, whipped

Combine milk, bread crumbs, eggs, ham, and pork. Pack into a 9 x 5 x 3 loaf pan. (Loaf may be frozen at this point.) Invert onto a shallow baking pan. Bake at 350° for 1½ hours (3 hours if frozen). Combine brown sugar, water, vinegar, and mustard. Baste loaf with glaze occasionally. Garnish platter with parsley and spiced apples. Serve with Horseradish Sauce.
Serves 12/Freezes.

Horseradish Sauce Mix horseradish, vinegar, mustard, salt, Worcestershire sauce, cayenne, and paprika. Fold into whipped cream and chill.
Yields 1 cup.
Mrs. Larry Temple (Louann Atkins)

Leg of Lamb with Pork Tenderloin

1	4½ to 5 lb. leg of lamb	Pepper
1	pork tenderloin	Rosemary
6	garlic cloves	Flour
Salt		

Have the butcher bone a leg of lamb and pull through a pork tenderloin. Insert slivers of garlic under the skin. Combine salt, pepper, rosemary, and flour, and dust meat well. Roast at 350° for approximately 30 to 35 minutes per pound (have butcher weigh meat after it is boned and stuffed), or until meat thermometer registers 185°. Serve with currant jelly sauce for lamb.

Currant Jelly Sauce for Lamb
1   c. chili sauce
1   c. currant jelly
½   c. butter
Mint leaves

Combine chili sauce, jelly, and butter; simmer for 30 minutes. Add mint leaves before serving.
Serves 10.
Mrs. Thomas Irvin Lowry (Katherine Sangster)

Lamb Chops Madeira in Choux Paste

6   loin chops, 2 inches thick
¾   c. Madeira
Salt and pepper
Spice Islands fines herbes or thyme

Choux Paste

1	c. water	1	c. unsifted flour
½	t. salt	4	eggs
½	c. butter		

Marinate chops in Madeira for 30 minutes. Drain and lightly sprinkle with salt, pepper, and fines herbes or thyme. Broil 2 inches from heat until browned on 1 side, approximately 7 minutes. Cool and set aside. Combine water, salt, and butter over medium heat. When butter melts and mixture boils, add flour and remove from heat. Stir until smooth; mixture should come away from sides of pan. Beat in eggs 1 at a time; paste will be smooth and shiny. (Choux paste can be prepared and refrigerated; allow it to reach room temperature before using.) Evenly spread ⅓ cup on each chop. Cover and chill for 12 to 24 hours. Bake at 425° for approximately 35 minutes, until brown.
Lamb covered with a puffy pastry.
Serves 6.
Mrs. Thomas Irvin Lowry (Katherine Sangster)

Dorothy's Shish Kebob

Marinade

Juice of 2 lemons	1 t. powdered ginger
¼ c. olive oil	1 clove garlic, pressed
2 T. minced onion	2 t. turmeric or curry powder
1 T. ground chili peppers	1 T. salt
1 t. coriander	

2 lb. lamb, cut into 1½ inch cubes	Bell pepper pieces
	Tomato pieces
Melted butter	Whole mushroom caps
Small onions	Long grain and wild rice

Combine marinade ingredients in blender and whirl. Marinate lamb for 2 hours; drain, and arrange on skewers. Broil or grill over charcoal basting with butter. Slightly parboil onions and bell pepper and broil them with tomato pieces and mushroom caps, basting with butter. Serve lamb and vegetables over rice.
Separate cooking of meat and vegetables insures that each achieves the proper doneness.
Serves 6.
Mrs. R. Kinnan Golemon (Jackie Burst)

Lamb Curry Williams

2 large onions, minced	1 t. coarsely ground pepper
¼ c. olive oil	1 c. chicken broth
¼ c. butter	1½ c. sweet vermouth
3 to 4 lb. lean lamb, cut into bite-size pieces	1½ T. cornstarch
2 large cloves garlic, crushed	4 t. curry powder, or to taste
Salt to taste	3 T. water
	Rice

Sauté onions in oil and butter. Add meat, brown and cook for 20 minutes. Blend in garlic, salt, pepper, broth, and vermouth. Cover and simmer for 1 hour. May refrigerate or freeze at this point. Make a paste of cornstarch, curry powder, and water. Blend into meat sauce and simmer 5 to 10 minutes more. Serve with rice.

Make your own curry powder, page 303.
Serves 8/Freezes.
Mrs. Sam Fason (Maydelle Foster)

Condiments for Curry

Grated coconut
Chopped chives
Grated orange and lemon peel
Rounds of green onions
Slivered almonds, browned in butter
Chopped unsalted peanuts
Chopped parsley
Dried currants soaked in brandy
Cashew nuts
Crumbled bacon
Raisins soaked in port or vermouth
Minced avocado sprinkled with lemon juice

Sieved egg yolk
Sieved egg white
Pine nuts
Quince, guava, or currant jelly
Shredded fresh pineapple
Fried bananas sprinkled with cinnamon and cloves
Chutney
Chopped green olives
Chopped candied ginger
Pitted ripe olives
Bombay duck (available canned in specialty sections of grocers) sautéed in butter, cooled, and crumbled

A selection of these condiments, plus beer and pappadams in place of bread, complete your curry dinner.
Mrs. R. Kinnan Golemon (Jackie Burst)

Butterflied Leg of Lamb

1 leg of lamb	1 t. salt
¾ c. vegetable oil	3 drops Tabasco
¼ c. dry sherry	¼ t. oregano
⅓ c. lemon juice	¼ t. thyme
2 T. grated onion	

Have butcher bone and butterfly lamb. Place lamb in a large, shallow baking dish. Blend remaining ingredients; pour over lamb. Cover and marinate 8 hours or overnight in refrigerator; turn occasionally. Place fat side up on broiling pan at least 6 inches from heat; broil approximately 20 minutes on each side. Brush occasionally with marinade. If broiled over a charcoal fire, meat will be crustier.
Serves 6 to 8.
Mrs. Homer Scace (Betty Gatch)

Lamb Avgolemono

2 lb. boneless lamb shoulder, cubed	1 stalk celery, each rib peeled and cut into 2 inch pieces
1 medium onion, finely chopped	2 eggs
2 T. butter	3 T. lemon juice
Salt and pepper to taste	¾ c. boiling chicken broth
¼ t. dill weed	

Sauté lamb and onion in butter until browned. Season with salt, pepper, and dill weed. Stir in 1 cup water, scraping pan well. Cover and simmer 1½ hours, until meat is tender. Add celery and simmer 15 minutes. Beat eggs until light. Add a dash of salt and beat in lemon juice. Slowly add hot broth, stirring constantly. Gradually add to lamb, stirring over low heat until thickened. Do not boil.
Serves 6.
Mrs. Jack W. Scarbrough (Betty Richer)

Moussaka

3 medium eggplant, peeled and
   cut into ½ inch slices
1¼ c. butter
3 large onions, chopped
2 lb. ground lamb
3 T. tomato paste
½ c. dry red wine
½ c. chopped parsley
¼ t. cinnamon

Salt and pepper to taste
6 T. flour
1 qt. milk, heated
4 eggs, beaten
Nutmeg
2 c. ricotta cheese
1 c. bread crumbs
1 c. grated Parmesan cheese

Brown eggplant in ½ cup of the butter; set aside. Sauté onions in ¼ cup of the butter until brown; stir in meat and cook 10 minutes. Combine tomato paste, wine, parsley, cinnamon, salt, and pepper; stir into meat and simmer over low heat, stirring often, until liquid has been absorbed. Melt remaining ¼ cup of butter and stir in flour and milk. When thickened, remove from heat. Cool slightly and beat in eggs, nutmeg, and ricotta cheese. Grease 2 3-quart casseroles and sprinkle lightly with some of the bread crumbs. Arrange alternate layers of eggplant and meat sauce, sprinkling each layer with Parmesan cheese and bread crumbs. Pour ricotta cheese mixture over top and bake at 375° for 1 hour. Allow to cool 20 minutes before serving.
Most flavorful if made a day in advance and reheated.
Serves 10/Freezes.
Mrs. Leon Bronson Dorsey, Jr. (Cathryn Seymour)

Chicken in Pastry

6	whole chicken breasts, boned and split	2	eggs, separated
	Seasoned salt to taste	3	8 oz. cans refrigerated crescent dinner rolls
	Seasoned pepper to taste	1	T. water
¼	c. grated orange peel	2	10 oz. jars red currant jelly
1	6 oz. package long grain and wild rice, cooked according to package directions for drier rice	1	T. prepared mustard
		3	T. port wine
		¼	c. lemon juice

Pound chicken with mallet to flatten; sprinkle with seasoned salt and pepper. Add orange peel to cooked rice. Beat egg whites until soft peaks form; fold into rice mixture. On a floured surface, roll 2 triangular pieces of roll dough together to form a circle. Repeat until there are 12 circles. Place a chicken breast in the center of each circle. Spoon ¼ cup of the rice mixture over the chicken; roll the chicken jellyroll fashion. Bring dough up around stuffed breast; moisten the edges of the dough with water and press together to seal. Place seam side down on a large baking sheet. Lightly beat egg yolks with water; brush over dough. Bake at 375° for 45 to 50 minutes; cover loosely with foil if dough browns too quickly. Heat currant jelly; gradually stir in mustard, wine, and lemon juice. Serve warm with chicken.
Surprisingly easy to prepare.
Serves 6 to 8/Freezes.
Mrs. David Gaffey Ford (Laura Lee Hill)

Charcoal Lemon Chicken

8	chicken broiler halves	3	T. Tabasco
½	c. butter, melted	2	T. celery salt
	Juice of 18 lemons (2 c.)	1	T. salt
½	c. plus 2 T. Worcestershire sauce	1	T. pepper
		1	T. onion salt

Marinate chicken overnight in combined ingredients. Broil over charcoal approximately 50 minutes, bone down, turning once to brown the skin.
Serves 8.
Mrs. Michael B. Cotten (Betty George)

Roast Chicken with Rice Dressing

2   whole chicken broilers,
    approximately 2¼ lb. each
Butter, at room temperature
Salt
½   c. chopped ham
2   chopped chicken livers

2   T. chopped almonds or
    pecans
3   c. cooked rice
1   T. minced parsley
¼   c. light dry sherry

Rub chickens with butter and sprinkle with salt. Sauté ham, livers, and nuts in 2 tablespoons butter. Stir into rice, toss with parsley, and stuff into cavities of chickens. Roast at 350° for 1 hour, basting with sherry every 15 minutes.
Serves 4 to 6.
Mrs. L. Allen Searight (Charleen Smith)

London Chicken

8   oz. Monterey Jack cheese
4   whole chicken breasts, boned,
    skinned, and halved
2   eggs, beaten
¾   c. dry bread crumbs
1   c. butter
½   c. chopped onion
½   c. chopped bell pepper
2   T. flour

1   chicken bouillon cube,
    dissolved in 1 c. boiling water
1   t. salt
1   6 oz. package long grain and
    wild rice, cooked
1   3 oz. jar sliced mushrooms
2   T. chopped pimiento
White wine

Cut cheese into 8 pieces. Pound chicken to ¼ inch thickness. Roll each chicken piece around a piece of cheese and secure with a toothpick. Dip in egg then roll in bread crumbs. Brown chicken in ½ cup of the butter over medium-low heat for 35 minutes. In another skillet, sauté onion and bell pepper in remaining butter until tender. Mix flour with bouillon, then stir into onion mixture. Cook until thick. Add salt, rice, mushrooms, and pimiento; stir. Pour mixture into a shallow, 2½ quart baking dish. Top with chicken. Bake, covered, at 400° for 20 minutes. If a moister rice mixture is desired, add a little white wine.
Serves 6 to 8/Freezes.
Mrs. Lindsey A. Williams, Jr. (Penelope Lord)

Baked and Broiled Chicken

¾ c. butter, at room
   temperature
1 T. Worcestershire sauce
2 T. lemon juice
1 t. salt

⅛ t. pepper
½ t. ground ginger
1 fryer, cut up, or
   4 chicken breasts

Mix butter and Worcestershire sauce; stir in lemon juice and seasonings. Brush mixture over chicken. Place skin-side down in baking pan. Cover with foil and bake at 350° for 45 minutes to 1 hour. After 35 minutes, turn chicken, baste with pan juices and bake uncovered until done. Broil 4 to 5 minutes until lightly browned.
Full-flavored juices a must over brown or white rice.
Serves 4.
Mrs. Jack Steinhauser (Cissy Wheat)

Red and Green Chicken

4 chicken breasts, boned and
   pounded
¼ c. butter

4 thick slices tomato
1 large avocado, sliced

Bechamel Sauce

2½ c. milk
1 large carrot, peeled and sliced
1 green onion, minced
1 rib celery, chopped
1 bay leaf

12 white peppercorns
Pinch nutmeg or mace
¼ c. butter
¼ c. flour
¾ c. heavy cream

Sauté chicken in ¼ cup butter until brown and arrange in a flat baking dish. Lightly sauté tomatoes in butter and place over chicken. Heat at 350° for 10 minutes. Arrange avocado slices over chicken and cover with warm Bechamel sauce. Return to oven for 2 minutes. Serve immediately.

Bechamel Sauce Heat milk, carrot, green onion, celery, bay leaf, and peppercorns. Simmer 10 to 15 minutes over low heat. Melt butter and stir in flour. Slowly strain milk into butter and flour, stirring constantly. Stir in cream; heat, but do not boil.
Serves 4.
Mrs. John Calhoun Miller (Karen Stromberger)

Herb Stuffed Broilers

1	c. finely chopped parsley	2	1½-lb. broilers, split
¼	c. finely chopped chives		Melted butter
1	t. tarragon		Salt and pepper
1	t. salt		
1	c. butter, at room temperature		

Combine parsley, chives, tarragon, and salt and blend into butter. Loosen skin of chickens and spread butter mixture over meat beneath skin. Brush both sides of chickens with melted butter and arrange, skin side up in a buttered pan. Sprinkle with salt and pepper. Roast at 425° for 35 minutes, basting frequently with pan juices, until golden brown. Arrange on serving platter and pour pan juices over chicken.
Serves 4 to 6.
Mrs. Homer Scace (Betty Gatch)

Chicken Tetrazzini

1	5 to 6 lb. hen	1	4 oz. jar diced pimientos
5	ribs celery with leaves	4	8 oz. cans sliced mushrooms, drained
1	onion, peeled	¼	t. cayenne
	Salt and pepper to taste	½	c. grated Parmesan cheese
1	12 oz. package spaghetti	1	t. sugar
1¼	c. butter	2	c. chopped parsley
1¼	c. flour	4	chicken bouillon cubes
1¼	t. salt		
5	c. light cream		
6 to 8	green onions, finely chopped		

Topping

3	tomatoes, peeled and thickly sliced	1	c. grated Parmesan cheese
2	c. buttered bread crumbs	2	T. oregano

Simmer hen in 4 quarts of water with celery, onion, salt, and pepper for 2 hours or until tender. Let cool in broth. Bone chicken and cut into bite-size pieces. Reserve broth. Cook spaghetti in chicken broth until just tender. Drain, but do not rinse. Make a thick white sauce using butter, flour, salt, and cream. Stir in remaining sauce ingredients; simmer over low heat for 10 minutes. Combine the chicken and sauce; mix with spaghetti. Place in 2 3-quart baking dishes. Top with tomatoes. Combine buttered bread crumbs, oregano, and Parmesan cheese. Sprinkle over tomato slices. Bake at 350° for 30 to 45 minutes or until bubbly. Brown quickly under broiler.

Serves 14 to 18/Freezes.
Mrs. James Swearingen (Jonilu Sellers)

Chicken in the Limelight

Grated peel and juice of 1 lime
1   chicken, cut into serving
    pieces
⅓   c. flour
1½ t. salt
½   t. paprika
¼   c. vegetable oil

2   T. brown sugar
½   c. chicken broth
½   c. dry white wine
Fresh mint
1   lime
1   avocado, sliced

Sprinkle lime juice over chicken; shake pieces in paper bag with flour, salt, and paprika. Brown in oil; arrange in single layer in baking dish. Combine lime peel with sugar and sprinkle over chicken. Add broth and wine. Place sprig of mint on each piece. Bake, covered, at 375° approximately 45 minutes to 1 hour. Cut 4 thin wedges from remaining lime. Squeeze rest of lime over avocado to prevent darkening; chill. When chicken is tender, transfer to warm platter, discarding mint. Garnish with lime wedges, avocado crescents, and fresh mint.

Serves 4.
Mrs. John C. Donovan (Anne Peterson)

Breast of Chicken in Mustard Sauce

6   large chicken breast halves
Salt and pepper to taste
¼   c. butter
¼   c. finely minced onion

½   c. sliced mushrooms
2   T. lemon juice
1   c. heavy cream
1   T. prepared mustard

Season chicken with salt and pepper. Melt butter in large skillet over medium heat; brown chicken. Add onion, reduce heat, and cook, covered, 15 minutes or until chicken is tender. Remove chicken to a warm serving platter. Add mushrooms to remaining drippings in skillet; sprinkle with lemon juice and sauté 2 to 3 minutes, stirring occasionally. Add cream, bring to a boil, and simmer 5 minutes. Stir in mustard; add salt and pepper to taste. Pour sauce over chicken.
Piquant and smooth.
Serves 6.
Mrs. Gray B. Jolink (Kingslea Thomas)

Moroccan Chicken

⅓   c. olive oil
1   large onion, thinly sliced
1   clove garlic, minced
1   T. finely chopped parsley
½   t. ground coriander
1   t. salt

½   t. coarsely ground pepper
1   chicken with giblets, cut
    in serving pieces
2   lemons, quartered
⅓   c. sliced pimiento stuffed
    olives

Heat oil in Dutch oven; stir in onion, garlic, parsley, coriander, salt, and pepper. Add chicken pieces and turn to coat with onion mixture. Arrange 4 lemon quarters on top. Cover and simmer, turning occasionally, for 1½ to 2 hours or until very tender. Remove chicken to a warm platter, arrange remaining lemon quarters on top and keep warm. Cook the liquid over high heat until reduced to a thick sauce. Add olives and pour over chicken.
Lively lemon-garlic flavor.
Serves 4.
Mrs. Hugh Rushing (Elaine Robinson)

Chicken Lasagne

8	oz. lasagne noodles	1	c. cream-style cottage cheese
1	10½ oz. can condensed cream of mushroom soup	⅓	c. sliced stuffed olives
		⅓	c. chopped onion
⅔	c. milk	¼	c. minced parsley
½	t. salt	3	c. diced cooked chicken
½	t. poultry seasoning	1½	c. soft bread crumbs, buttered
2	3 oz. packages cream cheese		

Cook noodles until tender. Drain and rinse with cold water. Mix soup, milk, salt, and poultry seasoning in saucepan and heat. Beat cheeses together. Mix olives, onions and parsley. Place half of the noodles in a buttered 9 x 13 baking dish and spread with half the cheese mixture, half the soup mixture and half the chicken. Repeat the layers. Top with crumbs. Bake in 375° oven for 30 minutes. Let stand for 10 minutes before serving.
Lasagne with a difference.
Serves 6 to 8/Freezes.
Mrs. Conrad P. Werkenthin (Clare Coates)

Chicken Livers Parisienne

16	slices bacon	3	c. sour cream, at room temperature
3	medium onions, chopped		
2	bell peppers, chopped		Salt and pepper to taste
¼	c. paprika	¼	c. chopped parsley
2½	lb. chicken livers	1	4 oz. jar pimientos, drained
2	c. sliced mushrooms		

Fry bacon until crisp; drain and crumble. Reserve ¼ cup bacon drippings. Sauté onions and peppers in drippings. Add paprika and cook for 1 minute. Add chicken livers and mushrooms; sauté over medium heat for 6 minutes or until liver is tender. Remove from heat; stir in bacon, salt, pepper, and sour cream. Serve over rice, toast points, split and toasted cornbread squares, unsweetened waffles, or English muffins. Garnish with parsley or pimientos.
Brunch or luncheon pièce de résistance.
Serves 12.
Mrs. Charles E. Bates (Linda Steinhauser)

Hop Po Gai Ding (Chicken with Walnuts)

4	lb. chicken breasts and thighs, skinned and boned	¼	c. vegetable oil
1	t. sugar	1	c. walnut halves
1	t. salt	¾	c. water
1	T. soy sauce	2	cloves garlic, minced
¼	c. sherry	½	t. ground ginger
Cornstarch		1	5 oz. can bamboo shoots, drained
1	egg, beaten	Hot, fluffy rice	

Cut chicken into bite-size pieces; soak in marinade, made by combining sugar, salt, soy sauce, and sherry, for 20 minutes. Remove chicken, reserving marinade. Sprinkle chicken lightly with cornstarch and dip lightly in egg. Heat oil in skillet; add walnuts and brown, turning often. Remove walnuts and set aside. Sauté chicken until brown. Add water, garlic, ginger, and marinade. Simmer, covered, 20 to 30 minutes. Stir in bamboo shoots and walnuts; simmer 5 minutes. Serve over hot, fluffy rice.
Serves 6/Freezes.
Mrs. Paul Secunda (Aileen Nation)

Chicken and Artichokes

6	lb. chicken breasts and thighs	¼	c. flour
1	T. salt	1	c. condensed chicken consommé
½	t. pepper		
1	t. paprika	1½	c. dry sherry
1½	c. butter	4	14 oz. cans artichoke hearts, drained
1	lb. mushrooms		

Season chicken with salt, pepper, and paprika. Brown chicken in 1 cup of the butter. Sauté mushrooms in the remaining ½ cup of butter. Sprinkle flour over the mushrooms; stir; add consommé and sherry. Simmer for 5 minutes. In a shallow casserole, combine chicken and mushroom mixtures. Bake, uncovered, at 350° for 1 hour. Add the artichokes during the final 15 minutes of baking.
Serves 12/Freezes.
Mrs. J. Chrys Dougherty (Mary Ireland Graves)

California Chicken Casserole

4	whole chicken breasts	½	c. chopped ripe olives
1	T. salt	2	slices pimiento, chopped
Parsley		½	c. sliced mushrooms
½	bell pepper, chopped	1	c. light cream
1	rib celery, chopped	½	t. salt
1	small onion, chopped	½	c. grated Swiss cheese
3	T. butter	½	c. slivered almonds
3	T. flour	Cooked rice or baked pastry
1	c. chicken broth		shells

Simmer chicken in water with salt and parsley until tender. Drain, reserving broth. Remove bones. Sauté vegetables in butter until tender. Stir in flour. Add chicken broth; cook until mixture thickens, stirring constantly. Add olives, pimiento, mushrooms, cream, salt, and cheese. Dice chicken and put in casserole. Pour sauce on top; sprinkle with almonds. Bake, uncovered, at 350° for 30 minutes. Serve over rice or in baked pastry shells.
Can easily be expanded for large groups.
Serves 6/Freezes.
Mrs. Bethea W. Brindley (Mary Ellen Kennedy)

Party Chicken Salad

8	c. diced cooked chicken	2	c. slivered almonds
½	c. lemon juice	1	T. onion juice
2	t. salt	2	c. grated sharp Cheddar
3 to 4 c. mayonnaise			cheese
5	c. diced celery	3	c. crushed potato chips

Combine all ingredients, except cheese and potato chips. Turn into shallow buttered casseroles. Mix cheese and potato chips and sprinkle over top. Bake at 375° for 20 to 25 minutes.
For ladies' luncheons in the winter.
Serves 20.
Mrs. Jim Abney (Lo Ann Burch)

Hot Chicken Salad

2 to 2½ c. cooked diced
   chicken breasts
1 8 oz. can water chestnuts,
   drained and sliced
2 pimientos, diced
½ c. slivered toasted almonds

½ c. sliced mushrooms
2 T. lemon juice
1½ c. mayonnaise
Salt and pepper to taste
½ c. grated Cheddar cheese
½ c. canned French fried onions

Combine chicken, water chestnuts, pimientos, almonds, mushrooms, lemon juice, and mayonnaise. Place in a buttered 2 quart casserole. Top with cheese and onions. Bake at 350° for 20 minutes or until golden.
Serves 6/Freezes.
Mrs. Shannon Ratliff (Gay Kokernot)

Chicken Spaghetti for 25

3 3½ lb. fryers
1 onion, sliced
Celery tops
4½ c. white wine
¾ c. butter
¾ c. flour
2 c. light cream
4½ c. sour cream
3 c. chicken stock
3 4 oz. jars pimiento

3 8 oz. jars mushroom pieces
Juice of 3 lemons
2 T. Worcestershire sauce
Dash cayenne
Salt and white pepper to taste
3½ c. grated Parmesan cheese
1½ lb. spaghetti
1 package Pepperidge Farms
   patty shells, baked

Place chicken, onion, celery tops, and 3 cups of the wine in a covered kettle and simmer until tender. Strain and reserve stock. Remove meat from fryers and dice. Melt butter in saucepan and add flour; cook for 1 minute. Add light cream, sour cream and 3 cups chicken stock; blend well. Add pimiento, mushrooms, lemon juice, Worcestershire, cayenne, salt, pepper, ¾ cup of the Parmesan cheese, and chicken. Cook spaghetti in the reserved chicken stock, 1½ cups of wine, and water to cover. Drain. Divide spaghetti among 3 8 x 12 pyrex baking dishes. Cover each with equal amounts of chicken sauce. Top with remaining Parmesan cheese. Crumble patty shells on top of each dish. Heat at 350° for 20 minutes or until bubbly.
Serves 25/Freezes.
Mrs. Jean Gilbert (Jean Summers)

Chicken Chinoiserie

1 c. butter, melted	1 c. soy sauce
Juice of 6 lemons	1 t. prepared horseradish
3 T. Worcestershire sauce	3 cloves garlic, crushed
Salt and pepper to taste	4 chickens, quartered

Mix ingredients; marinate chickens for several hours or overnight. Bake at 300° for 30 to 45 minutes or place over charcoals and grill until done.
Serves 16.
Mrs. Richard F. Brown (Ann Jarvis)

Victor Szebehely's Hungarian Chicken

2 chicken fryers, cut up	½ c. dry red wine
1 t. onion salt	10 slices bacon
1 t. garlic salt	2 c. finely chopped onion
1 t. white pepper	2 c. finely chopped bell pepper
1 t. black pepper	2 cloves garlic, minced
2 t. paprika (Hungarian, if possible)	¼ c. sour cream
2 10½ oz. cans beef or chicken broth	

Sprinkle chicken pieces with onion salt, garlic salt, white pepper, black pepper, and 1 teaspoon of the paprika. Pour broth and wine over chicken. Marinate 3 to 4 hours in refrigerator and 3 to 4 hours at room temperature. Fry 6 slices of the bacon; sauté onion in bacon drippings until golden. Add bell pepper and garlic; sauté until onion is brown. Remove from heat and sprinkle with 1 teaspoon paprika. Fry remaining 4 slices of bacon; then sauté chicken in bacon drippings, approximately 4 minutes per side. In a large Dutch oven, combine marinade, chicken, onion, bell pepper, garlic, and bacon. Simmer covered for 30 to 45 minutes, stirring every 10 minutes. Place chicken pieces on serving platter. Remove sauce from heat, stir in sour cream, and pour over chicken.
Sausage slices sautéed with the chicken add a spicy touch.
Serves 6/Freezes.
Mrs. Victor Szebehely (Jo Betsy Lewallen)

Chicken and Sausage Loaf

1 5 lb. hen	1 t. Worcestershire sauce
2 c. uncooked rice	1 t. salt
1 lb. bulk sausage	¼ c. melted butter
2 10½ oz. cans condensed	1½ c. dry bread crumbs
mushroom soup	
1 9 oz. can mushrooms,	
chopped	

Simmer chicken in water; cut into bite-size pieces. Cook rice in chicken broth and drain well. Fry sausage over low heat, pouring off excess grease. Combine sausage, rice, soup, mushrooms, Worcestershire sauce, and salt. Butter a shallow 3½ quart baking dish and spread half of the sausage mixture over the bottom. Cover with chicken and another layer of sausage. Mix butter with bread crumbs and sprinkle over casserole. Bake at 325° for 45 minutes. To serve, cut into squares. Serves 12 to 16/Freezes.
Mrs. Maury Hughes, Jr. (Phoebe Foster)

Chicken Élan

6 T. butter	½ c. toasted slivered almonds
6 T. flour	8 oz. egg noodles, cooked
1½ t. salt	3 T. minced parsley
½ t. celery salt	5 chicken breasts, cooked
1 t. Beau Monde	and diced
Marjoram to taste	1 c. mushrooms
2 c. chicken broth, heated	½ c. grated Cheddar or
2 c. heavy cream, scalded	Parmesan cheese
2 T. dry sherry	

Melt butter and add flour. Cook for 1 minute. Add seasonings and chicken broth, stirring constantly until thick; add cream and sherry. Stir in almonds, noodles, parsley, chicken, mushrooms and pour into a 3 quart buttered casserole. Top with cheese and bake at 350° for 40 minutes or until bubbly.
Serves 12/Freezes.
Mrs. Elora Jane Smith (Elora Jane Watt)

Chicken à l'Orange

6	chicken breast halves	1	t. salt
½	t. salt	¼	t. pepper
1	small onion, chopped	1	T. grated orange rind
1	c. sliced mushrooms	1½ to 3 T. flour	
1	c. orange juice	Parsley	
¼	c. sherry	Paprika	
½	c. water	Orange slices or crab apples,	
1	T. brown sugar		and parsley for garnish

Brown chicken under broiler for 10 minutes, 2 inches below heat. Remove to a shallow baking dish. Salt to taste. Arrange onion and mushrooms over chicken. Prepare sauce by mixing orange juice, sherry, water, brown sugar, salt, pepper, orange rind, and flour (enough to thicken). Simmer sauce until thick; pour over chicken and vegetables. Sprinkle with parsley and paprika. Bake at 375° for 45 minutes. Garnish with orange slices or crab apples, and parsley.
Serves 6.
Mrs. John C. Donovan (Anne Peterson)

Oven Barbequed Chicken

1½ T. catsup		½	t. salt
1½ T. vinegar		½	t. prepared mustard
1½ T. lemon juice		½	t. paprika
1	T. Worcestershire sauce	½	t. chili powder
2	T. water	½	t. cayenne
1	T. butter	Fryer, cut up	
1½ T. brown sugar			

Mix all ingredients, except chicken, and heat to boiling. Dip chicken in sauce. Line roasting pan with large enough piece of greased foil to fold over chicken. Place chicken on foil, pour remaining sauce, and seal. Bake at 500° for 15 minutes then reduce heat to 350° and bake for 1 hour longer. Do not open foil during cooking.
Economical and easy to make.
Serves 4.
Mrs. David Davenport (Diane Wilder)

Chicken Enchiladas with Sour Cream

1 lb. chicken breasts	3 4 oz. cans chopped
1 carrot	green chilies
1 sprig parsley	5 tomatoes, peeled and
Salt to taste	chopped
8 oz. Cheddar cheese, grated	2 medium onions, chopped
2 c. sour cream	Pinch oregano
1 clove garlic, minced	18 tortillas
¼ c. olive oil	Vegetable oil

Cover chicken, carrot and parsley with water and simmer until tender. Remove meat from bones and shred. Combine cheese and sour cream with the chicken. Sauté garlic in the olive oil. Add green chilies, tomatoes, onions, oregano, and salt. Cover with approximately ½ cup of water and cook, over low heat, until thick. Dip tortillas, one at a time, in vegetable oil until soft, approximately 2 seconds. Then dip tortillas into the sauce, fill with chicken mixture and roll. Place in a flat casserole and cover with remaining sauce. Bake at 350° for 10 to 15 minutes.

A mild version.

Serves 6.

Mrs. Jack Roche (Josephine Klotz)

Turkey Artichoke Casserole

2 T. chopped bell pepper	2 T. chopped parsley
2 T. chopped green onion, including tops	Dash Worcestershire sauce
¼ c. chopped celery	Dash Tabasco
2 T. chopped onion	Salt and pepper to taste
½ c. butter	1 4½ oz. can sliced
1 10½ oz. can condensed cream of mushroom soup	mushrooms, drained
2 c. sour cream	1 14 oz. can artichoke hearts, drained
1 c. grated Parmesan cheese	4 c. chopped turkey
1 2 oz. jar chopped pimiento, drained	

Sauté bell pepper, green onions, celery, and onion in butter. Add remaining ingredients. Bake in a 3 quart casserole at 350° for 45 minutes. *Makes you glad to have leftover turkey.*
Serves 6/Freezes.
Mrs. John C. Oliver (Mary Ellen Dooley)

Green Tomato Enchiladas

Sauce

12	tomatillos (green tomatoes) or 2 1-lb., 4 oz. cans tomatillos, undrained	½	c. chopped bell pepper
		2	T. vegetable oil
		2	T. flour
1	c. hot water (omit if canned tomatillos are used)	1	t. sugar
		1	t. salt
1	chicken bouillon cube	¼	t. pepper
½	c. chopped onions	1	T. chopped green chilies
2	cloves garlic, crushed	2	t. coriander

Filling

2	c. cooked, chopped chicken	1	t. cumin
2	c. grated Monterey Jack cheese	1	T. chopped parsley
			Salt and pepper to taste
1	c. cream-style cottage cheese	12	tortillas
		1	c. sour cream
1	t. coriander		

Sauce Place tomatillos, water, and bouillon in blender and whirl for 10 seconds. Sauté onions, garlic, and bell pepper in oil; stir in flour. Gradually stir in green tomato purée. Add remaining ingredients and simmer gently for 1 to 1½ hours.

Filling Combine all ingredients, except tortillas and sour cream. Dip tortillas in green tomato sauce to soften. Place filing, less than ½ cup each, on tortillas and roll up. Arrange in a buttered 9 x 13 baking dish. Bake at 350° for 20 to 25 minutes. Top with remaining heated sauce. Spoon sour cream over sauce and serve immediately.
Serves 4 to 6.
Mrs. James H. Albright (Mary Margaret Carlson)

Crabmeat in Ramekins

1½ c. fresh crabmeat
2 T. finely minced celery
2 T. finely minced onion
2 T. finely minced parsley
2 T. dry sherry
2 t. cornstarch
⅛ t. nutmeg
½ t. salt
¼ t. white pepper

⅛ t. cayenne
2 c. cream
4 eggs, lightly beaten
½ c. sliced mushrooms,
sautéed in butter
½ c. grated Swiss cheese
Butter
Grated Parmesan cheese

Combine crabmeat, celery, onion, parsley, and sherry. Refrigerate 1 hour. Mix cornstarch, nutmeg, salt, pepper, and cayenne. Add enough cream to form a smooth paste, then add remaining cream. Stir in eggs. Add mushrooms, cheese and crabmeat mixture. Pour into individual ramekins, buttered, and dusted with Parmesan cheese. Bake at 325° for 30 minutes.
Also a superb quiche when baked in a pie shell.
Serves 6.
Mrs. Wayland Rivers (Ann Staacke)

Shrimp Creole

1 lb. shrimp, cleaned and deveined
2 T. olive oil
1 c. chopped green onions, tops and bottoms
½ bell pepper, finely chopped
1 c. chopped celery (include some tender leaves)
1 T. chopped parsley
1 large garlic clove, pressed

1 heaping t. salt
1 t. paprika
¼ t. cayenne
Pinch oregano
¼ t. gumbo filé
2 bay leaves, crushed
1 16 oz. can tomatoes, chopped
1 8 oz. can tomato sauce
Cooked rice

Sauté shrimp in olive oil in large skillet until pink. Add onions, bell pepper, celery, parsley, garlic, salt, paprika, cayenne, oregano, gumbo filé, bay leaves, tomatoes, and tomato sauce. Bake, covered, at 350° for approximately 1 hour. Serve over rice.
Serves 4/Freezes.
Mrs. Richard T. Weber (Violetta Van Devanter)

Jambalaya Lafitte

1 T. shortening	½ c. chopped green onion tops
1 T. flour	
1 lb. ham, diced	2 cloves garlic, minced
1 lb. highly-seasoned link sausage, sliced	1 red pepper pod
	Salt and pepper to taste
1 lb. shrimp, peeled and deveined	1 c. uncooked rice
	1½ c. water
1 1 lb. 4 oz. can tomatoes	18 oysters, optional
	Minced parsley
¾ c. chopped onion	

Melt shortening in a heavy pot. Blend in flour and brown slightly. Add ham and brown. Mix in sausage, shrimp, and tomatoes. Cover and simmer for 20 minutes. Stir in remaining ingredients, except oysters, and simmer, covered, for approximately 20 minutes until rice is tender. Stir in oysters and simmer until edges curl.
Serves 8.
Mrs. Bob Miller (Eugenia Betts)

Port Aransas Boiled Shrimp

3 qt. water	2 lemons (squeeze, but put in whole lemon)
1 box crab boil	
½ c. salt	3 lb. unpeeled shrimp
2 cans beer	Melted butter or red sauce
2 whole jalapeños	

To 3 quarts of water, add crab boil, salt, beer, jalapeños, and lemons; boil 4 minutes. Add shrimp; bring to boil again. Simmer 3 to 7 minutes, depending on size of shrimp. Serve hot with melted butter or cold with red sauce.
Everyone peels his own.
Mrs. Al H. Robinson, III (Judy Elaine Bradley)

Paëlla

1½ c. uncooked rice
½ lb. chorizo or hot
  link sausage, sliced
¼ c. olive oil
Meat cut from 4 chicken
  legs
1 medium onion, chopped
1 clove garlic, minced
½ c. cubed ham
1 c. cubed fish fillets
2 c. clam juice or
  chicken broth

¼ t. thyme
Pinch saffron
1 T. tomato paste
Salt and pepper to taste
1 c. shrimp, peeled and
  deveined
Clams or mussels,
  optional
1 c. scallops
½ c. green peas
Pimiento strips
Chopped parsley

Soak rice in water to cover for 1 hour; drain well. Sauté sausage in olive oil; remove from pan. In same pan, brown chicken, onion, and garlic. Stir in rice and brown. Add sausage, ham, and fish fillets. Combine clam juice or broth with thyme, saffron, tomato paste, salt and pepper. Mix well and stir into chicken and ham. May be prepared ahead to this point. Bring mixture to a boil. Arrange in a large skillet or paëlla pan and bake at 425° for 7 to 10 minutes. Mix in shrimp, clams or mussels, scallops, and peas. Return to heat for 7 to 10 minutes. Garnish with pimiento and parsley.
Spanish culinary triumph.
Serves 8.
Mrs. Thomas F. Reese (Mary Lynn Roth)

Shellfish au Gratin

½ c. sliced mushrooms
¼ c. butter
1 c. medium cream sauce
½ c. cooked lobster
½ c. crabmeat

½ c. cooked, peeled shrimp
2 T. dry sherry
½ c. grated cheese,
  Cheddar or Swiss
Cooked rice

Sauté mushrooms in butter. Stir in cream sauce, seafood, and sherry. Pour into a 1½ quart casserole and sprinkle with cheese. Heat at 350° for approximately 15 minutes until lightly browned. Serve over rice.
Serves 4.
Mrs. Ford Smith (Kay Willis)

Pepper Shrimp

1 c. butter	1 T. Worcestershire sauce
3 T. freshly ground pepper	1 lb. jumbo shrimp in shells

Melt butter; stir in pepper and Worcestershire sauce. Arrange shrimp in one layer in a flat pan. Pour sauce over shrimp and stir. Roast, uncovered, at 350° for 30 minutes, stirring often.
A bib and large napkins are in order.
Serves 2.
Mrs. Roy Talley (Martha Charlotte Green)

Coquilles Saint Jacques

6 c. dry white wine	½ c. minced onions
3 to 4 sprigs parsley	1 T. minced parsley
¼ t. thyme	2 T. water
½ bay leaf	1 t. lemon juice
2 lb. scallops, rinsed and drained	¼ c. flour
	2 egg yolks, slightly beaten
½ t. salt	
½ c. butter	¼ c. heavy cream
½ lb. mushrooms, chopped	⅓ c. buttered bread crumbs

Heat wine in a saucepan. Add parsley, thyme, and bay leaf. Add scallops and salt to wine and simmer, covered, approximately 10 minutes or until tender. Remove parsley and bay leaf; drain scallops, reserving liquid, and cut scallops into fine pieces. Melt ¼ cup of the butter and stir in mushrooms, onions, parsley, water, and lemon juice. Cover and simmer 5 to 10 minutes. Strain liquid into seasoned wine and add vegetable mixture to scallops. Melt remaining butter and stir in flour; cook, stirring, over low heat until bubbly. Remove from heat and slowly add wine liquid. Return to heat and quickly bring to a boil, stirring constantly; continue cooking for 1 to 2 minutes. Remove sauce from heat and add gradually, stirring vigorously, to a mixture of the egg yolks and cream. Stir in scallops and vegetables. Mix well. Pour into 6 buttered baking shells, or ramekins, piling high in the center. Sprinkle with buttered bread crumbs. Place shells on a baking sheet and heat at 450° for 8 to 10 minutes.
Serves 6.
Mrs. C. Dale Parker (Marilyn Burns)

Charcoal Broiled Shrimp

½ c. paprika
¼ c. chili powder
2 T. garlic salt
¼ t. salt

2 lb. jumbo shrimp, peeled and deveined with tails on
Vegetable oil
Lemon slices

Combine paprika, chili powder, and salts. Sprinkle both sides of shrimp with seasoning mixture. Cover and refrigerate 2 to 4 hours. Brush shrimp with oil and place over charcoal fire. Grill for 15 minutes, turning twice on each side. Serve with lemon slices.
Serves 4.
Mrs. Thomas D. Kirksey (Gene Weisinger)

Redfish Court Bouillon

½ c. flour
½ c. olive oil
½ c. butter
4 lb. onions, chopped
1 stalk celery, chopped
2 bell peppers, chopped
6 cloves garlic, pressed
1 6 oz. can tomato paste
1 15 oz. can tomato sauce
3 qt. hot water
1 bunch parsley, chopped

1 bunch green onion tops, chopped
1 T. Worcestershire sauce
1 lemon, cut into 4 thick slices
2 to 3 c. burgundy wine
Salt and pepper to taste
5 bay leaves
6 lb. redfish fillets, cut in large pieces

In a large kettle, brown flour and oil. Blend in butter and brown well. Add onions, celery, bell peppers, and garlic. Sauté until soft. Stir in tomato paste and tomato sauce. Add water, parsley, and green onion tops, Worcestershire sauce, lemon, wine, salt, pepper, and bay leaves. Simmer for 40 minutes. Add fish and cook for another 30 minutes. May be made a day ahead and refrigerated.
Serves 14/Freezes.
Mrs. Robert G. Umstattd (Jeanne Smith)

Spaghetti Mario

2 to 4 cloves garlic, minced	8 oz. spaghetti, cooked
6 T. olive oil	and drained
6 T. butter	Freshly ground pepper
2 to 3 8-oz. cans minced	Chopped parsley
clams, undrained	Parmesan cheese

Sauté garlic in olive oil. Add butter and clams. Simmer 2 to 3 minutes until hot. Serve over spaghetti and sprinkle with pepper, parsley, and cheese.
A pantry stowaway for last minute guests.
Serves 4 to 6.
Mrs. Terrell James (Dianne Hill)

Italian Broiled Shrimp

2 lb. jumbo shrimp, peeled	4 t. lemon juice
with tails left on	Freshly ground pepper
3/4 c. flour	2 T. minced garlic
1/4 c. olive oil	1/4 c. minced parsley
1 1/4 c. melted butter	

Dry shrimp and dust with 1/4 cup of the flour. Mix olive oil and 1/4 cup of butter together in a large flat baking dish. Stir in shrimp and broil for 3 minutes. Stir remaining 1/2 cup flour into remaining 1 cup of the butter. Add all remaining ingredients and simmer for 5 minutes. Pour over shrimp and stir well. Broil 6 minutes, turning once.
Serves 6.
Mrs. Thomas D. Kirksey (Gene Weisinger)

Stuffed Redfish with Shrimp Sauce

1 whole redfish, approximately 4 pounds	Salt and pepper
Butter	Sliced lemons

Stuffing

1 c. chopped onions	¾ t. pepper
¼ c. chopped green onions	1 t. salt
¼ c. butter	1 t. chopped parsley
3 c. cubed bread	

Sauce

¼ c. flour	1½ t. salt
½ c. butter	1 t. pepper
½ c. chopped celery	1 lb. fresh shrimp, peeled and deveined
¾ c. chopped bell pepper	½ c. chopped parsley
1 garlic clove, minced	Cinnamon
1 c. chopped onions	
4 c. canned whole tomatoes	

Rinse fish in cold water and dry with paper towels. Cut deep gashes into fish at 1½ inch intervals. Rub fish with butter and sprinkle with salt and pepper. Insert lemon slices into gashes and set fish aside.

Stuffing Sauté onions in butter until soft. Soak bread in water and squeeze out; add to onions and cook over low heat for 15 minutes. Mix in seasonings and set aside to cool.

Sauce Stir flour into butter and cook over medium heat for 2 to 3 minutes. Add celery, bell pepper, garlic, and onions; sauté until soft. Stir in tomatoes, salt and pepper, and simmer until sauce thickens. Add shrimp and parsley; mix well. Fill cavity of fish with stuffing. Pour sauce over fish and sprinkle with cinnamon. Bake at 325° for 1 hour. Serves 4 to 6.

Mrs. Stephen S. Clark (Kate Eustis)

Barbequed Redfish

Heavy-duty aluminum foil
1   3 to 5 lb. redfish
1   c. butter
Juice of 4 lemons

3   T. Worcestershire sauce
Salt and pepper
Paprika
1   c. barbeque sauce

Make a long, double-thick platter of foil to cover the fish. Score fish on both sides and place on foil. Place pats of butter in scores. Sprinkle with lemon juice, Worcestershire sauce, salt, pepper, and heavily with paprika. Repeat on other side. Pour barbeque sauce over fish. Arrange fish over hot coals, with foil open, for 5 to 10 minutes. Close foil and top of barbeque pit, if possible. Cook for 20 minutes or until fish flakes.
Serves 6 to 8.
Mrs. Al H. Robinson, III (Judy Elaine Bradley)

Venison Scallopini

2	lb. venison backstrap, cut into ½ inch thick pieces	1	t. sugar
	Salt, pepper, and flour for dredging	½	c. sliced mushrooms
		1¼	c. tomato sauce with tomato bits
2	medium onions, sliced	1¼	c. hot water

Coat venison with salt, pepper, and flour. Fry in oil until golden brown; turn once and add onions. Drain fat from meat; place in an oiled casserole. Mix remaining ingredients; pour over venison. Bake, covered, at 350° for approximately 1½ hours.
Serves 6.
Mrs. Thomas P. Francis (Nelda Cummins)

Fork-Tender Venison

3	lb. venison, cubed	1	bunch carrots, peeled and cut into 1 inch pieces
	Meat tenderizer	1	c. diced onions
1½	c. flour	2	large cloves garlic, minced
1	t. paprika	1	bell pepper, cut into ½ inch pieces
1	t. salt		
1	t. pepper	2	T. minced parsley
1	c. vegetable oil		Pinch oregano
3	c. boiling water	1	t. Worcestershire sauce
3	beef bouillon cubes	2	T. molasses, optional
3	chicken bouillon cubes	3	c. cooked rice
2	c. sliced mushrooms		

Sprinkle meat with meat tenderizer and set aside for 2 to 3 hours. Combine flour, paprika, salt, and pepper. Dredge meat thoroughly in flour mixture and brown, a small portion at a time, in hot oil. Remove from pan and set aside. Stir flour left from dredging meat into pan drippings. Dissolve bouillon cubes in boiling water and pour over flour; stir well over medium heat. Simmer, stirring often, until slightly thickened. Return meat to pan and add remaining ingredients; stir. Bake, uncovered, at 350° for 2 hours. Serve over rice.
Serves 6.
Mrs. J. Travis Davis (Kathleen Penn)

Venison Marinade

1	c. finely chopped onions	Juice of 6 lemons (1 c.)	
2	c. butter	2	5 oz. bottles Worcestershire
1	14 oz. bottle catsup		sauce
1	6 oz. jar prepared mustard	1	T. Tabasco
½	c. vinegar	2	T. salt
1	t. paprika	1	t. garlic salt
1	t. chili powder		

Sauté onions in butter; add remaining ingredients and simmer for 30 minutes. Do not boil.
Yields 3 quarts.
Mrs. Robert H. McIntyre (Danya Nicholson)

Fiesta Venison

2   venison backstraps or
    1 venison ham
Cracked pepper

Dehydrated green onion
Worcestershire sauce

Sauce

1	c. butter	2	T. Worcestershire sauce
½	c. lemon juice	2	jalapeños, diced, seeds
2	t. salt		included
1	t. pepper		

Remove any excess muscle or fat on meat. If the ham is used, remove bone. At least 1 hour before cooking, sprinkle meat with pepper, green onion, and Worcestershire sauce. Combine all ingredients for sauce in a saucepan. Bring to a boil. Pour some of sauce over meat and rub into meat. Cook meat on barbeque pit over a slow fire, basting with sauce every 10 to 15 minutes. Grill meat for 45 to 60 minutes. To serve, slice meat and brush with remaining sauce.
Serves 8 to 10.
Mrs. William H. Page (Lolla McNutt)

Dot Carter's Venison Backstrap Sauté

1 venison backstrap
Salt, pepper, and
  flour for dredging

¼ to ½ c. currant jelly
¼ to ½ c. butter
2 T. sherry

Cut backstrap crosswise into 1 inch thick pieces. Pound pieces until they are ¼ inch thick; dredge in salt, pepper, and flour. Melt equal amounts of jelly and butter in a skillet (use larger amount if backstrap is large). Add sherry. Sauté meat in the jelly until brown; turn meat and brown other side.
Different from the usual treatment of venison.
Serves 4 to 6.
Mrs. Ronald S. Driver (Susan Page)

Venison Shoulder Roast

3 to 4 garlic cloves, slivered
1 venison shoulder roast
1 lb. carrots, peeled and diced
2 onions, chopped
4 ribs celery, chopped
1 14 oz. can tomatoes
1 10½ oz. can condensed
   consommé

1¼ c. dry red wine
2 bay leaves
¼ t. chopped parsley
¼ t. thyme
Cooked potatoes or rice

Pierce surface of roast in a number of places and insert slivers of garlic into gashes. Place meat in a large roasting pan; arrange carrots, onions, and celery on and around roast. Pour tomatoes, consommé, and wine over meat and vegetables. Sprinkle with spices. Roast, covered, at 350° for approximately 4 hours (age of deer will determine cooking time), until tender. Mash vegetables into cooking liquid to make a gravy. Serve with potatoes or rice.
Serves 8.
Mrs. W. T. Archer (Dorothy Newton)

Jack Corley's Venison Annandale

6 lb. venison cutlets or
  round steak
1½ c. flour
Salt and pepper to taste

½ c. vegetable oil or
  bacon drippings
2 medium onions, sliced

Lightly pound venison. Dredge in 1 cup of the flour and sprinkle with salt and pepper. Brown in hot oil or bacon drippings. Remove to a Dutch oven and cover with sliced onions. Make gravy with pan drippings, adding remaining ½ cup of flour. When browned, stir in 4 cups water and pour over venison. Cover and bake at 325° for 1 hour, turning cutlets twice.
Serves 8 to 10.
Mrs. Jack Corley (Frances Barton)

Burgundy Venison Stew

3 medium onions, peeled
  and sliced
½ c. bacon drippings
2 lb. boneless venison stew
  meat, fat removed and
  cut into ¾ inch cubes
¼ c. flour
1¾ c. Burgundy wine

1 10½ oz. can condensed
  beef broth
⅛ t. marjoram
⅛ t. thyme
Salt and pepper to taste
1 lb. mushrooms, sliced
Hot noodles, optional

Sauté onions in ¼ cup of the bacon drippings until golden brown. Remove and reserve onions. Brown venison, small portions at a time, in same pan, adding more bacon drippings as needed. Place browned meat in a 4 quart Dutch oven and sprinkle with flour. Add wine, broth, marjoram, thyme, salt and pepper. Simmer gently covered, for 3 hours. Stir in mushrooms and sautéed onions. Simmer 1 hour. Serve in soup bowls or over noodles.
Serves 6 to 8/Freezes.
Mrs. William Duncan (Betty Howell)

Quail with Cherry Sauce

½ c. flour
1½ t. salt
¼ t. garlic salt
½ t. paprika
8 quail breasts, skinned

¼ c. vegetable oil
1 1 lb. can pitted dark sweet
cherries, drained
1 c. sauterne

Combine flour, salt, garlic salt, and paprika in a paper bag. Add quail, 2 at a time, and shake to coat. Heat oil and brown quail. Add cherries and sauterne. Cover and simmer 35 to 45 minutes or until tender.
Dressed up quail.
Serves 4.
Mrs. John C. Donovan (Anne Peterson)

Dunkin' Quail

12 quail
¼ c. vegetable oil
1 onion, diced
3 green chilies, sliced
into rounds
2 tomatoes, diced
4 cloves garlic, minced

2 to 3 T. flour
2 10½ oz. cans condensed
chicken consommé
½ c. sliced mushrooms
Salt and pepper to taste
¼ c. sauterne or Chablis
French bread

Brown birds in oil and remove to deep casserole. Sauté onion in oil until almost tender. Add chilies, tomatoes, and garlic; simmer until tomatoes are soft and begin to fall apart. Sprinkle in flour, a little at a time, and stir for 5 minutes. Add consommé and mushrooms; season to taste with salt and pepper. Add wine. Pour sauce over birds; cover and bake at 325° for 45 minutes to 1 hour. Serve in bowls with sauce and French bread for dunking.
Dunkin' good!
Serves 4 to 6.
Mrs. Fisher A. Tyler (Eleanor Niggli)

Fried Quail for Saturday Breakfast

8 quail	½ c. flour
Milk	2 c. butter
4 eggs, beaten	Biscuits and honey
1½ c. cracker crumbs	

Soak quail in milk for 1 hour. Drain and dip in eggs, then combined crumbs and flour. In a large skillet, heat butter and gently brown quail. Simmer, covered, 10 to 20 minutes, until tender. Serve with biscuits and honey.
Serves 4.
Mrs. George Robinson, Jr. (Sue Cocke)

Roast Goose or Duck

1 goose or duck	1 clove garlic, chopped
Salt and pepper	1 strip of bacon
1 small apple, peeled, cored and chopped	1 c. guava jelly
¼ c. chopped celery	½ c. frozen orange juice, undiluted
½ c. chopped onion	½ c. Port wine
¼ c. raisins	Wild rice

Place goose or duck in a shallow roasting pan. Rub with salt and pepper. Combine apple, celery, onion, raisins, and garlic. Stuff bird with mixture. Place bacon over cavity. Cook at 500° for 30 minutes, then reduce to 350° for 1 hour 30 minutes longer, or until tender. Melt jelly and orange juice in a small sauce pan. Add wine. Pour mixture over bird while baking. Baste frequently. Serve with wild rice.
Serves 2.
Mrs. John Philip Ferguson (Mitzi Ann Riddle)

Sautéed Quail

16 quail	½ lb. mushrooms, sliced
1 c. flour	Salt and pepper to taste
1 c. butter	1⅓ c. dry sherry
1 medium onion, sliced	

Dredge quail in flour. Sauté in butter until brown, approximately 10 minutes. Stir in onion and mushrooms, sautéing until tender. Add salt, pepper, and sherry, mixing well. Bring to a boil; reduce heat and simmer, covered, for 20 minutes, until tender.
Serves 8.
Mrs. John Oscar Robinson (Nancy Newton)

Stuffed Pheasant

½ c. finely chopped onion	1 pheasant or 2½ to 3 lb. roasting chicken
2 T. butter	4 thick slices bacon
1 4 oz. can chopped mushrooms	10 T. dry sherry
½ c. uncooked rice	¼ c. melted butter
2 T. chopped parsley	3 T. flour
Salt and pepper to taste	2 c. chicken broth

Sauté onion in 2 tablespoons butter. Drain and reserve liquid from the can of mushrooms. Add enough water to make 1 cup. Add liquid to onion and bring to a boil. Slowly add rice, stirring constantly. Cover and cook over low heat until all liquid is absorbed, approximately 20 to 25 minutes. Stir in mushrooms and parsley. Season with salt and pepper. Stuff pheasant loosely with rice mixture; dress and place in baking pan, breast up. Lay slices of bacon over breast and legs. Roast, uncovered, at 350° for 1 hour 30 minutes or until tender. Baste with a mixture of ½ cup of the sherry and ½ cup melted butter. Remove pheasant to heated platter. Discard all but 3 tablespoons of drippings from pan. Blend in flour, then broth. Cook until thick. Add 2 tablespoons of the sherry. Season to taste with salt and pepper. Serve sauce on the side with pheasant.
Serves 2.
Mrs. Charles Michael Smith (Sally Thomas)

Barbequed Dove

Lemon Juice
Butter, at room temperature
Doves

Lemon-pepper
Bacon slices

Blend equal amounts of lemon juice and butter. Rub each dove with mixture, then sprinkle with lemon-pepper. Wrap each dove with one piece of bacon and secure with toothpick. Place over hot charcoals and grill until bacon is done, turning once.

Mrs. John H. Coates (Ann Cox)

Vegetables

Scalloped Artichokes

1 large onion, finely chopped	¼ t. thyme
1 bell pepper, finely chopped	½ t. salt
¼ c. vegetable oil	¼ t. basil or rosemary
16 cooked artichoke hearts	Dash Tabasco
2 eggs, beaten slightly	20 small crackers, crushed
1½ c. sour cream	

Sauté onions and bell pepper in oil until tender, but not brown. Pour into a 1½ quart buttered casserole and arrange artichoke hearts over onions. Combine eggs and sour cream; add seasonings and pour over artichokes. Sprinkle cracker crumbs on top. Heat at 350° for 25 minutes.
Serves 8.
Mrs. J. Chrys Dougherty (Mary Ireland Graves)

Artichokes alla Ricco's

¼ c. chopped onion	1 T. chopped parsley
2 c. olive oil	2 t. salt
6 T. butter	1 t. freshly ground pepper
3 c. seasoned Italian bread crumbs	8 fresh artichokes, trimmed and cooked
2 cloves garlic, mashed	Olive oil
2 T. wine vinegar	

Sauté onion in olive oil and butter. Remove pan from heat and toss bread crumbs, garlic, vinegar, parsley, salt, and pepper with olive oil mixture. Gently spread apart leaves of artichokes; pull out thistle-like core. With a long handled spoon, scrape out choke. Spoon stuffing into the center of the artichokes and press the remaining stuffing between the outer leaves. Arrange the artichokes snugly in a deep baking dish; pour 1 inch of boiling water around artichokes. Drizzle olive oil over the artichokes. Cover with foil and bake at 350° for 1 hour.
Serves 8.
Mrs. Charles E. Bates (Linda Steinhauser)

Opulent Asparagus

¼ c. butter
¼ c. flour
2 c. milk
Salt and pepper to taste
Dash cayenne
½ c. slivered, toasted
  almonds
1 3 oz. jar pimiento pieces,
  drained

2 10 oz. packages frozen
  asparagus or 1 lb. fresh
  asparagus, cooked until
  just tender
2 hard-cooked eggs, sliced
½ c. grated Swiss cheese
Paprika

Melt butter and stir in flour; add milk gradually, stirring constantly until thickened. Add salt, pepper, cayenne, almonds, and pimiento. Layer asparagus, egg slices, and cream sauce in a buttered 7 x 11 baking dish. Sprinkle with cheese and paprika. Bake at 350° for 30 minutes or until bubbly and cheese is melted.
Serves 6 to 8.
Mrs. Charles E. Bates (Linda Steinhauser)

Fresh Asparagus

You will need: asparagus, the best you can procure; outside lettuce leaves, found unfit for other uses and stored in a plastic sack in the vegetable bin of your ice box; lemon butter, if desired.

Wash asparagus gently under running water. Please do not plunge and soak. Do not cut this lovely succulent vegetable, but rather bend it gently and it will break where the spear becomes tender. Put the tough ends in the ice box for the soup pot. Lay the spears in the cold skillet, still wet from washing. Do not dry them. Bring out the stored lettuce leaves and rinse again and while still wet, lay them on top of the asparagus, leaving enough room for the lid to fit tightly on the skillet. Turn the fire to medium only long enough to heat the skillet and the lid to hot. Turn fire to low, but, if you hear a sizzle, turn to warm. Cook for about 5 or 6 minutes. Do not remove cover until ready to serve. If you serve on plates, or in a large serving dish, pick the prettiest setting you have for this vegetable. Have the lemon butter ready to serve on the side. When ready, remove lid, discard lettuce and place asparagus on dishes. It will have retained a bright green color and needs no seasoning, for the delicate and delicious spears have a wonderful taste that salt, pepper or the like, will only distort.

If you like this method of cooking asparagus, try it on fresh green garden peas, beans, zucchini, or crook neck yellow squash. This is an ideal way to fix spinach but you will not need the lettuce leaves for this. The secret of the beautiful color is that you do not uncover the skillet until ready to serve. It is the air that enters the cooking process that discolors and darkens the vegetables.
An editorial, not a recipe.
Mrs. James N. Ludlum (Dorothy Standifer)

Baked Barley

1 c. barley
½ c. butter
2 10½ oz. cans condensed chicken broth
1 4 oz. can sliced mushrooms, drained

Sauté barley in butter until lightly browned. Pour broth and mushrooms over barley; stir. Bake, covered, at 350° for 1 hour or until broth is absorbed.
Serves 4 to 6.
Mrs. Richard T. Weber (Violetta Van Devanter)

Green Beans with Horseradish Sauce

1 T. prepared horseradish
2 hard-cooked eggs, chopped
1 c. mayonnaise
1 t. Worcestershire sauce
Salt, pepper; garlic salt,
  celery salt, onion salt to taste

1½ t. chopped parsley
Juice of 1 lemon
3 9 oz. packages frozen green
  beans or 1½ lb. fresh green
  beans, cooked and drained

Combine all ingredients, except beans, and set aside. Sauce should be at room temperature. Pour sauce over hot beans, or pass separately.
Serves 6 to 8.
Mrs. John C. Donovan (Anne Peterson)

Frijoles Borrachos

2 c. dried pinto beans, rinsed
Salt
1 garlic clove, minced
Salt pork
2 T. bacon drippings

1 onion, chopped
2 green chili peppers, minced
2 tomatoes, minced
1 can beer

Soak beans in water overnight. Drain and cover with water; add salt, garlic, and salt pork. Simmer 2½ hours, until beans are soft. Drain beans and reserve liquid. Heat bacon drippings and sauté onion, peppers, and tomatoes until soft. Stir mixture into beans and simmer 5 minutes. Just before serving, pour beer and as much reserved liquid as desired into beans and serve hot. Beans can be mashed.
Title translates as Drunken Beans.
Serves 8 to 12/Freezes.
Mrs. Frank N. Ikard, Jr. (Carol Foster)

Susan Diggle Horton's Green Beans

4	c. frozen French-cut green beans	1	t. salt
½	lb. Swiss cheese, grated	¼	t. pepper
2	T. butter	1	t. sugar
2	T. flour	1	c. sour cream
½	t. grated onion	1	c. crushed cornflakes
		2	T. butter, melted

Place beans in buttered 1½ quart casserole; sprinkle with cheese. Melt butter and blend in flour. Add onion, salt, pepper, sugar, and sour cream. Simmer slowly for several minutes, stirring constantly. Pour sauce over beans and cheese. Stir cornflakes into melted butter until crumbs are coated. Sprinkle top of casserole with buttered cornflakes. Bake at 400° for 20 minutes.
A handsome layered effect.
Serves 8 to 10.
Mrs. George K. Meriwether (Sara May McCampbell)

Lima Beans Sauté

¼	c. butter	½	t. salt
1	6 oz. can water chestnuts, thinly sliced	¼	t. pepper
		¼	t. monosodium glutamate
2	T. wine vinegar	2	10 oz. packages lima beans, cooked and drained
2	t. dill weed		

Melt butter in skillet; add all ingredients except lima beans; sauté until water chestnuts are lightly browned. Add beans to the sauce and heat.
Serves 8.
Mrs. Frank M. Covert, III (Martha Woods)

Raunch Beans

1	lb. dried pinto beans	1	T. chili powder
1	8 oz. can tomato sauce	4	beef bouillon cubes
1	T. salt	2	T. bacon drippings
1	T. sugar	2	medium onions, chopped
1	T. ground cumin	1	4 to 5 inch smoked sausage,
1	t. pepper		diced

Sort and rinse beans thoroughly. Place beans in bowl with water to cover. Add tomato sauce, all seasonings, and bouillons cubes. Soak overnight. Stir occasionally. Heat bacon drippings in heavy Dutch oven; sauté onions and sausage. Pour in bean mixture. Boil. Reduce heat, cover, and simmer for approximately 8 hours. Beans should be covered by ¼ inch liquid the entire time. Stir occasionally. During the last two hours, mash some of beans against side of pot to thicken the pot likker. Beans are better if prepared the day before serving.
Serves 12/Freezes.

Fringe Benefit Bean Dip

Place 2 cups of the Raunch beans and enough pot likker to cover beans into blender. Split lengthwise, remove seeds and stems from 2 to 4 jalapeños. Add to beans. Blend until smooth. Serve with fried tortilla chips.
By way of Dr. James Albright.
Mrs. James H. Albright (Mary Margaret Carlson)

Teresita's Black Beans

1	lb. dried black beans	½ c. tomato sauce
1	bay leaf	1 t. ground cumin
1	onion, chopped	1 t. sugar
1	bell pepper, chopped	Salt and pepper to taste
3	cloves garlic, minced	⅓ c. dry sherry
½	c. vegetable oil	

Soak beans in water 3 to 4 hours or overnight; drain. Cover beans with water, add bay leaf, and simmer, covered, for 3 to 4 hours. Sauté onion, bell pepper, and garlic in oil until tender. Add onion mixture and all remaining ingredients to beans. Correct seasoning and simmer, uncovered, for 30 to 45 minutes, or until thick.
A Southwestern version.
Serves 12/Freezes.
Mrs. John C. Donovan (Anne Peterson)

Green Beans in Casserole

⅓ c. chopped onion
2 T. butter
1 c. sour cream
1 t. salt
¼ t. pepper
½ t. grated lemon rind
1 T. minced parsley

2 T. flour
1½ lb. fresh green beans or
   3 10 oz. packages frozen
   French-style green beans,
   slightly cooked and drained
½ c. buttered bread crumbs
½ c. grated American cheese

Sauté onion in butter. Combine sour cream, salt, pepper, lemon rind, parsley, and flour and add to onions. Stir in beans and mix well. Pour into a buttered 1½ quart casserole and sprinkle with bread crumbs and cheese. Bake at 300° for 30 to 40 minutes.
Distinctive with sour cream and lemon rind.
Serves 6.
Mrs. John Stayton (Gene Cherry)

Sweet and Sour Beets

2 t. cornstarch
4 t. honey
¼ c. cider vinegar

½ t. salt
1 16 oz. can diced beets,
   drained

Mix cornstarch, honey, vinegar, and salt in saucepan. Stir in beets. Simmer, covered, for 2 minutes.
Serves 6.
Mrs. Larry Temple (Louann Atkins)

Fresh Beets in Orange Sauce

6 to 8 small beets
¼ c. sugar
1½ t. cornstarch

¾ t. salt
½ c. orange juice
1 T. butter

Remove beet root and all but ½ inch of the stem. Boil until tender; peel and set aside. Combine sugar, cornstarch, salt, and orange juice; cook until thickened and add butter. Slice the beets into the sauce. Heat and serve. Better made ahead, refrigerated, and reheated. Carrots may be substituted for the beets.
Serves 4 to 6.
Mrs. William Green (Jeanie Mullins)

Broccoli with Mushrooms

1 bunch fresh broccoli
6 T. vegetable oil
½ lb. fresh mushrooms, slivered
   or quartered
1½ t. salt

Trim broccoli stems and cut into small strips. Break flowerets into bite-size pieces. Rinse in cold water. In a skillet heat oil until very hot; add broccoli and mushrooms. Sprinkle with salt. Stir fry until coated with oil. Cover and cook 2 minutes over medium heat. Uncover and cook 4 minutes longer. Serve immediately. Asparagus may be substituted for broccoli.
Serves 4 to 6.
Mrs. Frank N. Ikard, Jr. (Carol Foster)

Tomato-Broccoli Stackup

3 large tomatoes	1 10 oz. package frozen,
Salt	chopped broccoli, cooked
4 oz. Swiss cheese,	and drained
grated	¼ c. chopped onion

Slice tomatoes ¾ inch thick; sprinkle with salt. Set aside 2 tablespoons of the cheese for topping; combine remaining cheese with broccoli and onion. Arrange tomato slices on baking sheet; spoon broccoli mixture onto tomatoes. Sprinkle with cheese. Broil 10 to 12 minutes until cheese bubbles and tomato slices are hot.
Serves 4 to 6.
Mrs. Benjamin McPherson, Jr. (Marie Lois Leopold)

Gumbochu

6 slices salt pork, slivered	1 onion, chopped
and rinsed	Salt and freshly ground
1 T. bacon drippings	pepper to taste
⅓ c. uncooked rice	
½ head cabbage, coarsely	
chopped	

Brown salt pork in hot bacon drippings. Remove pork and add rice, stirring until slightly brown. Stir in cabbage and onion, cooking until glazed. Add a scant ¼ cup water and bring to a boil. Simmer, covered, over low heat, approximately 12 minutes. Sprinkle with salt and pepper.
Serves 4 to 6.
Mrs. Edward Clark (Ann Metcalf)

Hot Cabbage Crisp

1 T. vegetable oil or melted butter	1 small bell pepper, chopped
2 c. shredded cabbage	1 small onion, chopped
2 ribs celery, chopped	Salt and pepper to taste
	Cayenne to taste

Combine all ingredients in a skillet. Sauté approximately 5 minutes or until hot. Vegetables should be crisp. Serve immediately.
Serves 4.
Mrs. Howell M. Finch (Diane Hierholzer)

Red Cabbage

2 tart apples	½ t. pepper
2 T. butter	2 cloves
1 medium onion, chopped	1 bay leaf
4 c. water	Juice of ½ lemon
½ c. red wine vinegar	1 medium size head red cabbage, shredded
½ c. sugar	
½ t. salt	2 to 3 T. flour

Peel, core, and chop apples. Heat butter in a large pan and sauté onions and apples for 3 to 4 minutes. Add water, vinegar, sugar, salt, pepper, cloves, bay leaf, and lemon juice. Stir. Bring to a boil and add cabbage. Cover and simmer for 45 minutes. Just before serving, sprinkle in flour to absorb liquid.
Serves 6.
Mrs. Charles R. Crites (Mildred "Milly" Holmes)

Carrots Veronique

½ c. packed brown sugar	30 fresh seedless white grapes
½ c. butter, melted	1 T. chopped mint leaves
½ c. Cointreau	Fresh mint
2 15 oz. cans tiny whole Belgian carrots, drained	

Stir brown sugar into butter and bring to a boil. Pour in Cointreau and simmer 5 minutes. Add carrots, grapes, and chopped mint; simmer slowly for 5 minutes. Garnish with mint sprigs.
Serves 6.
Mrs. Charles E. Bates (Linda Steinhauser)

Ginger Glazed Carrots

1 bunch carrots, peeled and sliced julienne style	¼ c. butter
1 chicken bouillon cube dissolved in ¼ c. boiling water	1 T. lemon juice
	3 T. honey
	½ t. ginger
1 t. sugar	¼ t. nutmeg
	Chopped parsley

Simmer carrots in bouillon, sugar and 1 tablespoon of the butter for 12 to 15 minutes. Drain well. Combine remaining butter, lemon juice, honey, ginger, and nutmeg; pour over carrots and cook uncovered over medium heat for 3 minutes, tossing frequently. Sprinkle with parsley.
Serves 6 to 8.
Mrs. McNay Crossland (Sara McNay)

Carrot Ring

15 carrots, cooked until tender and drained	½ c. chopped parsley
8 hard-cooked eggs	Salt, pepper, and paprika to taste
1 bell pepper	¼ c. butter, melted
1½ T. finely grated onion	Parsley

In a food grinder, finely grind carrots, eggs, and bell pepper. Stir in onion, parsley, and butter. Add salt, pepper, and paprika; mix well. Pour into a buttered 6 cup ring mold (may be frozen at this point); bake at 350° for 25 to 30 minutes. Turn carrot ring out onto a platter; garnish with parlsey.
Center may be filled with green peas or broccoli.
Serves 8 to 10/Freezes.
Mrs. Jack Corley (Frances Barton)

Carrots in Cheese Sauce

2 lb. carrots, peeled and sliced	½ t. dry mustard
2 onions, minced	¼ t. pepper
1 T. butter	¼ t. celery salt
¼ c. flour	2 c. milk
1 t. salt	8 oz. Cheddar cheese, grated
	6 T. buttered bread crumbs

Simmer carrots until tender. Sauté onions in butter; add flour, seasonings and milk. Stir and cook until smooth and thickened. Arrange layers of carrots and cheese in a 1½ quart casserole; pour cream sauce over carrots and top with crumbs. Bake at 350° for 25 minutes, uncovered.
Serves 8.
Mrs. John C. Donovan (Anne Peterson)

Carrots Parmesan

20 large carrots, peeled and
    cut into thirds
1 t. sugar
3 c. heavy cream

1½ c. Parmesan cheese
Salt and pepper to taste
1 onion, grated
20 pecan halves

Boil carrots until tender in salted water to which sugar has been added. Drain and chop finely or put through food mill. Stir in cream, cheese, salt, and pepper. Pour into a buttered 2 quart casserole. Spread grated onion on top and arrange pecan halves over casserole. Heat at 350° for 45 minutes to 1 hour.
Company carrots.
Serves 8.
Mrs. Larry Temple (Louann Atkins)

Carrots Lyonnaise

4 T. butter
1 medium onion, thinly sliced
2 lb. carrots, peeled and
    cut into strips

Salt to taste
Lemon pepper to taste
Chopped parsley

Melt 3 tablespoons of the butter in skillet; sauté onion in butter until tender; remove onion and reserve. Add carrots and 1 more tablespoon butter. Toss carrots with the butter. Cover and cook for 15 minutes, or until tender. Remove cover, add onion, and simmer until liquid evaporates. Season, sprinkle with parsley, and serve hot.
Serves 8 to 10.
Mrs. W. R. Long, III (Carol Tyler)

Avery Corn Pudding

½ medium onion, finely chopped
1 bell pepper, finely chopped
3 T. butter
3 T. flour
2 c. milk
1 c. grated Cheddar cheese
Salt and pepper to taste

1 t. sugar
2 12 oz. cans whole kernel corn, drained
2 eggs, beaten
Buttered bread crumbs, optional
Paprika, optional

Sauté onion and bell pepper in butter until limp. Stir in flour, milk, and cheese; add salt, pepper, and sugar. Stir in corn and eggs; pour into buttered baking dish. Top with bread crumbs and paprika; bake at 350° for 30 to 40 minutes or until firm. Serve hot.
Serves 6/Freezes.
Mrs. Albert P. Jones (Annette Lewis)

Corn Pudding

1 12 oz. can cream-style corn
1 12 oz. can whole kernel corn, drained
1 c. tomato juice
1 c. grated Cheddar cheese
½ c. corn meal

¼ c. finely chopped onion
¼ c. finely chopped bell pepper
Salt and pepper to taste
2 eggs, beaten
½ c. milk
Paprika

Combine all ingredients, except paprika, reserving ½ cup of the cheese. Pour into a 1½ quart buttered casserole. Top with the remaining cheese; sprinkle with paprika. Bake in a hot water bath at 350° for 1 hour.
An untraditional version.
Serves 6 to 8.
Mrs. Grant W. Simpson (Mary Ellen Reese)

Eggplant with Mushroom Stuffing

1 large eggplant	1 c. finely chopped bell pepper
1 c. chopped fresh mushrooms	Salt and pepper to taste
3 T. butter	½ c. buttered bread crumbs

Cut eggplant in half lengthwise; scoop out the pulp leaving shells approximately 1 inch thick. Chop eggplant pulp and sauté with mushrooms in butter for 5 minutes. Stir in bell pepper and seasonings. Stuff shells with eggplant mixture and sprinkle with bread crumbs. Bake at 350° until bread crumbs are brown, approximately 30 minutes.
Serves 6 to 8.
Mrs. T. S. Painter, Jr. (Dorothy Bulkley)

Ratatouille

2 small or 1 medium eggplant, peeled and diced	Salt and pepper to taste
1 large onion, chopped	1 T. sugar
2 bell peppers, thinly sliced	1 T. wine vinegar
2 medium zucchini, sliced	¼ t. oregano
6 medium tomatoes, peeled and diced, or 2 16 oz. cans tomatoes, drained	¼ t. basil
	5 T. olive oil
	½ c. water
2 to 3 large cloves garlic, crushed	25 pitted ripe olives, optional
	¼ c. chopped parsley

Combine eggplant, onion, peppers, zucchini, tomatoes, garlic, salt, pepper, sugar, vinegar, oregano, and basil in Dutch oven; sprinkle with olive oil and water. Simmer, covered, over low heat until tender, approximately 1 hour. Remove cover and simmer 10 minutes to reduce liquid. Add olives and serve with parsley sprinkled on top. Serve hot or cold.
Serves 8.
Mrs. Charles E. Bates (Linda Steinhauser)

Spanish Hominy

1 onion, finely chopped	1 8 oz. can tomato sauce
1 bell pepper, finely chopped	1 4 oz. can mushrooms
¼ c. bacon drippings	Salt and pepper to taste
2 to 3 t. chili powder	2 29 oz. cans hominy, drained
1 t. cumin	1 c. grated Cheddar or Monterey
1 4 oz. can tomato paste	Jack cheese

Sauté onion and bell pepper in bacon drippings. Stir in chili powder and cumin. Add tomato paste, tomato sauce, mushrooms with liquid, salt, and pepper. Mix hominy with the sauce. Pour into a buttered casserole and top with cheese. Bake at 325° for 25 minutes.
Serves 8 to 10.
Mrs. Terrell James (Dianne Hill)

Mushroom Pie

6 T. butter	1½ c. chicken broth
2 lb. mushrooms, with stems	½ c. Madeira wine
removed	½ c. heavy cream, heated
Salt and pepper to taste	Pie dough for a 1 crust pie,
2 T. lemon juice	rolled to 11 x 7
3 T. flour	1 egg, beaten

In a large pan melt 4 tablespoons of the butter; add mushroom caps. Sprinkle with salt, pepper, and lemon juice; cook slowly for 10 minutes, stirring often. Remove mushrooms with slotted spoon; arrange in a 1 quart baking dish. To pan juices, add the remaining 2 tablespoons of butter and melt; add flour and stir. Slowly add chicken broth; simmer, stirring constantly, until sauce is smooth and thick. Stir in Madeira and cream. Pour sauce over mushrooms. Cover with pie dough; trim edges. Brush with egg; cut slits in the pastry. Bake at 450° for 15 minutes; reduce heat to 350° for an additional 10 to 15 minutes.
A roast beef complement.
Serves 8.
Mrs. Stephen Clark (Kate Eustis)

French Fried Mushrooms

2   eggs, beaten
Salt and pepper to taste
2   lb. whole mushrooms

1   c. dry bread crumbs
Vegetable oil
Salt and pepper to taste

Add salt and pepper to beaten eggs. Dip mushrooms in egg and then in bread crumbs. Fry until brown in deep fat. Drain; salt and pepper lightly. Serve immediately.
Serves 12.
Mrs. Charles E. Bates (Linda Steinhauser)

Mushrooms au Gratin

1   lb. fresh mushrooms
¼   c. butter
3   T. flour
¾   c. chicken broth
¼   t. marjoram
1   T. chopped parsley

¼   t. salt
⅛   t. pepper
¼   c. heavy cream
1   T. dry vermouth
2   T. grated Parmesan cheese
¼   c. soft bread crumbs

Remove stems from mushrooms; chop finely. Slice mushroom caps. Melt butter in large pan; sauté caps and stems, uncovered, for 10 minutes, stirring often. Stir in flour. Slowly add chicken broth, stirring until sauce is smooth. Add seasonings; simmer, stirring constantly, for 5 minutes. Blend in cream and vermouth; simmer for 3 minutes. Pour mixture into buttered 1 quart casserole; top with mixed cheese and bread crumbs. Bake at 350° for 15 minutes or until brown.
For very special guests.
Serves 4 to 6.
Mrs. Stephen Clark (Kate Eustis)

Okra and Tomatoes

1	lb. young, tender okra	1	t. salt
1	T. bacon drippings	¼	t. pepper
1	large onion, chopped	2	dashes cayenne
2	tomatoes, peeled, cored, and chopped	½	t. sugar

Rinse okra and dry well. Remove tops and slice pods crosswise in ¼ inch pieces. Heat bacon drippings in large aluminum or stainless steel skillet. Sauté okra 10 to 15 minutes, stirring occasionally, until it begins to look dry and loses its ropy texture. Stir in onions, cooking until they are clear and soft. Add tomatoes and seasonings; lower heat and continue cooking for several minutes.
Serves 4/Freezes.
Mrs. Russell Painton (Ann "Aggie" Mullins)

French Fried Onions

1	c. sifted flour	6	T. water
1	t. salt	2 to 3 large onions, peeled and sliced ¼ inch thick	
½	c. evaporated milk		
2	T. vegetable oil	Vegetable oil	
1	egg white		

Sift flour and salt together. Add milk, oil, and egg white. Beat until smooth. Add water. Separate onions into rings. Dip into batter so each ring is completely coated. Heat cooking oil to 375°. Fry a few rings at a time in the oil until golden brown. Sprinkle with salt.
Anything deep-fried would benefit from this perfect batter.
Serves 4 to 6.
Mrs. C. Dean Davis (Mollie Villeret)

French Epicurean Peas

4   slices bacon, chopped
1   T. chopped onion
1   T. flour
1   17 oz. can LeSueur brand peas,
    drained

1   c. light cream
½   c. chopped mushrooms
Salt and pepper to taste

Fry bacon until crisp. Sauté onions in bacon drippings until tender. Drain off all but 1 tablespoon bacon drippings. Blend in flour. Add peas and cream; simmer, stirring, over low heat until thickened. Stir in mushrooms, bacon, salt, and pepper.
Serves 6.
Mrs. Bethea W. Brindley (Mary Ellen Kennedy)

Green Pea Ring

2   lb. fresh or frozen green peas
2   T. butter
2   T. flour
½   c. light cream, heated
2   T. grated onion

1   t. salt
¼   t. nutmeg
⅛   t. cayenne
4   eggs, separated
½   c. cracker crumbs

Simmer peas in water until barely tender; drain and reserve liquid. Purée with ½ cup liquid. In a saucepan, make a white sauce of butter, flour, and cream. Add the onion and seasonings; allow sauce to cool slightly. Combine white sauce and puréed peas; add beaten egg yolks slowly and cracker crumbs. Beat egg whites until stiff and fold into the pea mixture. Line the bottom of a buttered 1½ quart ring-mold with buttered wax paper. Pour mixture into mold and bake at 350° for 40 minutes. Unmold and fill center of ring with artichoke hearts, Carrots Veronique, or rice pilaf.
Serves 8 to 12.
Mrs. Frank N. Ikard, Jr. (Carol Foster)

Cheese Stuffed Potatoes

6 Idaho potatoes, baked	½ c. heavy cream
½ c. cottage cheese	6 T. butter
2 T. grated onion	Salt and pepper to taste
2 T. chopped bell pepper	Paprika
¾ c. grated Cheddar cheese	

Cut an oval into each potato and scoop out inside. Combine potato pulp with remaining ingredients, except paprika, and blend thoroughly in a mixer. Refill shells and sprinkle with paprika. Heat at 350° for 20 minutes.

Serves 6/Freezes.

Mrs. John Philip Ferguson (Mitzi Ann Riddle)

Sweet Potato Soufflé

¾ c. maple syrup	2 t. grated orange peel
⅓ c. butter	4 eggs, separated
1 15½ oz. can mashed sweet potatoes or yams	

Heat together syrup and butter until hot. Combine syrup, potatoes, and orange peel. Mix well. Beat egg yolks and add to potato mixture. Beat egg whites to soft peak stage; fold into potatoes. Turn into a greased soufflé dish. Place in a hot water bath. Bake at 350° for 1 hour. Serve immediately.

Serves 4 to 6.

Mrs. Robb Southerland (Janis Barr)

Stuffed Baked Sweet Potatoes

2 sweet potatoes	2 T. chopped parsley
½ c. sour cream	2 T. finely chopped onion
2 T. butter	Melted butter
½ t. salt	

Bake sweet potatoes at 400° for 50 minutes, until they can be easily pierced with a fork. Cut in half and scoop out pulp. Mash or beat until free of lumps. Stir in sour cream, butter, salt, parsley, and onion. Pile lightly into potato shells and brush with melted butter. Heat at 400° for 25 minutes.
For a change, a sweet potato recipe that's not sweet.
Serves 4/Freezes.
Mrs. Larry Temple (Louann Atkins)

Charlie Potatoes

4 Idaho potatoes	Butter
2 t. chopped parsley	Salt and pepper to taste
2 t. minced dried onion	½ c. grated Cheddar cheese
2 t. prepared mustard	Paprika or parsley
Milk	

Bake potatoes at 425° for 1 hour or until done. Slice in half; scoop out meat, reserving shell. Mash well; add parsley, onion, and mustard. Beat in enough milk and butter to make potatoes fluffy. Season with salt and pepper; stir in cheese. Spoon into shells; sprinkle with paprika or parsley. Reheat at 300° until hot.
Serves 8/Freezes.
Mrs. Russell Painton (Ann "Aggie" Mullins)

Hot Sour Cream Potatoes

6 to 8 potatoes, cooked in jackets
½ c. butter
1   4 oz. jar pimiento pieces
½ c. diced onion

2   c. sour cream
Salt, pepper, cayenne, garlic
   salt, and paprika to taste

Peel and dice potatoes while warm. Add butter, pimientos, onion, and seasonings. Mix well and refrigerate for 1 hour. Stir in sour cream. Bake at 350° for 30 minutes.
Serves 8.
Mrs. Tom G. Ezell (Lilla Stevens Keyes)

Sesame Hash Browned Potatoes

¼ c. butter
1   T. finely chopped green onion
¼ c. sesame seeds
4   potatoes, baked, peeled,
   and diced

1   t. salt
½ t. freshly ground pepper
¼ c. heavy cream

Sauté onion in butter. Add sesame seeds and cook until lightly browned. Add potatoes, salt, pepper, and cream. Cook, stirring occasionally, until potatoes are golden brown.
Serves 4 to 6.
Mrs. Hugh Rushing (Elaine Robinson)

German Potatoes

⅓ c. butter
3 T. flour
1¼ c. chicken broth

2 T. vinegar
8 to 10 medium potatoes
1 bay leaf

In a skillet, melt butter, add flour, and cook until brown. Add broth and vinegar. Peel and cut potatoes in thin lengthwise slices. Place slices in gravy along with the bay leaf. Simmer, covered, 10 to 15 minutes or until tender.
Serves 6 to 8.
Mrs. Larry Temple (Louann Atkins)

Rice Indienne

½ c. raisins
¾ c. sauterne
¼ c. caraway seeds
2 c. hot, fluffy rice

Plump raisins in sauterne; drain. Toss rice with raisins and caraway seeds. Serve at once.
Serve with a curry dish.
Serves 4 to 6.
Mrs. Charles E. Bates (Linda Steinhauser)

Bayou Rice

1	c. broken vermicelli	1	c. rice
½	c. butter	2	10¾ oz. cans beef bouillon
3	ribs celery, chopped	½	c. sliced mushrooms
1	bunch green onions, chopped		Minced parsley
1	small bell pepper, chopped		

Sauté vermicelli in part of the butter and set aside. Sauté celery, onions, and bell pepper in remaining butter. Add rice, bouillon, and browned vermicelli to vegetables. Cook, covered, until rice is done, approximately 20 to 30 minutes. Toss with mushrooms and parsley.
Serves 8 to 10/Freezes.
Mrs. Lem Scarbrough, Jr. (Alice Ann Rotsch)

Italian Rice

¼	c. olive oil	¼	c. butter
1	clove garlic	1½	c. uncooked rice
½	lb. mushrooms, thinly sliced	3½	to 4 c. chicken broth
	Salt and pepper to taste	½	c. white wine
1	small onion, sliced	½	c. Parmesan cheese

Heat olive oil in skillet and add garlic and mushrooms. Sauté, stirring constantly, about 5 minutes. Season with salt and pepper. Discard garlic. In a separate skillet, sauté onion in butter until tender but not brown. Stir in rice and cook until rice is shiny. Add chicken broth ¼ cup at a time and simmer until broth is absorbed. Stir in wine and continue to cook until rice is creamy. Add mushrooms and cook until rice is tender. Stir in cheese and serve at once on warm platter.
Serves 4.
Mrs. Jack W. Scarbrough (Betty Richer)

Wild Rice with Pecans

6 T. butter	½ to 1 c. chopped pecans
½ lb. sliced mushrooms	1 c. wild rice, rinsed and
1 medium onion, chopped	drained
2 T. finely chopped	3 c. chicken broth
bell pepper	Salt and pepper to taste
1 clove garlic, minced	

Heat butter in a saucepan. Add mushrooms, onion, bell pepper, and garlic. Sauté for 5 minutes. Stir in pecans and cook 1 minute. Mix in rice and broth. Season with salt and pepper. Turn into a well-buttered 2 quart covered casserole. Bake at 350° for 1 hour.
Serves 8/Freezes.
Mrs. Charles Michael Smith (Sally Thomas)

Rice Dressing

1 lb. ground beef	6 c. cooked rice
1 lb. bulk pork sausage	Salt and pepper to taste
1 large onion, chopped	Dash garlic powder
2 to 3 ribs celery, chopped	½ c. chopped green onion tops
1 bell pepper, chopped	½ c. chopped parsley
2 link sausages, cut into	
small pieces and browned	

Brown ground meat and bulk sausage. Add onion, celery, and bell pepper; simmer until wilted. Season with salt, pepper, and garlic powder. Add link sausage to meat mixture and correct seasoning. Toss meat mixture with rice; add onion tops and parsley. May be served immediately or placed in a buttered, 2 quart casserole and heated at 250° for 30 minutes.
Double the meat mixture and serve as an entrée.
Serves 6 to 8/Freezes.
Mrs. C. Dean Davis (Mollie Villeret)

Orange Cashew Rice

3 T. butter	2 T. grated orange rind
⅔ c. diced celery	1¼ t. salt
2 T. finely chopped onion	1 c. uncooked rice
1½ c. water	1 11 oz. can mandarin oranges,
Juice from drained mandarin	drained with juice reserved
oranges plus orange juice	1 c. cashew nuts
to make 1 c.	Parsley

Melt butter; add celery, onion, water, orange juice, orange rind, and salt. Bring to boil; add rice slowly and cover. Reduce heat; cook 25 to 30 minutes or until rice is done. Gently stir in orange sections and cashew nuts. Garnish with parsley.
Serves 6.
Mrs. W. T. Archer (Dorothy Newton)

Rice Filled Bell Peppers

12 bell peppers	2 T. melted butter
1 c. uncooked rice	1 T. Worcestershire sauce
¼ lb. sharp or Old English	¼ t. sugar
cheese, grated	Salt and pepper to taste
1 clove garlic, minced	Buttered cracker crumbs

Slice off stem end of the peppers and remove membrane. Cook rice; rinse and drain. Add cheese, garlic, butter, Worcestershire, sugar, salt and pepper to the rice; toss lightly. Fill pepper shells with rice mixture. Top with crumbs. Place in baking dish and add a little water to the pan to prevent sticking. Bake at 350° for 30 to 45 minutes or until peppers are soft and crumbs are brown.
Good also as a tomato filling.
Serves 12.
Mrs. Beverly Sheffield (Lois Crow)

Spinach au Gratin

1 lb. spinach, finely chopped	4 slices bacon, crisply fried
1 T. lemon juice	¾ c. cracker crumbs
¾ c. grated Cheddar cheese	¼ c. melted butter
1 c. medium white sauce, heated	

Cook spinach for 2 to 3 minutes; drain and set aside. Add lemon juice and cheese to white sauce, stirring until cheese melts. Mix in spinach and pour into a buttered 1 quart baking dish. Crumble bacon over the top and sprinkle with cracker crumbs combined with butter. Heat at 350° for 20 minutes, until crumbs are browned.
Serves 4.
Mrs. Duke Matthews Covert (Lynne Carole Shapiro)

Spinach and Artichokes

½ c. chopped green onions with tops	2 8 oz. cans artichoke hearts in water, well-drained
½ c. butter	2 c. sour cream
2 10 oz. packages frozen chopped spinach, cooked and well-drained	Salt and pepper to taste
	½ c. grated Parmesan cheese

Sauté onions in butter; fold in spinach, artichoke hearts, and sour cream; add salt and pepper. Pour into 2 quart casserole and sprinkle with cheese; bake at 350° for 20 to 30 minutes.
Serves 4 to 6.
Mrs. Stephen Clark (Kate Eustis)

Spinach Balls

1	10 oz. package frozen spinach, cooked and drained	⅛	t. thyme
1	c. herb stuffing mix	⅛	t. pepper
¼	t. minced garlic	2	eggs, beaten
½	large onion, minced	6	T. melted butter

Combine all ingredients and chill until stiff enough to shape into bite-size balls. Bake at 350° for 20 minutes. Or bake at 350° 10 minutes; freeze; bake another 10 minutes to serve.
Serves 4 to 6/Freezes.
Mrs. Leon Bronson Dorsey (Cathryn Seymour)

Baked Spinach and Tomatoes

2	10 oz. packages frozen spinach, thawed and drained	3	tomatoes, halved
Salt and pepper to taste		4	slices bacon, fried and crumbled
4	oz. sliced, processed American cheese		

Spread spinach in a greased, 1½ quart baking dish; sprinkle with salt and pepper. Place ½ of cheese on spinach. Arrange tomatoes, cut side up, on cheese layer; sprinkle with salt and pepper. Place remaining cheese and crumbled bacon on top of tomatoes. Bake, uncovered, at 375° for approximately 20 minutes.
Serves 6.
Mrs. Lem Scarbrough, Jr. (Alice Rotsch)

Sesame Spinach

6   T. sesame seeds
3   10 oz. packages frozen,
    chopped spinach, thawed
    and very well-drained

½   c. butter
Salt and pepper to taste

Toast seeds at 350° until rich brown in color. Combine all ingredients and heat.
Spinach with a crunch.
Serves 6.
Mrs. Larry Temple (Louann Atkins)

Texas Crabgrass

1   medium onion, finely
    chopped
½   c. butter
1   package frozen, chopped
    spinach, cooked and drained
1   7 oz. can crabmeat or
    ½ lb. fresh or frozen
    crabmeat, cooked and flaked

¾   c. grated Parmesan cheese
¼   c. dry sherry or
    ¼ c. dry sauterne
Crackers

Sauté onion in butter. Add spinach, crabmeat, cheese, and wine. Serve as a vegetable for 4 to 6 persons or as a hot dip in chafing dish with crackers for 10 persons.
Mrs. Louis Southerland (Jean Reed)

Spinach Gnocchi

1	10 oz. package frozen, chopped spinach	1	t. salt
1	clove garlic, minced	1	t. basil
⅓	c. chopped onion	⅛	t. nutmeg
1	T. vegetable oil	¾	c. fine, dry bread crumbs
1	c. ricotta cheese	2	T. chopped parsley
2	eggs, beaten	½	c. grated Parmesan cheese
			Approximately ⅓ c. flour

Tomato Sauce

1	c. chopped onion	½	c. sauterne
1	clove garlic, minced	3	8 oz. cans tomato sauce with tomato bits
2	T. vegetable oil		Salt to taste
¾	t. oregano		
¾	t. rosemary, crumbled		

Cook spinach according to package directions; drain thoroughly, pressing out as much water as possible. Gnocci will not hold together if it is too liquid. Sauté garlic and onion slowly in oil until transparent, but not brown. Add spinach, ricotta cheese, eggs, salt, basil, and nutmeg; mix well. Blend in bread crumbs, parsley, and Parmesan cheese. Chill thoroughly. Shape rounded tablespoons into small cylinders approximately 2 tablespoons long; roll in flour. Cook a few at a time in boiling, salted water for 3 to 4 minutes until gnocchi rises to the top. Remove with slotted spoon; keep warm while cooking remaining ones. Serve hot with tomato sauce.

Tomato Sauce Sauté onion and garlic lightly in oil, stirring constantly. Add oregano, rosemary, sauterne, tomato sauce, and salt; simmer 20 minutes.

Gnocchi serves 4 to 6/Sauce yields approximately 3 cups.

Mrs. Clint Small, Jr. (Annie Laurie Jaeggli)

Spinach Cheese Pie

4	frozen patty shells	2	T. sliced green onions
6	eggs	1	T. chopped parsley
1	3 oz. package cream cheese, at room temperature	½	t. salt
			Dash pepper
¼	c. grated sharp, processed cheese	2	T. grated Parmesan cheese
			Tomato wedges, optional
1	10 oz. package frozen chopped spinach, cooked and well-drained		

Defrost patty shells in refrigerator for 2 hours. Roll out on lightly floured surface to fit a 10 inch pie plate, sealing edges together. Let rest 5 minutes; place in pie plate and flute edges. Combine eggs, cream cheese, and grated cheese; beat well. Stir in spinach, green onion, parsley, salt, and pepper. Pour into pastry shell; sprinkle with Parmesan cheese. Bake at 425° for 15 minutes or until edges of filling are set. Let stand 10 minutes before serving. If desired, top with tomato wedges and more Parmesan cheese; return to oven 3 to 5 minutes.
Serves 8.
Mrs. Thomas E. Nelson, Jr. (Carol Corley)

Mexican Squash

4 lb. yellow squash, sliced	1 medium onion, chopped
Dash salt	¼ c. milk
½ t. sugar	1 lb. Velveeta brand process
2 jalepeño peppers, chopped	cheese, grated

Combine in saucepan squash, salt, sugar, peppers, and onion; simmer in a small amount of water until tender. Remove from heat and drain well by mashing in a colander. Pour into a 2 quart casserole; add milk and cheese. Bake at 350° for 30 minutes, or until cheese is bubbly.
Serves 6 to 8/Freezes.
Mrs. David Gaffey Ford (Laura Lee Hill)

Holiday Acorn Squash

2 acorn squash	2½ T. dry sherry
2 T. butter	4 orange shells
3 T. frozen orange juice	Nutmeg
concentrate	Holly leaves

Cut the squash in half and bake at 400° for 30 minutes or until soft. Remove the seeds. Scoop the pulp from the squash into a bowl. Add the butter, orange juice, and sherry. Fill orange shells with squash mixture. Keep warm in oven until ready to serve, then sprinkle with nutmeg and top with a holly leaf.
Festive.
Serves 4.
Mrs. Frank N. Ikard, Jr. (Carol Foster)

Baked Squash

6 to 8 medium yellow squash,
  sliced
1 3 oz. package cream cheese,
  at room temperature

½ t. garlic salt
Cracker crumbs
2 T. melted butter

Simmer squash in salted water until tender, and drain. Place cream cheese and squash in casserole. Mash cheese and squash together; add garlic salt and mix well. Top with cracker crumbs and melted butter. Bake at 350° for 15 to 20 minutes or until bubbly.
Simplicity is the keynote.
Serves 6.
Mrs. Laurens B. Fish, Jr. (Julia Corley)

Pineapple Acorn Squash

3 acorn squash, halved and
  seeded
Salt to taste
1 T. cream sherry
1 8¾ oz. can crushed
  pineapple, drained

1 apple, unpeeled and chopped
2 T. brown sugar
2 T. butter

In a shallow, 7 x 11 buttered baking dish, place squash, cut-side down; bake at 350° for 40 to 45 minutes. Turn cut-side up and sprinkle with salt. Combine sherry, pineapple, apple, and brown sugar; fill each squash-half with this mixture and dot with butter. Return to oven; bake at 350° for 30 minutes or until squash is tender.
Serves 6.
Mrs. James M. Dunnam (Anne Jeffers)

Bacon-Stuffed Yellow Squash

12 well-shaped yellow squash
6   slices bacon, crisply fried
    and crumbled, with drippings
    reserved
1   c. chopped onions
Salt and pepper to taste

Dash Worcestershire sauce
½   c. bread crumbs
Dash cayenne
Paprika
Butter

Remove tips from squash; boil until tender, but still firm, and drain. Slice in half lengthwise; scoop meat from large end, reserving flesh. Arrange shells in flat, 3 quart pyrex dish. Mash reserved squash in mixing bowl; set aside. Sauté onions in bacon drippings; add mashed squash, salt, pepper, and Worcestershire sauce. Stir over medium heat for several minutes. Add bread crumbs, bacon, and cayenne; stir. Stuff shells with mixture. Sprinkle with paprika; top with a small pat of butter. Bake at 325° for 30 minutes.
Serves 6 to 8.
Mrs. Roy M. Talley (Martha C. Green)

Squash with Water Chestnuts

8   small yellow squash or
    zucchini, sliced
2   eggs, separated
½   c. heavy cream
1   5 oz. can water chestnuts,
    diced

¼   c. butter, melted
1   t. salt
½   t. pepper
Bread crumbs

Simmer squash until tender. Drain and purée in blender. Beat cream into egg yolks and mix with squash, water chestnuts, butter, salt, and pepper. Beat egg whites until stiff and fold into squash mixture. Pour into a 2 quart buttered soufflé dish and sprinkle with bread crumbs. Bake at 350° for 30 minutes.
Intriguing texture contrast.
Serves 6 to 8.
Mrs. McNay Crossland (Sarah McNay)

Cheese-Stuffed Zucchini

4 medium zucchini, ends
   trimmed and halved lengthwise
1 egg, lightly beaten
½ c. cooked rice
1 c. cream-style cottage cheese
¼ c. chopped onion

1 T. chopped parsley
½ t. salt
4 drops Tabasco
4 slices processed American
   cheese, each cut into 8 strips

Parboil zucchini in boiling salted water approximately 15 minutes or until squash just begins to soften; drain. Scoop out pulp, mash, and drain. Arrange shells in a shallow buttered 2 quart baking dish. Mix egg, rice, cottage cheese, onion, parsley, salt, Tabasco, and zucchini pulp. Spoon into shells, mounding slightly. Bake at 375° for 30 minutes or until filling is set. Place 4 cheese strips on each zucchini half in a crisscross pattern. Bake 5 minutes or until cheese melts.
Serves 4.
Mrs. Howard Rose, Jr. (Patsy Patteson)

Zucchini and Corn

2 lb. zucchini, sliced
1 large onion, chopped
2 T. butter
2 12 oz. cans whole kernel
   corn, drained
½ lb. American or Old
   English processed cheese,
   cubed or grated

1 4 oz. can green chilies,
   seeded and chopped
Salt and pepper to taste

Sauté squash and onion in butter until just tender. Rinse corn and drain well. Add corn, cheese, and green chilies to squash and onions. Cook over low heat until cheese is melted, stirring occasionally. Season with salt and pepper. Bake in 2 quart casserole at 350° for 30 minutes.
Serves 8 to 10.
Mrs. Warren Freund, Jr. (Karen Thatcher)

Sour Cream Zucchini

2 T. butter	1 T. grated onion
6 medium zucchini, thinly sliced	1 c. sour cream
½ t. salt	Grated Parmesan cheese or
¼ t. celery seed or	1 c. buttered bread crumbs,
1 t. Beau Monde seasoning	optional

Melt butter in saucepan; add zucchini, salt, celery seed or Beau Monde, and onion. Cover and simmer for 5 minutes or until squash is tender but still crisp. Gradually mix in sour cream. Heat thoroughly, but do not boil. This may be served immediately as is or arranged in a casserole, sprinkled with cheese or bread crumbs, and baked for 10 minutes at 350° just to heat.
Serves 6 to 8.
Mrs. Mac Umstattd (Catherine Houston)

Zucchini Provençale

10 zucchini, cut into ⅛ inch slices	2 6 oz. cans tomato paste
⅔ c. coarsely chopped onion	1 garlic clove, minced
¼ lb. mushrooms, sliced	1 t. salt
3 T. olive oil	½ t. monosodium glutamate
⅔ c. grated Parmesan cheese	⅛ t. pepper

Cover and cook zucchini, onion, and mushrooms in hot olive oil for 10 to 15 minutes, stirring occasionally. Remove from heat and stir in half of the cheese. Combine remaining ingredients except cheese, and blend into zucchini mixture. Pour into a buttered 2 quart casserole and sprinkle with remaining cheese. Heat at 350° for 20 to 30 minutes.
Serves 8.
Mrs. T. Hardie Bowman (Nancy Price)

Winedale Cold Stewed Tomatoes

1 T. cornstarch	¼ c. sugar
1 28 oz. can tomatoes, drained	½ t. salt
with liquid reserved	½ t. basil

Soften cornstarch in small amount of tomato liquid; combine with tomatoes, sugar, salt, and basil in a saucepan. Bring to boil and simmer 2 to 3 minutes, stirring constantly, until it loses the milky look. Chill. *Good served with country dinner of ham, black-eyed peas, and corn-bread.*
Serves 4.
Mrs. Wayland Rivers (Ann Staacke)

Onion-Sauced Tomatoes

1 medium onion, chopped	⅛ t. Tabasco
1 bell pepper, chopped	1 t. salt
¼ c. butter	1 bay leaf
4 tomatoes, peeled	⅓ lb. Swiss cheese, diced
2 t. tarragon vinegar	

Sauté onion and bell pepper in butter until tender. Slice off and chop top one-third of tomatoes and add to onion and pepper. Stir in vinegar, Tabasco, salt, and bay leaf and simmer, stirring occasionally, for 5 minutes. Remove bay leaf. Slice each remaining tomato, almost to the base, into 6 wedges. Arrange in a buttered 1 quart baking dish and spoon tomato-onion mixture into tomatoes and top with cheese. Bake, covered, at 350° for 15 minutes.
Baked tomatoes with pizazz.
Serves 4.
Mrs. Duke Matthews Covert (Lynne Carole Shapiro)

Sautéed Cherry Tomatoes and Small Onions

12 cherry tomatoes	Sugar
2 T. butter or olive oil	12 small white onions, peeled
Salt	¼ c. butter

Sauté tomatoes in 2 tablespoons of butter or olive oil. Sprinkle with salt and sugar. Cook tomatoes over moderate heat, shaking pan frequently, until skins are shiny and lightly caramelized. Cut a shallow cross in base of each onion to help keep the shape during cooking. Cook the onions in 1 inch of water, covered, until almost tender. Drain; pat dry with a paper towel. Sauté onions in ¼ cup butter; sprinkle with salt and sugar. Cook until tender and lightly caramelized. Arrange the two vegetables around a meat dish or mix together as a side dish. *Rubies and pearls.*
Mrs. Jack W. Scarbrough (Betty Richer)

Turnip and Onion Casserole

2 lb. turnips, peeled and thinly sliced	2 T. butter
3 c. thinly sliced onions	Crumbled bacon or parsley
Salt and pepper	
1 chicken bouillon cube, dissolved in ½ c. boiling water	

Arrange alternate layers of turnips and onions in a buttered 2½ quart casserole. Sprinkle lightly with salt and pepper. Pour bouillon over vegetables and dot with butter. Bake, covered, at 400° for 1 hour, 15 minutes. Garnish with bacon or minced parsley before serving.
Serves 6.
Mrs. Russell Painton (Ann "Aggie" Mullins)

Scalloped Turnips

3   c. thinly sliced peeled
    turnips, approximately 1½ lb.
½   c. sliced onion
⅓   c. diced celery
⅔   c. sliced bell pepper
1   t. salt

Dash pepper
1   T. butter
½   c. diced Cheddar cheese
½ to 1 T. cornstarch
¼   c. cold water

Bring 1 cup of water to boil in a large saucepan. Add turnips, onion, celery, bell pepper, salt and pepper. Reduce heat to low; cover and simmer 20 to 30 minutes or until turnips are tender. Do not drain. Add butter and cheese. Combine cornstarch and cold water; stir until smooth. Add to turnip mixture. Cover, simmer, and stir occasionally, until cheese melts.
Serves 4.
Mrs. Russel Painton (Ann "Aggie" Mullins)

Garden Patch

1   c. butter
1   lb. carrots, peeled and sliced
1   head cauliflower, broken
    into flowerets
⅓ to ¾ c. brown sugar,
    according to taste

½   lb. zucchini, sliced
    into rounds
1   bell pepper, diced
12 mushrooms
Salt to taste

Melt butter; add carrots and cook 2 minutes over medium heat. As vegetables are added, continually stir. Add cauliflower and cook 6 minutes; add brown sugar, stirring until it melts. Add zucchini and bell pepper and cook 5 minutes; add mushrooms and cook 4 minutes. Add salt to taste. Cover and cook a few minutes longer if softer vegetables are desired.
For those who enjoy vegetables on the sweet side.
Freezes.
Mrs. Frank N. Ikard, Jr. (Carol Foster)

Vegetable Mélange

1 onion, chopped	8 yellow squash, sliced
2 T. butter	1 clove garlic, pressed
3 large tomatoes, unpeeled and quartered	Salt and pepper

Brown onions in butter; add tomatoes, squash, and garlic. Sprinkle generously with salt and pepper. Simmer, covered, for 20 minutes and serve at once.

Must be prepared at the last minute and not overcooked.

Serves 6.

Mrs. George E. Heyer (Hallie Dewar)

Vegetables with Anchovy Butter

8 medium carrots, each cut into 4 lengthwise strips	6 medium zucchini, each cut into 4 lengthwise strips
1 stalk celery, each rib cut into strips	Grated Parmesan cheese
½ lb. fresh green beans, snapped	

Anchovy Butter

1 c. butter	1 T. chopped parsley
1 clove garlic, pressed	Pinch tarragon
4 anchovy fillets	Freshly ground black pepper

Simmer vegetables separately until just crisp; do not overcook. As each vegetable is done, run under cold water to stop the cooking process. Arrange vegetables side by side in a long baking dish. This may be prepared ahead and set aside. Prepare anchovy butter by melting butter in a saucepan; add other ingredients and cook until anchovies fall apart. Anchovy butter may be prepared and set aside. Before serving, pour anchovy butter over vegetables; sprinkle with Parmesan cheese. Bake, uncovered, at 350° for 15 minutes or until hot and bubbling.

Serves 6.

Mrs. Larry Temple (Louann Atkins)

Chinese Vegetables

1   lb. broccoli
½ t. sugar
1½ t. cornstarch
1½ t. soy sauce
½ c. chicken broth
¼ c. vegetable oil

¼ t. salt
1   medium onion, thinly sliced
1   9 oz. package frozen cut
      green beans, thawed
¼ lb. mushrooms, sliced
¼ c. dry white wine

Remove broccoli stems and use only flowerets, broken into bite-size pieces. Mix sugar, cornstarch, soy sauce, and broth and set aside. Heat oil and salt. Add broccoli, onion, and beans; sauté and stir until broccoli is just tender. Add mushrooms and wine. Cover and cook for approximately 3 minutes. Stir in cornstarch mixture and cook until thickened. Serve immediately.

Serves 4 to 6.

Mrs. Hugh Rushing (Elaine Robinson)

Breads

Sarah Penn Harris' Wheat Bread

2 c. warm water
1 package dry yeast
¼ c. honey, molasses, or
   brown sugar
5 c. whole wheat flour

¼ c. butter, melted
2 T. vegetable oil
2 t. salt
½ c. wheat germ

Dissolve yeast in water; add honey, molasses, or brown sugar. Cover and let stand 15 minutes. Stir in flour. Cover with a damp cloth and leave for 10 to 20 minutes. Grease two small loaf pans with part of butter and oil; add remaining butter and oil, along with salt and wheat germ, to the dough. Knead for 5 minutes. Shape into 2 loaves. Bake at 200° for 15 to 20 minutes, until double in bulk, then 300° for 15 minutes, then 375° for 30 minutes.
Austinites will remember.
Yields 2 loaves/Freezes.
Mrs. Bradley Fowler (Sally Pope)

Naturally Good Rye Bread

2 t. salt
2 T. dark corn syrup or
   molasses
2 T. vegetable oil
1 c. scalded milk

1 yeast cake
1 c. lukewarm water
3½ c. all-purpose flour
2 c. rye flour

Combine salt, corn syrup, oil, and milk. Dissolve yeast in water. When milk mixture is cool, stir in yeast and all-purpose flour. Slowly add rye flour, kneading until smooth and elastic. Place in an oiled bowl. Cover and let rise until doubled. Punch down and let rise again approximately 1 to 1½ hours. Shape into 2 long loaves and, with scissors, cut slashes every 2 inches. Let rise until doubled. Bake at 375° for 40 minutes, brushing with vegetable oil after 35 minutes.
Yields 2 loaves/Freezes.
Mrs. Willard Y. Ferrick (Alice Heiligenthal)

Whole Wheat Bread

6   c. whole wheat flour
2   packages dry yeast
1/4 c. honey or 2 T. brown sugar
1   T. salt
2/3 c. nonfat dry milk

2 1/2 c. warm water (120° to 130°)
1/4 c. butter, melted
Cornmeal
Melted butter or vegetable oil

In a large bowl combine 2 cups of the flour, yeast, brown sugar or honey, salt, and dry milk; stir well. Add water and butter; mix well. Add 2 more cups of flour and mix; add last 2 cups of flour and mix. Knead dough 10 minutes or until smooth and elastic. Cover with a bowl and let rest 20 minutes. Punch down and cut in half. Shape into 2 loaves; place in well-greased loaf pans which have been sprinkled on the bottom and sides with cornmeal. Brush tops with butter or vegetable oil. Cover loosely with plastic wrap and place in refrigerator for 2 to 24 hours. When ready to bake, remove from refrigerator and let stand, uncovered, for 10 minutes. Bake at 400° for 50 minutes to 1 hour. Remove from pan immediately and cool on wire rack.
Freezes.
Mrs. Charles Crites (Mildred "Milly" Holmes)

Lou Neff's Cheese Bread

3 1/2 c. flour
1   T. dry yeast
1/2 c. milk
1/2 c. water
1/2 c. vegetable oil

1/4 c. sugar
1   t. salt
2   eggs
1 1/2 c. grated sharp cheese
1/2 t. coarsely ground pepper

Combine 1 1/2 cups of the flour with yeast. Heat milk, water, oil, sugar, and salt over low heat, stirring to blend; do not boil. Add liquid mixture to flour and yeast, beating until smooth. Blend in remaining ingredients and flour; beat until smooth and elastic. Spoon into 2 well-greased 1 pound coffee cans. Cover with lids and let rise approximately 1 hour; remove lids. Batter should be 1/4 to 1/2 inch below top of can. Bake at 375° for 30 to 35 minutes. Allow to cool 15 minutes before removing from cans.
A no-knead bread that makes convenient round slices.
Yields 2 loaves/Freezes before rising or after baking.
Miss Nancy Louise Neff

Oatmeal Bread

1 ⅔ c. boiling water
1 ¼ c. quick-cooking rolled
    oats
¼ c. shortening
½ c. molasses
1 T. salt

2 yeast cakes
½ c. warm water
2 eggs
6 to 6 ½ c. flour
Melted butter

Combine boiling water, oats, shortening, molasses, and salt in a large bowl; cool to lukewarm. Dissolve yeast in warm water; stir into oat mixture. Add eggs and beat at low speed for 30 seconds, scraping sides of bowl. Beat 3 minutes at high speed. Stir in flour gradually by hand until it is not sticky and a stiff dough is formed. Knead until smooth, approximately 4 to 5 minutes. Put in 2 greased loaf pans. Cover and let rise in a warm place until double in bulk, approximately 1 ½ to 2 hours. Brush tops with melted butter. Sprinkle with additional oats, if desired. Bake at 350° for approximately 35 to 45 minutes. Remove immediately from pan for a crustier crust.
Yields 2 loaves/Freezes.
Mrs. James H. Albright (Mary Margaret Carlson)

Monkey Bread

2 packages dry yeast
1 c. lukewarm water
1 egg, slightly beaten
½ c. sugar

2 t. salt
3 ½ c. flour
½ c. butter, melted

Dissolve yeast in warm water. Add egg, sugar, and salt. Blend in enough flour to make a soft dough. Cover bowl with a damp cloth and let rise until double in size, approximately 2 hours. Roll dough on a floured surface to ¼ inch thick. Cut the dough with a biscuit cutter and dip each biscuit into the melted butter. Layer biscuits, overlapping them, in a bundt pan. Cover pan with a damp cloth and let rise until double in size. Bake at 375° for 20 to 25 minutes. If bread browns too fast while baking, cover top with foil.
Freezes.
Mrs. Bill Armer (Maedene Maedgen)

Edwina's Angel Rolls

5 c. flour	1 c. shortening
¼ c. sugar	1 package dry yeast
1 T. baking powder	¼ c. warm water
1 t. baking soda	2 c. buttermilk
1 t. salt	½ c. butter, melted

Sift dry ingredients; cut in shortening; dissolve yeast in warm water and add with buttermilk to dry ingredients. Mix well. Knead on a floured surface until smooth and satiny; roll out ¼ inch thick on a floured board. Cut with round cutter, dip in melted butter, fold in half, and place on cookie sheet. At this point you may:
1. Bake at 400° for 12 to 15 minutes.
2. Put in refrigerator to bake later in day.
3. Put in freezer; when frozen put in plastic bag.
Leftover dough may be rolled very thin and spread with melted butter, sugar, and cinnamon, then rolled up, sliced, and baked as cinnamon rolls.
Freezes.
Mrs. Alden Barton Smith (Barbara Mae Leonard)

Sour Dough Starter

1 package dry yeast	2 c. flour
2½ c. warm potato water	1 T. sugar
or plain water	1 t. salt

Mix and leave in warm place for 2 days or until mixture stops fermenting. Each time a 1 cup portion is taken out, add ½ cup water, ½ cup flour and 1 teaspoon sugar. Leave in a warm place for 2 days, then refrigerate. Do not use starter if it turns orange.
Mrs. Kenny Jastrow (Susan Thomas)

Sour Dough Bread

1 package dry yeast	1½ t. salt
1½ c. warm water	5 c. flour, approximately
1 c. sour dough starter	½ t. baking soda
2 t. sugar	

In a large bowl, soften yeast in warm water. Blend in starter, sugar, and salt. Add 3½ cups of the flour. Beat 3 to 4 minutes, cover and let rise in warm place 1½ hours. Combine soda with the remaining 1½ cups flour, then add to dough. Add enough additional flour to make a stiff dough. On a lightly floured board, knead for 8 to 10 minutes. Shape dough into 2 round loaves. Place on lightly greased baking sheet. Make diagonal cuts across the top of loaves. Let rise 1½ hours, or until doubled in size. Bake at 400° for 35 to 40 minutes. Brush with butter and cool on a wire rack.
Yields 2 loaves/Freezes.
Mrs. Kenny Jastrow (Susan Thomas)

Laurens' Sour Dough Pancakes

1½ c. sour dough starter	1 t. baking soda
2 eggs, separated	¼ c. flour
2 t. salt	2 T. melted shortening
1 T. sugar	

Blend starter, egg yolks, salt, sugar, baking soda, flour, and shortening. Beat egg white until stiff; fold into batter. Cook on a hot, lightly greased griddle.
Yields approximately 18.
Mrs. Laurens B. Fish, Jr. (Julia Corley)

Sally Lunn

½ yeast cake or 1½ scant
    t. dry yeast
½ c. lukewarm milk
½ c. butter

¼ c. sugar
2 eggs, separated
½ t. salt
2 c. flour

Dissolve yeast in milk. Cream butter and sugar; add beaten egg yolks and salt. Alternately add flour and milk mixture. Fold in well-beaten egg whites. Pour into a greased 8 inch square pyrex pan. Cover and let rise 2½ to 3 hours or until doubled. Bake at 350° for 25 to 30 minutes. Serve hot.

Leftovers are excellent buttered and toasted.

Yields 9 squares.

Mrs. Maury Hughes, Jr. (Phoebe Foster)

Cinnamon Puffs

1 yeast cake
¼ c. lukewarm water
1 c. milk
¼ c. sugar
½ c. shortening

1 t. salt
2 eggs, beaten
3¼ c. flour
Melted butter
Brown sugar

Topping
¼ c. sugar
1 t. cinnamon

Dissolve yeast in water. Scald milk, then add sugar, shortening, and salt. Cool mixture to lukewarm. Add 2 cups of the flour and mix well. Stir in yeast, eggs, and remaining flour. Beat until smooth. Cover and let rise until doubled, approximately 1 hour. Put 1 teaspoon melted butter and 1 teaspoon of brown sugar in each muffin cup. Stir dough down and drop by spoonfuls into muffin tins. Sprinkle with topping. Let rise until light, about 45 minutes. Bake at 350° for 10 to 12 minutes or until brown.

A muffin marvel.

Yields 36/Freezes.

Mrs. Thomas F. Sedberry (Ellen Warren)

Bran Rolls

½ , c. sugar
½ c. shortening
½ c. All-Bran stirred into
 ½ c. boiling water
1 yeast cake, dissolved in
 ½ c. lukewarm water

1 egg, beaten
1 t. salt
Approximately 3 c. flour

Cream sugar and shortening. Add bran mixture and let cool until lukewarm. Stir in yeast, egg, and salt. Blend in enough flour to make a stiff dough. Place in refrigerator until ready to shape. Approximately an hour and a half before baking, shape into cloverleaf rolls and place in greased muffin tins. Let rise. Bake at 400° for approximately 20 minutes.
Yields 20 rolls/Freezes.
Mrs. Edward Clark (Anne Metcalf)

Rolled Butter Rolls

¼ c. sugar
1 t. salt
½ c. butter, at room
 temperature
2 eggs, at room temperature

1 c. warm water
1 package dry yeast dissolved
 in 3 T. warm water
4 c. sifted flour
½ c. melted butter

Mix sugar, salt, butter, eggs, and water. Add the yeast mixture. Stir in enough flour to make a soft dough. Cover with damp tea towel or plastic wrap; refrigerate overnight. Approximately 3 hours before serving, turn dough onto a well-floured surface. Roll out into a large circle. Spread with melted butter. Let stand for a few minutes. Cut into 16 triangles. Roll each triangle from large to small end. Bake on ungreased baking sheet at 350° for 20 minutes or until golden brown.
Yields 16 rolls/Freezes.
Mrs. Robert Teten (Catherine Nash)

Cracked Wheat Bread

2 to 3 c. whole wheat flour	1¼ c. water
2 packages dry yeast	3 T. butter
3 T. sugar	1 c. cracked whole wheat
4 t. salt	cereal
¾ c. low fat milk	2 to 3 c. white flour

Combine 2 cups of the whole wheat flour with yeast, sugar, and salt in a large mixing bowl. Over low heat, warm the milk, water, and butter. Add milk mixture to dry ingredients a little at a time. Beat for 2 minutes at medium speed. Scrape the bowl; stir in cereal and beat 2 minutes. Add 2 cups of the white flour and mix by hand. Continue adding small, but equal, amounts of wheat and white flour, mixing by hand to make a soft dough. Knead on a lightly floured board for 10 minutes. Place dough in a large, greased bowl, turning dough once to grease top. Let rise until double in bulk, approximately 1 hour, in a draft-free, warm place with a damp towel covering bowl. Punch dough down; place on lightly floured board and cut the dough in half. Roll each half into a 12 x 8 rectangle. Starting with the short end, roll the dough; seal seams and ends. Grease 2 loaf pans; place loaves with seams down in pans. Allow to rise in draft-free, warm place until doubled in volume, approximately 1 hour. Bake at 400° for 30 minutes. Remove from pans immediately; cool on wire racks.
Yields 2 loaves/Freezes.
Mrs. Charles Crites (Mildred "Milly" Holmes)

Cheese and Pepper Bread

1 t. sugar dissolved in ¼ c. warm water	5½ c. sifted flour
1 package dry yeast	1½ c. warm water
¼ c. sugar	2 T. butter at room temperature
1 t. salt	1 egg, slightly beaten
1 t. freshly ground pepper	1 c. grated sharp Cheddar cheese
½ t. basil	
½ c. non-fat dry powdered milk	

Add yeast to sugar water; let stand for 10 minutes. Combine sugar, salt, pepper, basil, powdered milk, and 1½ cups of the flour; add the well-stirred yeast and mix well. Add warm water, butter, egg, and remaining flour (up to 4 cups) to make a fairly stiff dough. Knead on a floured board until smooth and elastic. Place in bowl, cover, and let rise approximately 1 to 1½ hours in a warm place until doubled. Turn out onto lightly-floured board; press with palms of hands to flatten dough. Cover with ½ cup of the cheese; knead cheese into dough. Add remaining ½ cup cheese; knead into dough. Shape into 2 loaves; place in greased loaf pans. Cover; let rise in warm place until doubled, approximately 1½ hours. Bake at 400° for 15 minutes; lower temperature to 350° and bake 35 to 40 minutes or until bread shrinks slightly from sides of pan. Turn out immediately and cool on wire rack.
Discovered in Harry's Bar in Venice.
Yields 2 loaves/Freezes.
Mrs. James A. Williams (Priscilla Nichols)

Swedish Bread

5	c. milk	5	lb. flour (whole wheat,
¾	c. sugar		white, or combination of ⅔
¾	c. shortening		white and ⅓ whole wheat);
1	T. salt		the amount of flour must
3	yeast cakes		be determined by feel of
¾	c. molasses		dough—approximately 15
			to 20 c.

Combine milk, sugar, shortening, and salt; scald and cool to lukewarm. Add yeast and molasses; mix well. Stir in a portion of the flour, adding gradually until dough is stiff. Knead in remaining flour on floured surface until dough is no longer sticky. Return dough to buttered bowl and cover with damp towel. Let rise in a warm place until doubled in size (approximately 1 to 1½ hours). Knead again. Shape into 8 loaves; place in 8 greased loaf pans. Let rise again until doubled in size (approximately 1 to 1½ hours). Bake at 325° for 30 minutes or until brown.
A bountiful return for your effort.
Yields 8 loaves/Freezes.
Mrs. John C. Donovn (Anne Peterson)

Hungarian Coffee Cake

1	c. sugar	2	eggs, beaten
1	c. packed brown sugar	1	c. buttermilk
3	c. sifted flour	1	t. baking soda
¼	t. salt	1	c. chopped pecans
1	c. butter		Cinnamon

Mix sugars, flour, and salt in bowl and cut in butter. Reserve 1 cup for topping. Mix eggs with buttermilk, to which soda has been added. Combine dry mixture and egg mixture. Pour into a greased, floured 9 x 13 pan. Sprinkle with reserved topping, pecans, and cinnamon to taste. Bake in a 350° oven for 40 to 45 minutes.

Freezes.

Mrs. W. T. Archer (Dorothy Newton)

Cranberry Coffee Cake

½	c. butter, at room temperature	1	t. salt
		1	c. sour cream
1	c. sugar	1	t. almond extract
2	eggs, unbeaten	1	c. whole cranberry sauce
1	t. baking powder	¾	c. chopped walnuts or pecans
1	t. baking soda		
2	c. sifted flour		

Almond Topping

¾ c. confectioners' sugar
2 T. warm water
½ t. almond extract

Cream butter and sugar gradually. Add eggs one at a time, beating well. Sift dry ingredients together; add alternately with sour cream to batter, ending with dry ingredients. Add almond extract. Grease and flour a bundt or tube pan. Put ½ the batter into pan; add ½ the cranberry sauce, spreading evenly. Repeat with remaining batter, then remaining cranberry sauce. Sprinkle with nuts; bake at 350° for 55 minutes. Cool 5 minutes, if topping is desired, and spread topping on while warm.

Topping   Mix sugar, water, and almond extract.

Freezes.

Mrs. Frank N. Ikard, Jr. (Carol Foster)

Pineapple Coconut Coffee Cake

2 c. sugar	Dash salt
2 c. sifted flour	2 c. crushed pineapple with
1 t. baking soda	juice

Icing

½ c. butter	1 c. chopped pecans
½ c. sugar	1½ c. flaked coconut
¾ c. evaporated milk, undiluted	

Combine sugar, flour, soda, salt, and pineapple. Pour into a greased and floured 9½ x 13 pan. Bake at 350° for 30 to 40 minutes.

Icing   In saucepan, combine butter, sugar, and evaporated milk. Simmer, stirring constantly, for 10 minutes. Add pecans and coconut. Spread over cake.
Stays moist.
Freezes.
Mrs. Sam Fason (Maydelle Foster)

Sausage Coffee Cake

3 c. packed brown sugar	2 t. cinnamon
1 lb. bulk sausage, uncooked	¼ t. salt
1 egg, beaten	1 c. strong black coffee
3¼ c. sifted flour	2 t. vanilla
2 t. baking soda	½ c. raisins or chopped dates
1 T. baking powder	1 c. pecans
1 t. nutmeg	

Mix sugar with sausage; add egg and mix well. Sift dry ingredients together; add to sausage mixture alternately with coffee. Add vanilla; beat well. Stir in fruit and nuts. Pour into well-greased tube pan. Bake at 350° for 1¼ hours.
A dark, heavy cake, satisfying on a wintry day.
Freezes.
Mrs. Larry Temple (Louann Atkins)

Orange Honey French Toast

2   eggs, beaten slightly
½   c. orange juice
¼   c. honey

8   slices whole grain bread
¼   c. butter

Combine eggs, orange juice and honey. Dip each slice of bread into mixture and brown each side in buttered skillet, adding butter as needed.
Serves 4.
Mrs. Thomas B. Cowden (Margaret Craig)

Molasses Muffins

½   c. plus 2 T. butter, at
     room temperature
½   c. sugar
2   eggs
2   c. sifted flour
¼   t. cinnamon
⅛   t. ginger

1   t. baking soda
½   c. buttermilk
¼   c. molasses
½   c. raisins, plumped
½   c. chopped pecans,
     optional

Cream butter and sugar. Add eggs, one at a time, and beat. Sift flour with cinnamon and ginger. Stir soda into buttermilk. Add flour and milk alternately to butter mixture. Stir in molasses, raisins and/or pecans. Bake in greased muffin tins at 400° for 15 to 20 minutes.
Yields 3 dozen/Freezes.
Mrs. William F. Weldon (Morey McGonigle)

Semester Muffins

1	10 oz. box raisin bran	4	eggs, beaten
3	c. sugar	1	c. melted shortening,
5	c. sifted flour		cooled
5	t. baking soda	1	qt. buttermilk
2	t. salt		

Mix raisin bran, sugar, flour, baking soda and salt. Add eggs, shortening and buttermilk. Mix well. Store in covered container in refrigerator for 24 hours before using. When ready to use, do not stir. Fill greased muffin tins ⅔ full and bake at 400° for 15 to 20 minutes.
This batter will keep for six weeks in refrigerator.
Yields 5 to 6 dozen.
Mrs. Harry Whittington (Mercedes Baker)

Orange Muffins

1	c. sugar	2	c. sifted flour
½	c. butter		Grated rind and juice of
2	eggs		1 orange
1	t. baking soda	1	c. pecans
1	c. buttermilk	1	c. raisins

Cream ⅔ of the sugar with butter. Add eggs one at a time. Add soda to buttermilk and stir into creamed mixture alternately with flour. Grind together orange rind, pecans, and raisins and add to flour mixture. Pour into small greased and floured muffin tins. Bake at 425° for approximately 15 minutes. Combine remaining sugar with orange juice; pour over hot muffins while still in tins.
Moist hours after baking.
Yields 36 small muffins/Freezes.
Mrs. William Milstead (Jacqueline Wheeler)

Orange Bread

Rind of 4 navel oranges
1 t. baking soda
2 c. sugar
2 eggs
⅔ c. milk

¼ c. vegetable oil
3½ c. sifted flour
3½ t. baking powder
½ t. salt
1 c. finely chopped pecans

Boil orange rind 5 minutes in 1 cup water and baking soda. Rinse 3 times. With scissors, cut rind into very small slivers. Place in a saucepan with ½ cup water and 1 cup of the sugar and boil 3 minutes. Cool. Stir in eggs, milk, and oil. Blend flour, baking powder, salt, pecans and 1 cup of the sugar in a large bowl. Stir in orange mixture. Mix well. Pour batter into 3 small well-greased loaf pans. Bake at 325° for 45 minutes. *Incomparable.*

Yields 3 loaves/Freezes.
Mrs. Stanley Finch (Emily Rice)

Persimmon Bread

1 c. sugar
1 t. baking soda
½ t. salt
½ t. cinnamon
1½ c. sifted flour
1 t. baking powder
½ t. nutmeg
1 egg

½ c. milk
1 c. raisins
2 T. melted butter
½ c. nuts, chopped
Persimmons, peeled and
    pureed, to yield 1 c.
    pulp

Sift together the dry ingredients and spices. Beat egg in milk; add with the remaining ingredients to the flour mixture. Mix well and pour into greased loaf pan. Bake at 350° for 1 hour.

Yields 1 loaf.
Miss Sue Campbell

Carrot Mincemeat Bread

1 c. chopped pecans	1 lb. carrots, grated
1½ c. sifted flour	(approximately 5 c.)
1 c. sugar	¾ c. vegetable oil
1 t. baking soda	1 t. baking powder
¼ t. salt	½ t. cinnamon
2 eggs	
1 9 oz. package condensed	
mincemeat	

Combine all ingredients and beat 3 minutes. Pour into 2 small greased and floured loaf pans. Bake at 350° for 1 hour. Turn heat off and leave in oven an additional 10 minutes.
A bread this rich will serve many.
Yields 2 small loaves/Freezes.
Mrs. Shannon Ratliff (Gay Kokernot)

Peach Nut Bread

1 c. packed, light brown	1¾ c. peach preserves
sugar	2½ c. sifted flour
½ c. sugar	½ t. baking soda
1 c. butter, at room	1 t. baking powder
temperature	¼ t. salt
4 eggs, slightly beaten	1½ t. cinnamon
1½ t. vanilla	2 c. chopped pecans

Cream sugars and butter; add eggs, vanilla, and preserves. Sift dry ingredients together and add to preserves mixture; add pecans. Bake in 2 greased loaf pans at 325° for approximately 1 hour.
Experimenting with other preserves provides limitless variations.
Yields 2 loaves/Freezes.
Mrs. P. Frank Lake (Emily Ware)

Double Boiler Bread

2	T. baking powder	1	c. chopped dates
1	t. salt	4	t. caraway seeds
2	c. sifted flour	1½	c. milk, warmed
½	c. yellow cornmeal	2	T. butter, melted
2	T. sugar		

Sift baking powder, salt, and flour together; add cornmeal, sugar, dates, and caraway seeds. Stir mixture into warm milk and add butter. Pour into greased and floured double boiler and cook over hot water, covered, 1 to 2 hours. (Overcooking will not harm it.) Should be firm when turned out. Serve hot or cold with butter and honey.
Freezes.
Mrs. Howard Barr (Margaret Pressler)

Cranberry Nut Bread

2	c. fresh cranberries	1	t. salt
¾	c. chopped pecans	½	t. baking soda
2	T. butter	1	egg, beaten
2	c. sifted flour	⅓	c. orange juice
1	c. plus 2 T. sugar	¼	c. water
1¾	t. baking powder	1	t. grated orange rind

Grease the bottom only of a loaf pan. Line bottom with greased wax paper. Cut cranberries in half. Add pecans and set aside. Melt butter and cool. Sift together flour, sugar, baking powder, salt and baking soda. Combine the egg, orange juice, water and the melted butter. Make a well in the dry ingredients and add the liquid ingredients all at one time. Stir only enough to moisten dry ingredients. Blend in cranberries, nuts, and orange rind. Do not overmix. Bake at 350° for 1 hour, 10 minutes. Cool 10 minutes in pan on wire rack. Remove from pan and cool.
Very berry!
Yields 1 loaf/Freezes.
Mrs. Larry Temple (Louann Atkins)

Honey Walnut Bread

1	c. milk	2½ c. sifted flour	
1	c. honey	1 t. salt	
½	c. sugar	1 t. baking soda	
¼	c. butter, at room temperature	½ c. walnuts, coarsely chopped	
2	egg yolks		

Scald milk in saucepan; add honey and sugar. Stir, over medium heat, until sugar is dissolved. Cool. Beat in the butter and egg yolks. Sift dry ingredients together, then stir into the batter. Mix well. Fold in walnuts. Pour batter into a greased and floured loaf pan. Bake at 325° for 1 hour. Cool in pan for 15 minutes, then turn out on a wire rack to finish cooling. *Subtle sweetness.*
Yields 1 loaf.
Mrs. Jack W. Scarbrough (Betty Richer)

Lemon Bread

⅓ c. butter, melted	3 T. lemon extract	
1½ c. sugar	Grated rind and juice of	
2 eggs	1 lemon	
1½ c. sifted flour	½ c. almonds, ground in blender	
1 t. baking powder	½ c. milk	
1 t. salt		

Mix butter and 1 cup of the sugar; beat in eggs. In a separate bowl, combine dry ingredients. Stir lemon extract, lemon rind, and ground almonds into milk. Add flour mixture and milk alternately to egg mixture; stir well. Pour into 2 greased, lightly floured, small loaf pans. Bake at 350° for 50 minutes. Remove from oven. While hot, drizzle lemon juice which has been mixed with the remaining ½ cup of sugar over the loaves. Cool in pans.
Yields 2 small loaves/Freezes.
Mrs. John P. Watson (Barbara Lee Calhoun)

212 / Quick Breads

Crisp Waffles

¾ c. flour
Scant ¼ c. cornmeal
¾ t. baking powder
½ t. baking soda

½ t. salt
2 T. vegetable oil
1 egg, beaten
1 c. buttermilk

Mix all ingredients and cook in waffle iron.
Cornmeal makes the crunch.
Mrs. John Morehead (Susan Kline)

Arkansas Cheese Bread

1 large loaf French bread,
  unsliced
6 T. butter, at room
  temperature
4 green onions, finely
  chopped

2 t. poppy seeds
3 T. prepared mustard
Sliced Swiss cheese
2 to 3 slices bacon

Trim crusts from bread; slice diagonally. Mix together 4 tablespoons butter, onions, poppy seeds, and mustard; spread on bread slices. Place slices of cheese on each bread slice, not allowing cheese to extend over edges of bread. Press slices of bread together into a loaf; spread top of loaf with 2 tablespoons butter, lay bacon slices across top, wrap in foil, and bake at 350° for 30 to 40 minutes until bread browns on edges slightly.
An excellent alternative to garlic bread.
Serves 8 to 10/Freezes.
Mrs. P. Frank Lake (Emily Ware)

Cottage Cheese Pancakes

1 c. cottage cheese, at room temperature	6 T. butter, melted
6 eggs, at room temperature	Jelly
6 T. whole wheat or all-purpose flour	

Mix cottage cheese, eggs, flour, and butter in blender. Use ¼ cup batter for each pancake and cook on a hot, lightly greased griddle. Serve with jelly.

A high-protein breakfast.

Yields approximately 24 pancakes.

Mrs. Willard Y. Ferrick (Alice Heiligenthal)

Sweets

Apple Spice Cake

4	apples, peeled, cored, and diced	1	t. vanilla
2	t. baking soda	3	c. sifted flour
1	c. butter, at room temperature	1	t. cinnamon
2	c. sugar	1	t. nutmeg
3	eggs	1	t. ground cloves
		1	c. raisins
		2	c. chopped pecans

Mix apple and baking soda; let stand while mixing other ingredients. Cream butter and sugar; add eggs and vanilla. Sift flour, cinnamon, nutmeg, and cloves together; add to butter mixture. Add apples, raisins, and nuts. Pour into a greased, floured tube pan. Bake 1 hour at 350°.

Freezes.

Mrs. Charles Crites (Mildred "Milly" Holmes)

Banana Birthday Cake

1	c. butter, at room temperature	2	t. baking soda
3	c. sugar	½	c. sour cream
4	eggs	3	c. sifted flour
6	very ripe bananas, mashed		

Butter Icing
½ c. butter, at room temperature
3 c. sifted confectioners' sugar
3 to 4 T. heavy cream
1 t. vanilla

Cream together butter and sugar; add eggs one at a time, beating thoroughly after each addition. Beat in bananas. Mix baking soda and sour cream; add to banana mixture. Add flour; mix well. Bake in 3 greased and floured 8 inch cake pans at 325° for 25 to 35 minutes. When cool, frost layers with butter icing.

Butter Icing Cream together butter and confectioners' sugar; add cream and vanilla, mixing well.

Freezes.

Mrs. Wayland Rivers (Ann Staacke)

Pineapple Cake

2   c. sugar
2   c. sifted flour
1   t. baking soda
2   eggs, slightly beaten

1   16 oz. can crushed pineapple, undrained
1   t. vanilla
Heavy cream, whipped

Coconut-Pecan Icing

1   c. sugar
½   c. evaporated milk
½   c. butter

1   c. chopped pecans
1   c. grated coconut
1   t. vanilla

Sift together dry ingredients; add eggs, pineapple, and vanilla and mix well. Bake in 9 x 13 greased and floured pan at 350° for 30 minutes or until brown and pulling from sides of pan. Spread with icing while both are warm. Cut into squares and serve with a dollop of whipped cream on each square.

Icing   Combine sugar, milk, and butter in saucepan; boil 2 minutes. Remove from heat; stir in pecans, coconut, and vanilla.
Freezes.
Mrs. John L. Carlson (Kartherine Anne Spence)

Pineapple Walnut Cake

½   c. butter
1½ c. sugar
4   eggs, separated
1   c. sifted cake flour
2   t. baking powder

Pinch salt
2   t. vanilla
⅓   c. milk
¾   c. walnuts

Filling

1   c. heavy cream
1½ t. confectioners' sugar
1   c. crushed pineapple, drained
¼   t. vanilla

Grease and flour 2 8-inch cake pans. Cream butter and ½ cup of the sugar. Beat in the egg yolks, one at a time. Sift together the flour, baking powder, and salt. Add 1 teaspoon of the vanilla to the milk. Add milk and dry ingredients alternately to the creamed mixture. Spread batter evenly into pans. Beat the egg whites to soft peaks. Add the remaining 1 cup of sugar slowly, beating until whites are stiff and glossy. Add the remaining teaspoon of vanilla with the final addition of the sugar. Spread the meringue equally over each portion of the batter and sprinkle with equal quantities of the nuts. Bake at 325° for 25 minutes or until meringue is browned and cake is done. Let cool 10 minutes in pans, then remove to wire rack. Arrange the cakes with plain sides toward each other and pineapple filling in between.

Filling   Stiffly whip the cream with the sugar. Stir in pineapple and vanilla. Chill briefly before spreading.
A showpiece.
Mrs. Larry Temple (Louann Atkins)

Italian Cream Cake

½ c. butter, at room temperature	1 t. baking soda
½ c. shortening	1 c. buttermilk
2 c. sugar	1 t. vanilla
5 eggs, separated	1 3½ oz. can grated coconut
2 c. sifted flour	1 c. chopped pecans

Cream Cheese Frosting

¼ c. butter, at room temperature	1 t. vanilla
1 8 oz. package cream cheese,	½ c. chopped pecans
at room temperature	½ c. grated coconut
2 c. sifted confectioners' sugar	

Cream butter and shortening; add sugar, beating until smooth. Add egg yolks, one at a time, beating well after each addition. Combine flour and soda; add alternately with buttermilk. Stir in vanilla; add coconut and pecans. Fold in stiffly beaten egg whites. Bake in 3 greased and floured 9 inch cake pans at 350° for 20 to 25 minutes. Cool and frost with Cream Cheese Frosting.

Cream Cheese Frosting   Cream butter and cream cheese; add sugar, mixing well. Add vanilla. Spread between layers and on top of cake. Sprinkle with pecans and coconut.
Freezes.
Mrs. Bill Armer (Maedene Maedgen)

Fresh Coconut Cake

¾ c. shortening
1½ c. sugar
¾ c. milk
2 c. sifted flour

2 t. baking powder
¼ t. salt
3 egg whites
¼ t. almond extract

Icing
½ c. water
2 T. white corn syrup
1 c. sugar

1 egg white
Coconut
Almond extract

Cream shortening and sugar. Sift dry ingredients and add alternately with milk to creamed mixture. Beat egg whites and fold into batter. Add almond extract. Pour into 2 greased layer cake pans which have been lined with wax paper. Bake at 350° for 20 to 25 minutes.

Icing Cook water, syrup, and sugar to a soft ball stage. Beat egg whites. Pour syrup over egg whites, beating constantly. Add 2 drops of almond flavoring. Frost cake and sprinkle with coconut.
Old-fashioned and luscious.
Freezes.
Mrs. Herman Heep (Minnie Taylor)

Fig Preserve Cake

1 c. buttermilk
1 c. vegetable oil
3 eggs
1½ c. sugar
2 c. sifted flour
1 t. baking soda

1 t. salt
½ t. cinnamon
½ t. allspice
1 t. vanilla
1 c. chopped pecans or walnuts
1 c. fig preserves, chopped

Glaze
½ c. buttermilk
1 c. sugar
6 T. butter
½ t. baking soda

Blend buttermilk, oil, and eggs. Beat in sugar. Add flour, soda, salt, cinnamon, and allspice. Stir in vanilla, nuts, and preserves. Pour into a greased and floured 10 inch tube pan or bundt pan. Bake at 325° for 55 minutes. Remove from pan and glaze while still warm.

Glaze   Blend all ingredients and cook to the soft ball stage.
A cake favorite; try it using fig preserves, page 299.
Freezes.
Mrs. Kenny Jastrow (Susan Thomas)

Buttermilk-Date Cake

1 8 oz. package dates, pitted and chopped	1 t. vanilla
1 t. baking soda	1 egg
1 c. boiling water	1 ½ c. sifted flour
½ c. shortening	¼ t. salt
1 c. sugar	1 c. chopped pecans

Buttermilk Icing

¼ c. flour	1 c. sugar
¼ c. butter, melted	1 c. chopped pecans
1 c. buttermilk	1 t. vanilla

Sprinkle dates with soda; cover with boiling water and let stand for 30 minutes. Cream shortening and sugar until light. Add vanilla and egg; beat well. Sift flour and salt together. Add flour mixture and date mixture alternately to creamed mixture, beating after each addition. Stir in pecans. Bake at 350° for 30 minutes in greased and lightly-floured 9 x 13 baking pan. Let cool in pan.

Icing   Melt butter; stir in flour; slowly add buttermilk; simmer, stirring, until slightly thickened. Add sugar and continue cooking until sugar is dissolved. Stir in pecans and vanilla. Spread on cake while icing is still warm.
Freezes.
Mrs. J. Travis Davis (Kathleen Penn)

Oatmeal Cake

1¼ c. boiling water	1 c. packed brown sugar
½ c. butter	1¼ c. sifted flour
1 c. rolled oats	1 t. baking soda
2 eggs	½ t. cinnamon
1 c. sugar	½ t. salt

Coconut Topping

½ c. sweetened condensed milk	1 3½ oz. can grated coconut
½ c. butter	1 c. chopped pecans
1 c. sugar	1 t. vanilla

Combine boiling water, butter, and oats; let stand 20 minutes. Add eggs; mix well. In separate bowl combine sugar, brown sugar, flour, baking soda, cinnamon, and salt; add to oat mixture. Bake in greased 9 x 13 pan at 350° for 30 minutes. Cool before adding topping.

Topping Bring to a boil milk, butter, and sugar. Remove from heat; add coconut, pecans, and vanilla. Spread on cake; place under broiler 5 minutes to brown.

Freezes.

Mrs. Thomas P. Francis (Nelda Cummins)

Vanilla Wafer Cake

1 c. butter, at room temperature	½ c. milk
2 c. sugar	1 7 oz. package grated coconut
6 eggs	1 c. chopped pecans
12 oz. vanilla wafers, crushed	1 c. heavy cream, whipped

Cream butter and sugar; beat in eggs, one at a time. Add crushed vanilla wafers and milk alternately. Fold in coconut and pecans. Pour into ungreased tube pan. Bake at 325° for 1 hour, 15 minutes. Serve with a dollop of whipped cream.

A no-flour cake.

Freezes.

Mrs. Banner Gregg (Isabel Hutchins)

Pumpkin Spice Cake

3	c. sugar	2	t. baking powder
1	c. shortening	1	t. ground cloves
3	eggs	1	t. nutmeg
1	16 oz. can pumpkin	1	t. cinnamon
3	c. sifted flour	1	t. allspice
1	t. baking soda	1	t. vanilla

Brown Sugar Glaze

½	c. brown sugar	1	T. milk, or more for
2	T. melted butter, cooled		spreading consistency
1	c. confectioners' sugar, sifted		Pecan halves

Cream together sugar and shortening; add eggs and pumpkin. Sift together dry ingredients; add to creamed mixture. Add vanilla. Bake in a bundt or tube pan, greased and floured, at 350° for 1 hour to 1 hour 15 minutes. Cool for 30 minutes; remove from pan.

Glaze   Blend ingredients together and drizzle over cooled cake. Decorate with pecan halves.
A natural for Halloween. Improves with age.
Freezes.
Mrs. Kenny Jastrow (Susan Thomas)

Pecan Cake

2	c. sugar	½	t. cinnamon
⅔	c. butter	¼	t. nutmeg
	Grated rind of 1 orange	2	t. baking powder
4	eggs, separated	1	c. milk
2⅓	c. sifted flour	2	c. pecans, ground in blender

Cream sugar and butter; add orange rind. Beat in egg yolks 1 at a time. Sift together flour, cinnamon, nutmeg, and baking powder; add alternately with milk. Stir in ground pecans. Beat egg whites until soft peaks form and fold into mixture. Pour into a greased and floured tube pan and bake at 350° for 45 minutes.
Surprisingly light.
Freezes.
Mrs. Barbara Alford (Bobbie Shaw)

Rodeo Cake

1½ c. sugar	1 c. mayonnaise
2 c. sifted flour	1 c. cold water
1 t. baking soda	2 t. vanilla
¼ c. cocoa	

Frosting
2   c. sifted confectioners' sugar
3   T. cocoa
3   T. butter
3   T. hot coffee

Sift sugar, flour, baking soda, and cocoa together. Add mayonnaise. Mix water with vanilla and stir into other ingredients. Bake in a 9 x 13 sheet cake pan at 350° for 25 minutes. Allow cake to cool before frosting.

Frosting   Combine all ingredients. If frosting is too thick, thin with cream or evaporated milk. Spread over cake before frosting cools and thickens. Stays moist for a week.
A devils' food cake served at the Junior League Family Rodeo.
Yields 30 squares/Freezes.
Mrs. Larry Temple (Louann Atkins)

Chocolate Pound Cake

1 c. butter, at room temperature	7 1½ oz. Hershey brand milk
2 c. sugar	chocolate bars, melted
1 c. buttermilk	1 5½ oz. can chocolate syrup
1 t. baking soda	2¾ c. sifted flour
4 eggs, separated	¼ t. salt

Cream butter and sugar; add buttermilk and soda, mixing well; add egg yolks, one at a time, mixing well. Sift flour and salt together. Add chocolate bars and chocolate syrup alternately with flour and salt. Beat egg whites; fold into mixture. Bake in greased and floured tube pan at 325° for 1 hour, 15 minutes to 1½ hours.
Freezes.
Mrs. Ford Smith (Kay Willis)

Chocolate Angel Food Cake With Peppermint Filling

1 c. sifted cake flour	½ t. vanilla
3 T. cocoa	2 c. peppermint ice cream
½ t. salt	2 c. heavy cream
1¼ c. egg whites (10 to 12 eggs), at room temperature	Red food coloring
	1 t. rose or almond extract
1¼ t. cream of tartar	Chocolate sauce
1½ c. sifted sugar	

Sift flour, cocoa, and salt together 3 times. Beat egg whites with cream of tartar until stiff, slowly adding sugar. Sift flour mixture into egg whites and fold gently. Add vanilla. Spoon into an ungreased tube pan. Bake at 350° for approximately 35 minutes. Immediately invert pan on a funnel until cake is cool. Split cake in half and spread with slightly softened ice cream. Replace top. Whip cream with a few drops of the food coloring and extract and spread over cake. Freeze. Place cake in refrigerator 1½ hours before serving. Slice and serve with chocolate sauce.
Delight a birthday honoree.
Freezes.
Mrs. Edward Robinson, Jr. (Mercedes Jensen)

Chocolate Sauce

1 6 oz. package semi-sweet chocolate pieces	½ c. light corn syrup
	¼ c. hot water
¼ c. butter	¼ c. creme de cacao
1 c. sifted confectioners' sugar	1 t. vanilla
Dash salt	

Melt chocolate over low heat; stir in butter until melted. With a mixer, beat in remaining ingredients. Serve warm or cold.
Yields 2 cups.
Mrs. Howard Rose, Jr. (Patsy Patteson)

Sock-It-To-Me Cake

1	box yellow butter cake mix	4	eggs
½	c. sugar	½	c. chopped pecans
¾	c. vegetable oil	2	T. brown sugar
1	c. sour cream	1½	t. cinnamon

Glaze

3	T. butter, at room temperature	1	c. sifted confectioners' sugar
3	T. milk	1	t. vanilla

Combine cake mix, sugar, oil, and sour cream. Beat in eggs one at a time. Pour half of mixture into a greased and floured bundt pan. Sprinkle the batter with the pecans, brown sugar, and cinnamon. Add the remaining half of the batter. Bake at 350° for 1 hour. Combine glaze ingredients and ice cake while it is warm. Continue to scoop glaze off of plate and spoon onto cake until it begins to congeal.
Freezes.
Mrs. W. B. Hahn (Martha Ethridge)

Ice Box Gingerbread

½	c. shortening	2	t. cinnamon
½	c. sugar	1	t. nutmeg
1	c. molasses	½	t. salt
1½	t. baking powder	2	t. baking soda dissolved in 1 c. boiling water
2½	c. sifted flour		
1	t. ginger	2	eggs

Cream shortening and sugar; add molasses. Combine dry ingredients; add alternately with the hot water and soda. Beat in eggs. Bake in a greased and floured 9 x 13 pan at 350° for 25 to 30 minutes.
Batter will keep in refrigerator for several weeks.
Serves 20.
Mrs. C. Dean Davis (Mollie Villeret)

Marble Cake

1	c. shortening	1	t. vanilla
3	c. sugar	1	5½ oz. can chocolate syrup
6	eggs	1	c. sifted confectioners' sugar
3	c. sifted cake flour	2	t. butter, at room
½	t. salt		temperature
¼	t. baking soda	2	T. milk
1	c. buttermilk		

Cream shortening and sugar. Add eggs, 1 at a time, beating well after each addition. Sift together flour, salt, and soda and add to creamed mixture, alternately with buttermilk. Blend in vanilla. Pour half of the batter in a greased and floured 10 inch tube pan. Stir chocolate into remaining batter and pour into pan, folding gently to create marbled effect. Bake at 350° for 1 hour, 10 minutes. Cool on wire rack. Combine confectioners' sugar, butter, and milk. Drizzle over top of cake.
Freezes.
Mrs. Gary Merritt (Kay McKay)

White Chocolate Cake

1	c. butter	1	t. baking powder
2	c. sugar	1	c. buttermilk
½	lb. white chocolate	1	c. chopped pecans
4	eggs	1	c. flaked coconut
2½	c. sifted cake flour	1	t. vanilla
¼	t. salt		

Cream butter and sugar. Add melted chocolate and beat in eggs, 1 at a time. Sift flour, salt, and baking powder. Add alternately with buttermilk. Fold in pecans, coconut, and vanilla. Bake in a bundt pan at 350° for 1 hour 15 minutes.
Freezes.
Mrs. Timothy H. Ritter (Mary Catherine "Cappy" Johnson)

Curtis' Grand Finale Cheesecake

1⅓ c. fine vanilla wafer crumbs
⅓ c. melted butter
⅓ c. sugar
1 t. cinnamon
5 8 oz. packages cream cheese, at room temperature
1¾ c. sugar
3 T. flour

¾ t. grated lemon rind
¾ t. grated orange rind
¼ t. salt
¼ t. vanilla
5 eggs plus 2 egg yolks, at room temperature
¼ c. heavy cream

Topping
Seedless green grapes
Canned apricot halves, drained
⅓ c. apricot preserves
1 T. rum or orange juice

Combine vanilla wafer crumbs, butter, sugar, and cinnamon. Press onto the bottom of a 9 inch springform pan; chill. With a mixer, beat cream cheese until light and fluffy. Combine sugar, flour, rinds, salt, and vanilla; gradually add to cheese, beating constantly. One at a time, add eggs and yolks, beating well after each addition. Gently stir in cream. Pour into prepared pan and bake at 500° for 10 minutes. Reduce heat to 200° and bake for 1 hour. Turn heat off and allow cheesecake to cool in oven. Remove from oven and let stand at room temperature for 30 minutes. Chill several hours or overnight and remove rim of pan before decorating with topping.

Topping Cut off one end of grapes so they will stand up. Arrange grapes and apricots on top of cheese cake. Heat preserves with rum or orange juice. Strain and spoon over fruit. Another beautiful topping can be made by substituting fresh strawberries glazed with strawberry preserves and cointreau or orange juice.
Serves 16.
Mrs. John Philip Ferguson (Mitzi Ann Riddle)

Pound Cake

1½ c. butter, at room temperature
3   c. sugar
9   eggs
3   c. sifted flour

½ t. almond extract
1 t. vanilla
Juice of 1 lemon

Cream butter and sugar. Add eggs, one at a time, beating 1 minute after each addition. Gradually beat in flour; stir in remaining ingredients. Pour into a buttered 10 inch tube pan. Bake at 350° for 1 hour, 20 minutes.
First among many.
Freezes.
Mrs. Jack Gray (Margaret Bellmont)

Praline Cheese Cake

1   c. graham cracker crumbs
3   T. sugar
3   T. butter, melted
3   8 oz. packages cream cheese,
      at room temperature
1½ c. packed, dark brown sugar

2 T. flour
3 eggs
1½ t. vanilla
½ c. finely chopped pecans
Maple syrup
Whole pecans

Combine crumbs, sugar, and butter. Press into bottom of 9 inch, springform pan. Bake at 350° for 10 minutes. Combine cream cheese, brown sugar, and flour; beat at medium speed in mixer until well blended. Add eggs, one at a time, mixing well after each addition. Blend in vanilla and pecans. Pour mixture over crumbs; bake at 350° for 50 to 55 minutes. Loosen cake from rim of pan. Cool before removing; chill. Brush with maple syrup and garnish with pecan halves.
Truly a 4 star recipe.
Serves 10 to 12.
Mrs. J. Chrys Dougherty (Mary Ireland Graves)

White Fruit Cake

2 c. butter, at room temperature
2 c. sugar
4 c. sifted flour
1 t. baking powder
9 eggs
3 T. lemon extract

1 lb. dates, finely chopped
1 lb. candied cherries, finely chopped
½ lb. candied pineapple, finely chopped
1 lb. pecan pieces

Glaze
2 c. orange juice
2 c. sugar
2 T. grated orange rind

Cream butter and sugar. Sift flour and baking powder; add ⅓ of flour, 4 of the eggs, and lemon extract. Add another ⅓ of the flour, 5 remaining eggs, then the last ⅓ of the flour. Stir in dates, cherries, pineapple, and pecans and blend. Pour into 1 large tube pan plus 1 loaf pan or 4 loaf pans. Bake at 325° for 2 hours. Mix orange juice, sugar, and orange rind. Heat until sugar melts and pour over warm fruit cake.
Mrs. Glenn H. Tooke, Jr. (Lila Ann Parker)

Gingerless Gingerbread

1 c. sugar
½ c. shortening
2 eggs
2 c. sifted flour
1 t. salt
1 t. baking soda

1 t. cinnamon
1 t. allspice
1 c. Bre'r Rabbit brand syrup
1 c. boiling water
Butter or whipped cream

Cream together sugar and shortening until light and fluffy. Beat in eggs, one at a time. Sift together dry ingredients and add alternately with syrup to creamed mixture. Slowly add boiling water. Mix well. Grease and flour a 9 x 13 sheet cake pan. Bake at 350° for 45 to 50 minutes. Serve with butter or whipped cream.
Freezes.
Mrs. Sam Kimberlin, Jr. (Alison Gray)

Lucille's Date-Nut Fruit Cake

2	'lb. dates, chopped	1½ t.	baking powder
1	lb. pecans, chopped	1½ t.	salt
1	c. sugar	1 t.	vanilla
4	eggs, separated		Pecan halves
2	T. water		Cherries
1	c. sifted flour		

Combine in large bowl dates, pecans, and sugar. Beat together egg yolks and water; add to date mixture, mixing well. Sift together flour, baking powder, and salt; add to date mixture. Beat egg whites until stiff, adding vanilla while beating; add to date mixture mixing well. Put greased wax paper in bottom of a greased and floured cake pan. Pour batter in pan, smoothing top. Garnish with pecan halves and cherries. Bake at 300° for 1 hour and 20 minutes.
Freezes.
Mrs. Thomas E. Fairey (Judith Gund)

Upside Down Cake

1	c. packed light brown sugar	4	eggs, separated
½	c. butter	1	c. sugar
1	15¼ oz. can sliced pineapple, drained with liquid reserved	1	c. sifted cake flour
		2	t. baking powder
1	c. pecans	1	t. vanilla

Melt brown sugar and butter in cast iron skillet. Arrange pineapple slices and nuts on bottom. Cream yolks and sugar together. Add 6 tablespoons pineapple liquid, flour, baking powder, and vanilla. Stiffly beat egg whites and fold into batter. Pour over pineapple and nuts. Bake at 350° for 40 minutes or until cake pulls away from sides. Cool 10 minutes in the pan, then invert onto platter.
Freezes.
Mrs. Lem Scarbrough, Jr. (Alice Ann Rotsch)

Fail-Safe Pie Crust

1¼ c. shortening
3　c. sifted flour
1　t. salt

1　egg, well-beaten
5　T. water
1　T. vinegar

Sift together flour and salt; cut in shortening. Combine egg, water, and vinegar and add to flour mixture. Lightly blend until flour is just moist. Divide into 4 balls and refrigerate, covered, using as needed. Roll out. Bake at 375° for 10 to 15 minutes.
Yields 4 8- or 9-inch pie shells/Freezes.
Mrs. Thomas Irvin Lowry (Katherine Sangster)

Pecan Crust

1½ c. ground pecans
¼　c. butter, at room temperature
6　T. sugar

Blend pecans with butter and sugar. Spread and pat firmly into a lightly greased 9 inch pie pan. Bake at 400° for 10 minutes. Watch closely as it scorches easily.
A rich base for any cream pie.
Freezes.
Mrs. Glenn Foster (Marcia Ungren)

Sesame Seed Pastry

1¼ c. sifted flour
½　t. salt
⅓　c. shortening

1　T. sesame seeds
3 to 4 T. ice water

Sift flour and salt together. Cut shortening into flour; add sesame seeds. Add ice water; blend gently with a fork until thoroughly moistened. Roll out pastry; place in a 9 inch pie pan. Bake at 400° for approximately 10 minutes.
Gives a lift to entrée or dessert pies.
Mrs. Travis Eckert (Carol Foust)

Pecan Pie

1 c. light corn syrup	1 t. vanilla
½ c. sugar	3 eggs, slightly beaten
¼ c. butter	¾ c. pecan pieces
Pinch salt	1 9 inch pie shell, unbaked

Combine corn syrup, sugar, and butter; bring to a boil. Cool slightly and add salt and vanilla. Stirring constantly, mix slowly with eggs. Pour into pie shell and sprinkle with pecans. Bake at 350° for 40 minutes.
Mrs. Albert Louis Wade, Jr. (Nancy Butcher)

French Apple Pie

Pastry for two-crust 9 inch pie	2 T. lemon juice
5 c. peeled, cored, thinly sliced apples	1 c. packed brown sugar
½ t. cinnamon	2 T. butter
½ t. nutmeg	3 T. flour
½ c. seedless raisins	½ c. pecans, chopped
½ c. sugar	¼ c. milk

Hard Sauce
½ c. butter
1½ c. confectioners' sugar
1 t. Cognac or rum

Place apples in pastry-lined pie pan. Combine cinnamon, nutmeg, raisins, and white sugar. Spread spice mixture over the apples; sprinkle with lemon juice. Blend the brown sugar, butter, and flour; spread over pie filling. Sprinkle with the pecans. Add 3 tablespoons of the milk, cover with the pastry top, prick with a fork, and brush the pastry with the remaining tablespoon of milk. Bake at 450° for 10 minutes; reduce heat to 350° and bake for 30 minutes.

Hard Sauce Cream butter and sugar. Add 1 tablespoon boiling water; add liquor and serve over warm pie.
Mrs. Frank N. Ikard, Jr. (Carol Foster)

Slice-O-Lemon Pie

2 8 inch pie crusts, unbaked	3 eggs
1¼ c. sugar	1 lemon
2 T. flour	Sugar
⅛ t. salt	Cinnamon
¼ c. butter, at room temperature	

Line an 8 inch pie pan with half of the pastry. Combine sugar, flour, and salt. Add the butter and mix thoroughly. Reserve 1 teaspoon of egg white, then beat the 3 eggs together. Add to the sugar mixture and blend. Grate 1 teaspoon of rind from the lemon; then peel the remaining skin from the lemon, making certain to remove all the white. With a very sharp knife, slice the lemon paper-thin, removing seeds. Add ½ cup water, grated rind, and lemon slices to the sugar mixture. Blend well. Pour into the pastry-lined pan. Top with remaining pastry. Cut slits in top. Brush with reserved egg white. Sprinkle with sugar and cinnamon. Bake at 400° for 35 minutes.
Lemon pie with two crusts.
Mrs. James A. Williams (Priscilla Nichols)

Angel Pie

4½ T. cornstarch	3 T. sugar
¾ c. sugar	½ t. vanilla
1½ c. boiling water	1 9 inch pie crust, baked
¼ t. salt	½ c. heavy cream, whipped
3 egg whites	Grated bitter chocolate

Mix cornstarch and sugar in double boiler. Add boiling water, stirring constantly; cook until thick and clear, approximately 10 minutes. In a separate bowl add salt to egg whites; beat until stiff. Add sugar and vanilla, beating until eggs are creamy. Pour hot cornstarch mixture over egg whites slowly, beating constantly. Cool slightly; fill pie crust. Chill for 2 hours. Just before serving, top with whipped cream and chocolate.
Mrs. Charles F. Herring (Doris Wallace)

Apricot Pie in Spice Crust

Crust
1   c. sifted flour
½   t. salt
1   T. sugar
¼   t. cinnamon

⅛   t. cloves or nutmeg
⅓   c. shortening
1   T. lemon juice
2 to 3 T. cold water

Filling
1   c. dried apricots
½   c. pineapple juice
4   egg whites

⅛   t. salt
1   c. sugar

Combine flour with salt, sugar, cinnamon, and cloves or nutmeg. Cut in shortening. Stir in lemon juice and water. Roll out on floured board. Line 9 inch pie pan with the pastry and bake. Cool.

Filling   Stew apricots in pineapple juice until very soft. Sieve or purée mixture. Cool. Beat egg whites with salt until stiff, then gradually add sugar. Carefully fold in apricots. Spoon mixture into pie shell and bake at 250° for 25 to 30 minutes or until lightly browned. Cool.
Apricots at their best.
Mrs. Charles E. Bates (Linda Steinhauser)

Peaches and Cream Pie

1½ c. vanilla wafer crumbs
1   T. sugar
¼   c. melted butter
2   T. orange juice
1   T. lemon juice

8   oz. marshmallows
1   c. crushed fresh peaches
1   c. heavy cream, whipped
3   peaches, peeled and sliced

Combine crumbs, sugar, and butter. Pat evenly over sides and bottom of a 9 inch pie pan. Heat orange and lemon juices to a rolling boil. Add marshmallows, stirring until dissolved. Cool. Stir in peaches and fold in cream. Pour into crust; chill or freeze until firm. Just before serving, arrange freshly sliced peaches on top of pie.
Freezes.
Mrs. Jerry Prestridge (Joyce Michels)

Cranberry Pie

1½ c. sugar
2 t. flour
¼ t. salt
¼ c. water
4 c. cranberries

1½ t. grated lemon rind
Juice of 1 lemon
2 T. butter
Pastry for 2-crust 9 inch
  pie, unbaked

In a saucepan, combine all ingredients. Stir over medium-low heat until butter melts. Cool; pour into pie shell. Cover with strips of lattice pastry and bake at 425° for 25 minutes.
Brilliant.
Mrs. Benjamin McPherson, Jr. (Marie Lois Leopold)

Strawberry Pie

2 3 oz. packages cream cheese,
  at room temperature
4 c. fresh strawberries,
  stemmed
1 9 inch pie shell, baked

¾ c. sugar
⅓ c. cornstarch
¼ t. salt
¼ c. water
1 c. heavy cream, whipped

Mash cream cheese and 4 of the strawberries until fluffy. Spread evenly over bottom and sides of pie shell. Mix sugar, cornstarch, and salt in a saucepan. Gradually stir in water and cook 2 minutes, stirring constantly. Add 2 cups of the remaining strawberries, which have been sliced in half. Stirring constantly, simmer slowly until mixture is clear and thickened, approximately 5 minutes. Cool. Fold in remaining whole strawberries and pour filling into pie shell. Chill. Serve topped with whipped cream.
Mrs. Larry Temple (Louann Atkins)

Blueberry Pie

1 T. unflavored gelatin	1 c. sour cream
¼ c. cold water	2½ c. blueberry pie filling,
1 14 oz. can sweetened	chilled
condensed milk	1 9 inch crumb crust
⅓ c. lemon juice	

Sprinkle gelatin over cold water; heat until dissolved. Combine condensed milk and lemon juice; stir in gelatin and fold in sour cream. Mix in 1¼ cups of the pie filling and pour into crust. Chill 2 to 3 hours. Spread remaining blueberry filling over pie.
Mrs. Ronald Schultz (Jo Anna Murray)

Pumpkin Chiffon Pie

1 T. unflavored gelatin	½ t. cinnamon
¼ c. cold water	½ t. nutmeg
3 eggs, separated	¼ t. salt
1 c. sugar	1 9 inch pie shell, baked
1¼ c. canned pumpkin	1 c. heavy cream, whipped
½ c. milk	Confectioners' sugar

Sprinkle gelatin over water; set aside. In top of double boiler combine egg yolks, ½ cup of the sugar, pumpkin, milk, cinnamon, nutmeg, and salt; cook over hot water until thick. Stir in gelatin until dissolved; chill. Whip egg whites until stiff but not dry. When pumpkin mixture begins to set, stir in remaining ½ cup sugar; fold in egg whites. Pour into pie shell and chill until set. Top with whipped cream, sweetened if desired.
Mrs. John C. Donovan (Anne Peterson)

Pecan Crunch Pie

3   eggs
½   t. baking powder
1   c. sugar
1   t. vanilla
11 graham crackers (4 sections
    each), crushed

1   c. chopped pecans
1   c. heavy cream, whipped with
    ½ t. sugar

Beat eggs and baking powder; add sugar slowly, beating until very stiff. Add vanilla. Fold graham crackers into batter; fold in pecans. Spread in heavily buttered 9 inch pie pan. Bake at 350° for 30 minutes. Cool; chill for 4 to 5 hours. Just before serving, top with whipped cream.
Mrs. Thomas F. Reese (Mary Lynn Roth)

Lemon-Alaska Pie

9   T. butter, melted
Grated peel of 1 large lemon
½   c. lemon juice
¼   t. salt
1½ c. sugar

6   eggs
1   qt. vanilla ice cream
1   10 inch deep dish pie
    shell, baked
⅓   c. sugar

In the top of a double boiler, combine butter, lemon peel and juice, salt and 1½ cups sugar. Beat together 3 eggs with 3 egg yolks, reserving remaining egg whites. Stir into lemon mixture and place over boiling water. Beat constantly with wisk until smooth, approximately 5 minutes. Chill mixture. Spread half of ice cream in pastry shell and freeze until firm. Spread half of lemon mixture on top of ice cream layer; freeze until firm. Repeat with remaining ice cream and lemon sauce. Beat 3 egg whites until stiff and add ⅓ cup sugar. Top pie with meringue, completely sealing edges. Place on wooden board and slightly brown at 475°. Serve immediately or freeze; remove from freezer 10 minutes before serving.
Freezes.
Mrs. J. Dudley Youman (Sandy Geyer)

Lemon Chess Pie

2	c. sugar	¼	c. milk
1	T. flour	2	T. grated lemon rind
1	T. cornmeal	¼	c. lemon juice
4	eggs	1	9 inch pie shell, unbaked,
¼	c. butter, melted		or Sesame Seed Pastry, page *230.*

Combine sugar, flour, and cornmeal. Add remaining ingredients; beat until smooth. Pour into pie shell; bake at 350° for approximately 35 to 40 minutes or until golden brown and almost set.
From the Deep South.
Mrs. Jerry Prestridge (Joyce Michels)

Ice Cream Pie

1	pt. vanilla ice cream, slightly softened	4	egg whites
1	pt. chocolate ice cream, slightly softened	¼	t. vanilla
		⅛	t. cream of tartar
1	9 inch graham cracker crust	¼	c. sugar

Chocolate Sauce

4	squares German's sweet chocolate	½	c. heavy cream
4	squares unsweetened chocolate	1	c. sugar

Layer ice cream in crust. Beat egg whites with vanilla and cream of tartar until soft peaks form. Add sugar gradually, beating until stiff and glossy and sugar is dissolved. Spread meringue over ice cream to edges of crust. Place under broiler for 30 seconds to 1 minute or until meringue is browned. Freeze for several hours. To serve, drizzle warm chocolate over each serving.

Chocolate Sauce Combine ingredients in top of double boiler; cook over water, stirring constantly, until thick. If necessary, add more cream.
A chocolate sundae with meringue.
Mrs. Richard T. Weber (Susan Blyth Donoghue)

Meringue Chess Pie

1½ c. sugar
1 T. cornstarch
6 T. butter
4 eggs, separated

1 c. milk, warmed
1 t. vanilla
1 9 inch pastry shell, unbaked
¼ t. cream of tartar

Cream 1 cup of the sugar with cornstarch and butter; add egg yolks, one at a time, beating well. Stir in milk and vanilla. Pour into pastry shell that has been chilled 2 hours or brushed with egg whites. Place in 350° oven and reduce temperature to 325°; bake 1 hour or until almost firm. Top with meringue: beat 4 egg whites, at room temperature, until frothy; add cream of tartar and continue beating until stiff; add remaining ½ cup sugar, a little at a time, beating well after each addition. Bake at 425° for 5 to 6 minutes until lightly browned.

Mrs. John Calhoun Miller (Karen Stromberger)

Buttermilk Pie

½ c. butter, at room temperature
2 c. sugar
3 eggs
3 rounded T. flour

1 c. buttermilk
1 t. vanilla
1 9 inch pastry crust, unbaked

Cream butter and sugar; add eggs and beat well. Add flour and mix well; add buttermilk and mix well; add vanilla and stir. Pour into pastry shell and bake at 350° for 50 to 60 minutes until set.

Freezes.

Mrs. Frank N. Ikard, Jr. (Carol Foster)

Sweet Potato Chiffon Pie

3 eggs, separated
1¼ c. sugar
1½ c. mashed, cooked sweet
   potatoes, cooled
1 c. milk
½ t. salt
2 t. cinnamon

½ t. nutmeg
1 T. unflavored gelatin softened
   in ¼ c. cold water
1 T. lemon juice
1 9 inch pie shell, baked
1 c. heavy cream, whipped
1 t. vanilla

Beat egg yolks; combine with ½ c. of the sugar, sweet potatoes, milk, salt, cinnamon, and nutmeg. Cook until thickened, stirring constantly. Stir in gelatin and chill. When mixture begins to set, add lemon juice. Beat egg whites until stiff, but not dry; gradually beat in ½ cup of the remaining sugar. Fold into potato mixture. Pour into pie shell; chill thoroughly. Top with whipped cream mixed with the remaining ¼ cup sugar and vanilla.

Mrs. C. Dean Davis (Mollie Villeret)

Raisin Pecan Pie

1	c. pecan halves	2 T. butter
1	c. raisins	1 c. cold water
1	c. sugar	1 8 inch pastry shell, unbaked
1½	T. flour	Vanilla ice cream or
Grated rind and juice of 1 lemon		whipped cream

Combine all ingredients in a saucepan and cook until thickened. Pour into pastry shell and bake at 450° for 10 minutes; reduce temperature to 400° and bake for 30 minutes. Serve with ice cream or whipped cream.

Mrs. Howard Rose, Jr. (Patsy Patteson)

Maple Pecan Pie

3	eggs	¼ c. melted butter
¾	c. packed brown sugar	1 c. chopped pecans
2	T. flour	1 9 inch pie shell, unbaked
1¼	c. maple-flavored pancake syrup (pure maple syrup is too rich)	

Beat eggs lightly. Add sugar, flour, syrup, and butter; blend well. Stir in pecans. Pour into pie shell and bake at 375° for 40 to 45 minutes.

A New England version.

Mrs. Thomas B. Cowden (Margaret Craig)

Blueberry Cobbler

½ t. baking powder
½ t. salt
4 c. sifted flour

1½ c. shortening
½ c. ice water

Filling
3 lb. blueberries, fresh or frozen
1⅓ c. sugar
½ c. butter
Vanilla ice cream

Mix baking powder, salt, and flour. Cut shortening into flour mixture. Blend in water until smooth. Form into ball. Roll half the dough into a rectangle which will cover the bottom and sides of a 9 x 13 baking dish. Line the dish with the dough and pierce bottom and sides with fork. Bake at 350° until slightly brown, approximately 12 minutes. Cool

Filling   In a saucepan, heat blueberries to a simmer; do not add water. Slowly add sugar, then butter. Pour blueberry mixture into the cooled crust. Make strips from remaining dough and criss-cross on top. Sprinkle top with sugar and dabs of butter. Bake at 400° for 25 minutes or until golden brown. Serve hot with vanilla ice cream.
Fresh fruit, such as peaches, may be substituted.
Serves 12.
Mrs. Al H. Robinson, III (Judy Elaine Bradley)

Blushing Peach Fried Pies

2 sticks or 1 package pie crust
   mix (a short, homemade crust
   will crumble in frying)
1 29 oz. can peach slices, drained
1 T. red cinnamon candies

2 T. sugar
1½ T cornstarch
Vegetable oil
Confectioners' sugar

Prepare pastry for 2 crust pie as directed on package, except after rolling pastry, cut into 16 rounds, 4½ inches in diameter. Stir together peaches, candies, sugar, and cornstarch in saucepan and heat until candies dissolve. Place 1 tablespoon fruit mixture on ½ of each pastry round; moisten edge and fold over fruit. Press edges with fork to seal.

In deep fat fryer or heavy skillet heat 3 to 4 inches oil to 375°. Fry pies, a few at a time, in hot oil, turning once until golden brown, approximately 5 minutes. Drain on paper towels; sprinkle with confectioners' sugar. Serve hot or cool.
Yields 16 pies/Freezes.
Mrs. William Scott Swearingen (Jann Turner)

Rocky Road Fudge Pie

½	c. butter	1	t. vanilla
¾	c. sugar	1	c. miniature marshmallows
2	eggs	½	c. chopped walnuts, optional
2	1 oz. squares unsweetened chocolate, melted and cooled	1	9 inch graham cracker crust
		1	c. heavy cream, whipped

Cream butter and sugar. Add eggs, chocolate, and vanilla. Beat until fluffy. If mixture seems thin, chill, then beat again until fluffy. Fold in marshmallows and walnuts. Spoon into graham cracker crust and chill until firm. Serve with whipped cream.
Spectacular.
Mrs. Duke Matthews Covert (Lynn Carole Shapiro)

Christmas Rum Pie

4	egg yolks	2	T. rum
1	scant c. sugar	1	9 inch pie shell, baked
1	T. unflavored gelatin		Bitter sweet chocolate curls
1	t. vanilla		Pistachio nuts, finely chopped
2	c. heavy cream, whipped		

Beat egg yolks until light; stir in sugar. Sprinkle gelatin over ½ cup cold water to soften and dissolve over low heat. Pour gelatin mixture into egg and sugar mixture, stirring constantly. Add vanilla to whipped cream and fold into egg mixture. Flavor with rum. Cool, but do not allow to set; pour into pie shell. When set, sprinkle top of pie heavily with chocolate curls and nuts. Chill at least 2 hours.
Mrs. John P. Watson (Barbara Lee Calhoun)

Hattie Ford's Chocolate Meringue Pie

½ c. unsweetened cocoa
¼ c. cornstarch
1½ c. sugar
3 eggs, separated
¼ t. salt

2 c. milk
2 t. vanilla
6 T. sugar
1 9 inch pie shell, baked

Combine cocoa, cornstarch, 1½ cups sugar, egg yolks, salt, and milk in top of double boiler. Cook over water until thick, stirring constantly. Add vanilla; pour into pie shell. Beat egg whites until stiff, adding 6 tablespoons sugar gradually while beating. Spread over filling; bake at 325° for 15 to 20 minutes or until meringue browns.
Old fashioned, dark, and good.
Mrs. Thomas C. Wommack (Virginia Ford)

Coconut Cream Pie

1 c. sugar
1 . heaping T. cornstarch
Pinch salt
1 c. light cream
2 eggs, separated

1 c. milk
1 t. vanilla
3½ oz. grated coconut
1 8 or 9 inch pie shell, baked
¼ t. cream of tartar

Mix ¾ cup of the sugar, cornstarch, and salt. Add cream and mix. Stir in egg yolks and milk and cook, stirring constantly, over very low heat. As mixture thickens, add ⅔ of the coconut and continue to cook until thickened. Remove from heat and pour into pie shell. Beat egg whites and cream of tartar. Slowly add sugar, beating, until peaks form. Spread over coconut cream; sprinkle with remaining coconut and bake at 300° for 15 to 25 minutes until golden brown.
Mrs. Gary Craig (Corrie Ann Crofts)

Chocolate Crinkles

¼ c. butter
2 1 oz. squares unsweetened
   chocolate
1 c. sugar
2 eggs

1 t. vanilla
1 c. sifted flour
1 t. baking powder
Sifted confectioners' sugar

Melt butter and chocolate over low heat until smooth; remove from heat. Beat in sugar, then eggs, one at a time. Stir in vanilla. Sift flour and baking powder together; add to the mixture. Chill for 20 minutes. Mold dough into balls, then roll in confectioners' sugar. Place on a greased cookie sheet and bake at 375° for 5 minutes; do not overcook. Cookies will be soft.
Yields 2 to 3 dozen/Freezes.
Mrs. William F. Turman (Sally Williams)

Chocolate Covered Butter Cookies

½ c. butter, at room temperature
½ c. brown sugar
1 egg yolk, beaten
1 c. sifted flour
½ t. vanilla
1 8 oz. Hershey brand milk
   chocolate bar

½ 8 oz. Hershey brand dark
   chocolate bar
1 4 oz. Baker's brand German's
   chocolate bar
½ c. broken pecan pieces

Cream butter and brown sugar; add egg yolk, flour, and vanilla and mix well. Spread on ungreased jelly roll pan approximately ¼ inch thick and bake at 350° for 15 minutes. Melt chocolate in top of double boiler. When cookie is done, spread on chocolate while both are warm. Sprinkle with pecans; place in freezer. When frozen, break into pieces with point of knife. Best served shortly after removing from freezer.
The universal favorite of our testers.
Yields 4 dozen/Freezes.
Mrs. Robert Morrison (Verna Mae Hardy)

Sesame Cookies

1½ c. packed light brown
    sugar
¾ c. vegetable oil
2 egg whites
1 t. vanilla

1 c. sesame seeds, toasted
1¾ c. sifted flour
¼ t. baking powder
¼ t. salt

Combine sugar, oil, egg whites, and vanilla. Stir in sesame seeds, flour, baking powder, and salt. Drop by half-teaspoonfuls onto a greased cookie sheet. Bake at 375° for 10 minutes. Remove from cookie sheet while hot.
Yields 5 dozen/Freezes.
Mrs. Robert H. McIntyre (Danya Nicholson)

Health Nut Cookies

½ c. butter, at room temperature
1 c. packed brown sugar
1 egg
1 t. vanilla
1 c. sifted whole wheat flour
½ t. baking soda
½ t. baking powder

½ t. salt
2 T. wheat germ
1 c. rolled oats
½ c. chopped pecans
½ c. white raisins
½ c. chopped dried apples or
    apricots

Cream butter and sugar. Add egg and vanilla; beat until light and fluffy. Mix flour, baking soda, baking powder, salt, and wheat germ. Add to creamed mixture; blend well. Stir in oats, pecans, raisins, and dried fruit. Drop by teaspoonfuls onto a greased cookie sheet. Bake at 350° for 8 to 12 minutes or until lightly browned.
Yields 4 dozen/Freezes.
Mrs. Larry Temple (Louann Atkins)

Cinnamon Crisps

1 c. butter, at room temperature
1 c. sugar
1 egg, separated

1 T. cinnamon
2 c. sifted flour
¾ c. finely chopped pecans

Cream butter and sugar. Add egg yolk. Add cinnamon and flour, sifted together. Spread as thinly and evenly as possible on a cookie sheet. Brush with unbeaten egg white and press pecans on top. Bake at 350° for 20 minutes. Cut while hot and allow to cool in the pan.
You can't stop at one.
Yields approximately 6 dozen/Freezes.
Mrs. W.R. Long, III (Carol Tyler)

Potato Chip Cookies

1 c. butter, at room temperature	¾ c. crushed potato chips
½ c. sugar	Pecan halves, optional
1 t. vanilla	Confectioners' sugar, optional
1½ c. sifted flour	

Cream butter and sugar. Add vanilla, flour, and potato chips. Drop on ungreased cookie sheet. Bake at 325° for 15 to 20 minutes. If desired, place pecan half on cookie before baking, or sprinkle with confectioners' sugar after baking.
Yields 2 dozen/Freezes.
Mrs. Thomas P. Francis (Nelda Cummins)

Raisin Nut Cookies

¾ c. butter, at room temperature	1 T. cinnamon
1 c. sugar	¼ c. milk
1 c. packed brown sugar	1 t. vanilla
3 eggs, beaten	2 15 oz. packages seedless
4 c. sifted flour	raisins
1 t. baking soda	4 c. chopped pecans

Cream together butter and sugars. Add eggs. Sift flour, soda and cinnamon together, then add to mixture alternately with milk. Add vanilla and mix well. Stir in raisins and pecans. Drop by teaspoonfuls onto a greased cookie sheet. Bake at 350° for 10 to 15 minutes.
Yields 3 dozen/Freezes.
Mrs. Rox Covert (Elizabeth Rogers)

Frosted Cashew Clusters

½ c. butter, at room temperature
1 c. packed brown sugar
1 egg
½ t. vanilla
2 c. sifted flour

¼ t. salt
¾ t. baking soda
⅓ c. sour cream
1½ c. chopped, salted
    cashew nuts

Frosting

½ c. butter, at room temperature
3 T. light cream
¼ t. vanilla

2 c. sifted confectioners'
    sugar

Cream butter and sugar. Beat egg and vanilla together; add to creamed mixture. Sift dry ingredients together; add to creamed mixture with sour cream, mixing well. Fold in cashews. Drop by teaspoonfuls onto greased cookie sheet. Bake at 400° for 8 to 10 minutes; cool and frost.

Frosting   Lightly brown butter in saucepan; add cream, vanilla, and sugar. Beat until smooth.
Yields 3 to 4 dozen/Freezes.
Mrs. Walter Reifslager, Jr. (Janet Sadler)

Oat Cakes

4 c. rolled oats
4 c. sifted flour or sifted
    whole wheat pastry flour
1½ c. sugar

1½ t. salt
1½ t. baking soda
2 c. shortening
¾ c. water

In a large bowl, blend oats, flour, sugar, salt, and baking soda. Cut in shortening. Stir in water. Sprinkle board with oats and flour. Roll dough ¼ inch thick and cut with cookie cutter *or* roll dough into balls and press with a glass than has been dipped in sugar. Place on a greased cookie sheet and bake at 375° for 10 minutes.
A Scottish recipe for a not-too-sweet cookie.
Yields approximately 16 dozen cookies/Freezes.
Mrs. Charles Sikes (Carole McIntosh)

Coconut Chews

¾ c. butter, at room temperature
¾ c. sifted confectioners' sugar
1½ c. sifted flour
2 eggs
1 c. packed brown sugar
2 T. flour

½ t. baking powder
½ t. salt
½ c. chopped pecans
½ t. vanilla
½ c. coconut

Frosting

1½ c. sifted confectioners' sugar
2 T. butter
3 T. orange juice
1 t. lemon juice

Cream butter and confectioners' sugar. Blend in 1½ cups flour. Press into bottom of a buttered 9 x 13 pan. Bake at 350° for 12 to 15 minutes. Mix remaining cookie ingredients and pour over hot crust. Bake 20 minutes. Combine ingredients for frosting; spread while warm. Cool. Cut into small squares.
Yields approximately 3 dozen/Freezes.
Mrs. Charles R. Crites (Mildred "Milly" Holmes)

Lou Neff's Sand Tarts

2 c. butter (do not substitute), at room temperature
¾ c. sifted confectioners' sugar
4 c. sifted flour

1 T. cold water
1½ t. vanilla
2 c. chopped pecans
Sifted confectioners' sugar

Cream butter and sugar; add flour and water and blend well. Stir in vanilla and pecans. Roll into small balls and place on ungreased cookie sheet. Bake at 325° for 5 to 8 minutes or until brown. Roll in confectioners' sugar while still warm.
Published previously in "House and Garden Magazine" as part of a description of Neff family Christmas traditions.
Yields 16 dozen/Freezes.
Miss Nancy Louise Neff

Post Toastie Macaroons

4 egg whites
1 c. sugar
4 to 5 c. corn flakes
1 c. pecans, chopped

Beat egg whites until almost stiff and gradually beat in sugar. Add remaining ingredients. Drop by teaspoonfuls onto an ungreased cookie sheet. Bake at 250° for 1 hour. Remove from sheet while hot.
Yields approximately 75 cookies/Freezes.
Mrs. Tom McCrummen (Marian Marley)

English Toffee Cookies

1 c. shortening
1 c. packed brown sugar
1 egg, separated
1 t. vanilla

2 c. sifted flour
½ t. salt
2 t. cinnamon
1 c. ground pecans

Cream shortening and sugar. Add beaten egg yolk and vanilla. Sift dry ingredients and blend into creamed mixture. Pat dough to ⅛ inch thickness on a well-greased cookie sheet. Coat with egg white. Sprinkle with pecans. Bake at 300° for 30 minutes. Cut into 1½ inch squares.
Yields 3 dozen/Freezes.
Mrs. Jack McKay (Tinka Reilly)

Rich Butter Cookies

2 c. butter, at room temperature
2 c. sugar
1 egg

1 t. vanilla
4 c. sifted flour
1 t. baking powder

Cream butter and sugar; add egg and vanilla, mixing well. Stir in remaining ingredients. Form into a roll, wrap in wax paper, and refrigerate overnight. Slice thin; bake at 350° for approximately 10 to 12 minutes on an ungreased cookie sheet.
Yields 5 dozen/Freezes.
Mrs. Charles Michael Smith (Sally Thomas)

Rolled Butter Cookies

2 c. butter (do not substitute), at room temperature	6 c. sifted flour
	Grated rind and juice of ½ lemon
1 c. sugar	1 t. baking powder
2 eggs, separated	Colored sugar

Whip butter, then cream with sugar. Beat in egg yolks. Combine flour with lemon rind and baking powder. Add to the creamed mixture and stir in lemon juice. Separate into several balls. Place in a large bowl, cover and refrigerate until chilled. Take one ball of dough at a time from the refrigerator and let it get soft enough to work with. Roll as thinly as possible between 2 sheets of wax paper (lightly flour bottom sheet). Remove top sheet and cut into desired shapes. Beat egg whites slightly and brush over cookies; sprinkle with colored sugar. Remove cookies to greased baking sheet with spatula, frequently dipping spatula into flour. Bake at 350° until barely beginning to brown.
Yields approximately 10 dozen cookies.
Mrs. Howell M. Finch (Diane Hierholzer)

Rum Butter Sweets

½ c. butter	1 t. rum extract
½ c. sifted confectioners' sugar	1¼ c. sifted flour
¼ t. salt	

Icing

1 3 oz. package cream cheese, at room temperature	½ t. rum extract
	½ c. chopped pecans
1 c. sifted confectioners' sugar	½ c. coconut
1 t. vanilla	

Cream butter and sugar; add salt and rum flavoring. Gradually add flour, mixing well. Shape dough into marble-size balls. Place on ungreased baking sheet; make an indentation in the center of each. Bake at 350° for 12 to 15 minutes or until delicately brown. Blend the icing ingredients; fill indentation while cookies are warm.
A pretty tea cookie.
Yields 4 dozen/Freezes.
Mrs. George E. Robinson, Jr. (Sue Cocke)

St. Patrick's Day Meringues

2   egg whites
Pinch salt
½   t. cream of tartar
¾   c. sugar

Few drops green food coloring
1   6 oz. package chocolate
    mint chips

Beat egg whites, salt, and cream of tartar until soft peaks form. Slowly, add sugar, beating until stiff. Add food coloring; fold in chocolate mint chips. Drop by teaspoonfuls onto a cookie sheet covered with wax paper. Place in 375° oven, turning off heat immediately. Leave in oven overnight; do not open door.
Yields 2 dozen small meringues.
Mrs. Thomas F. Reese (Mary Lynn Roth)

Apricot Confections

1   lb. dried apricots, rinsed
Juice and rind of 1 orange
2   c. sugar

1   c. chopped pecans
Sifted confectioners' sugar
    or grated coconut

Coarsely grind apricots and rind from orange. Combine apricots, orange juice, rind, and sugar. Cook over low heat for 8 minutes, stirring constantly. Remove from heat and add pecans. Cool slightly; form into small balls and roll in confectioners' sugar or coconut.
A Southern Christmas tradition.
Yields approximately 4 dozen/Freezes.
Mrs. Vernon L. Elledge, Jr. (Sharon Prentice)

Nut Dainties

½   c. butter, at room temperature
1   T. sugar
1   t. vanilla
1   c. sifted cake flour

1   c. ground pecans or walnuts
Confectioners' sugar or melted
    Hershey bars

Cream butter and sugar; stir in vanilla, flour, and nuts. Roll into marble-size balls. Place on greased cookie sheet; bake at 300° for 40 minutes. While hot, roll in confectioners' sugar and again when cool; or dip in melted Hersheys. Good served with ice cream.
Yields 2 dozen/Freezes.
Mrs. Milner S. Thorne (Polly Perry)

Thumbprint Cookies

1   c. butter, at room temperature
2   c. sugar
3   extra large eggs, separated
1   t. vanilla

4   c. sifted flour
Dash salt
1   t. baking powder
1½ c. finely ground pecans

Filling
1½ c. confectioners' sugar
Assorted food colors
½   c. light cream

Alternate filling
Jelly or marmalade

Cream butter and sugar in mixer. Add egg yolks and vanilla; cream again. After this do not use mixer. Sift together flour, salt, and baking powder. Gradually add to egg mixture. When well mixed, roll into small balls; dip in unbeaten egg whites, then in powdered nuts. Place on greased cookie sheet; make indentation with thumb in center of each cookie. Bake at 325° for 10 minutes; remove from oven; press with thumb again; return to oven for approximately 5 more minutes. While hot, dust with confectioners' sugar. Place on paper towels to cool.

Filling   Divide sugar into small dishes. Add enough cream to make a thick icing; add desired food coloring to each dish. Place icing in depression of each cookie. The jelly or marmalade may be used rather than the icing.
Yields approximately 5 dozen/Freezes.
Mrs. Conrad P. Werkenthin (Clare Coates)

Oatmeal Tollhouse Cookies

¾ c. shortening or butter,
   at room temperature
1½ c. packed brown sugar
1 egg
¼ c. water
1 t. vanilla
1 c. sifted whole wheat flour
½ c. non-fat dry powdered
   milk

1 t. salt
½ t. baking soda
2 c. rolled oats, uncooked
1 c. wheat germ
1 6 oz. package chocolate
   chips
½ c. chopped pecans

Beat together shortening, sugar, egg, water, and vanilla. Sift together flour, dry milk, salt, and soda; add to egg mixture. Blend in oats, wheat germ, chocolate chips, and pecans. Form small balls or drop by teaspoonfuls onto greased cookie sheet. Bake at 350° for 15 minutes.
For nutritious snacking.
Yields approximately 3 dozen/Freezes.
Mrs. James Chrisman Phillips (Meg Phillips)

Chocolate Chip Squares

1 c. butter, at room temperature
¾ c. sugar
¾ c. brown sugar
1 t. vanilla
½ t. water
2 eggs

2¼ c. unsifted flour
1 t. baking soda
1 t. salt
1 12 oz. package semi-sweet
   chocolate chips
1 c. chopped pecans

Cream butter, sugar, brown sugar, vanilla, and water. Add eggs; blend well. Add flour, ½ cup at a time, mixing after each addition; add soda and salt. Stir in chocolate chips and pecans with a spoon. Pour into greased 15 x 10 jelly roll pan and bake at 350° for 15 to 20 minutes, or until brown. Cut into squares when cooled.
Similar to the old favorite Toll House cookie recipe. Moist as a cake and great for a mother in a hurry.
Yields approximately 3 dozen/Freezes.
Mrs. Frank Ikard, Jr. (Carol Foster)

Melting Moments

1 c. butter, at room temperature	1 t. almond extract or 2 t. vanilla
½ c. sugar	2 c. sifted flour
½ t. salt	2 t. baking powder

White Icing
1 egg white
5 T. butter, at room temperature
Approximately 1 c.
   confectioners' sugar

¼ t. vanilla or ⅛ t.
   almond extract

Cream butter and sugar until very light and fluffy. Add salt, flavoring, flour, and baking powder; beat until light and fluffy. Roll into very small balls, indent top of each, and bake at 350° for 12 to 15 minutes. Combine icing ingredients and fill each indentation with icing; refrigerate after icing.
Yields 3 dozen/Freezes.
Mrs. Howard Rose, Jr. (Patsy Patteson)

Walnut Bars

Bottom Layer
½ c. butter
¼ c. packed brown sugar
1 c. sifted flour

Top Layer
1¼ c. packed brown sugar	½ t. baking powder
¼ c. sifted flour	½ c. grated coconut
2 eggs, well beaten	1 c. chopped walnuts

Blend ingredients for bottom layer together and press into greased, 8 inch square pan. Bake at 325° for 15 minutes. Mix ingredients for top layer togeter and spread over bottom layer. Bake at 325° for 45 minutes. While warm, cut into very small squares.
A very rich cookie.
Yields 2 to 2½ dozen squares/Freezes.
Mrs. Grant W. Simpson (Mary Ellen Reese)

Chocolate Peppermint Squares

First Layer

2   squares unsweetened
chocolate
½   c. butter
2   eggs, beaten

1   c. sugar
½   c. sifted flour
1   c. chopped pecans,
optional

Second Layer

1½ c. confectioners' sugar
3   T. butter, at room temperature

1½ T. cream or milk
1   t. peppermint flavoring

Third Layer

1½ squares unsweetened
chocolate
1½ T. butter

First layer Melt chocolate and butter over low heat; blend well. Combine eggs and sugar; beat until sugar is dissolved. Stir in flour, chocolate mixture, and nuts. Line an 8 inch square pan with buttered foil, allowing extra length to extend over the edges of the pan for easy removal later. Pour in batter and bake at 350° for 20 minutes or until toothpick inserted into center comes out clean. Let cool.

Second layer Beat sugar and butter together; beat in cream and peppermint flavoring. Spread on cooled first layer. Allow to set before adding third layer.

Third layer Melt chocolate and butter together over low heat; blend well. Pour over second layer, tilting pan so that chocolate mixture covers completely. Let cool. Lift out of pan by foil. Cut into 36 squares. Chill or freeze.

This reads as if it were difficult to make, but it is very easy.
Yields 36 squares/Freezes.
Mrs. James H. Albright (Mary Margaret Carlson)

Scotch Shortbread

1   c. butter (do not
substitute), at room
temperature

½   c. sugar
2½ c. sifted flour

Cream butter and sugar. Add flour and work into butter and sugar with hands. Pat into an ungreased 11½ x 7½ pan; dough should be approximately ½ inch thick. Prick with a fork and bake at 300° for 35 to 45 minutes. Cut into small bars before shortbread cools.
Simple and exquisite.
Yields approximately 2 dozen/Freezes.
Mrs. John Thomas (Martha Helen Hall)

Butterscotch Bars

½ c. butter	1 t. baking powder
1 c. packed light brown sugar	1 t. vanilla
1 egg, beaten	¾ c. chopped pecans
1 c. sifted flour	

Melt butter and sugar over low heat; cool and add egg. Add flour and baking powder, mixing well; add vanilla and pecans. Bake in 9 x 9 square pan at 325° for approximately 30 minutes. Cut into strips while warm.
Yields approximately 2½ dozen/Freezes.
Mrs. Albert Louis Wade, Jr. (Nancy Butcher)

Cheesecake Squares

⅔ c. packed brown sugar	¼ c. sugar
2 c. sifted flour	1 egg
⅔ c. butter, melted	1 c. sour cream
1 8 oz. package cream cheese, at room temperature	½ t. vanilla

Combine brown sugar and flour in large bowl; stir in butter, blending until light and crumbly. Press mixture into an ungreased 9 x 13 pan and bake at 350° for 15 minutes. Combine remaining ingredients and beat in mixer until smooth. Pour over baked layer and bake at 350° for 30 minutes. Cool and slice into squares. May be made ahead and refrigerated.
Yields approximately 40 squares/Freezes.
Mrs. David Gaffey Ford (Laura Lee Hill)

Miss Casey's Cookies

¾ c. shortening	2 t. baking soda
1 c. sugar	1 t. cinnamon
¼ c. molasses	1 t. ground cloves
1 egg	1 t. ginger
2 c. sifted flour	Sugar

Cream shortening and sugar; add molasses and egg and beat well. Sift dry ingredients together and add, beating until smooth. Roll into small balls, dip in sugar, and place on ungreased cookie sheet 2 inches apart. Bake at 350° for 7 to 8 minutes for a chewy cookie or 10 minutes for a crisp cookie.

Given to her English class by Miss Bertha Casey, an outstanding English teacher in the Austin Public Schools for many years.

Yields 3½ dozen/Freezes.

Mrs. John Thomas (Martha Helen Hall)

Applesauce Squares

2 c. sifted flour	1 c. sugar
1 t. baking soda	1 c. applesauce
1 t. cinnamon	1 t. vanilla
½ t. nutmeg	1 c. coarsely chopped dates
½ t. allspice	1 c. coarsely chopped walnuts
½ t. salt	Juice of 1 lemon
½ c. butter, at room temperature	1 c. sifted confectioners' sugar

Sift together flour, soda, cinnamon, nutmeg, allspice, and salt. In a large bowl, beat butter until smooth; gradually add sugar, ½ cup at a time, and beat until light and fluffy. Beat in applesauce, ¼ cup at a time, and vanilla. Carefully mix flour mixture into butter mixture, stirring only until flour is absorbed. Fold in dates and walnuts. Pour into greased, 9 x 11 baking pan; bake at 350° for approximately 30 minutes. After cooling on wire rack for 5 minutes punch holes in cake with a fork. Drizzle with glaze made by stirring lemon juice and confectioners' sugar together. Cut into squares.

Yields approximately 2 dozen/Freezes.

Mrs. Tom Schulze (Linda McDaniel)

Rum Fudge Brownies

½ c. butter
4 oz. unsweetened chocolate
4 eggs
½ t. salt
2 c. sugar
1 t. vanilla

1 c. sifted flour
1 c. coarsely chopped pecans
  or walnuts
2 T. light rum
¼ c. confectioners' sugar

Melt butter and chocolate over low heat; cool. Beat eggs with salt until light and foamy. Continue beating and add sugar, a tablespoon at a time, and vanilla. Fold chocolate, flour, and nuts into the egg mixture. Pour into a greased and floured 9 x 9 pan. Bake at 350° for 30 minutes. Cool for 15 minutes; sprinkle with rum. When cool, sift confectioners' sugar over brownies.

Adult brownies.
Yields 16 brownies/Freezes.
Mrs. Sam Kimberlin, Jr. (Alison Gray)

Lemon Bars

1 c. butter (do not substitute), at
  room temperature
1 c. sifted flour
½ c. sifted confectioners' sugar

Topping

4 eggs, slightly beaten
2 c. sugar
6 T. lemon juice

6 T. flour
½ t. baking powder

Cut butter into the 1 cup of flour and confectioners' sugar. Pat mixture on the bottom of a 9 x 12 pan. Bake at 350° for 25 minutes. For topping, combine eggs, sugar, lemon juice, 6 tablespoons flour, and baking powder. Pour mixture over the hot crust and bake 25 minutes. Sprinkle with additional confectioners' sugar. Cool and cut into fingers.
Yields approximately 3 dozen/Freezes.
Mrs. Shannon Ratliff (Gay Kokernot)

Aggression Cookies

3   c. packed light brown sugar   1   T. baking soda
3   c. butter, at room temperature   6   c. rolled oats
3   c. sifted flour

Place all ingredients in a bowl and knead until well-blended. Form in marble-sized balls; place on ungreased cookie sheet. Flatten with bottom of buttered, sugar-dipped glass. Bake at 350° for 10 to 12 minutes. May be refrigerated and baked as needed, because these cookies are better freshly baked.
So called because these cookies welcome your aggressive behavior— the more the dough is worked, the better the cookie.
Yields 15 dozen.
Mrs. Wayland Rivers (Ann Staacke)

Date-Nut Balls

1   c. chopped dates   1   egg, well beaten
1   c. chopped pecans   2   c. Rice Krispies cereal
1   c. sugar   ½   t. vanilla
½   c. butter   Confectioners' sugar
1   T. light corn syrup

Combine dates, pecans, sugar, butter, corn syrup, and egg in a deep, heavy saucepan; cook over medium heat 10 minutes, stirring constantly. Do not overcook. Remove from heat and stir in cereal and vanilla; set aside to cool. When cool enough to handle, form into small balls and roll in confectioners' sugar.
Yields 5 dozen/Freezes.
Mrs. James H. Albright (Mary Margaret Carlson)

Date Nut Bars

1½ c. sifted flour	4 eggs, beaten
1 t. baking powder	2 c. chopped pecans
1 t. salt	1 1 lb. package pitted
2 c. packed brown sugar	dates, chopped
½ c. melted shortening	

Sift together flour, baking powder, and salt. Combine with brown sugar, shortening, and eggs. Add nuts and dates. Pour into a greased 9 x 13 baking pan. Bake at 350° for 25 minutes.

Yields approximately 48 bars/Freezes.
Mrs. John C. Oliver (Mary Ellen Dooley)

Carrot Bars

4 eggs, well beaten	2 c. sifted flour
2 c. sugar	2 t. baking soda
¾ c. vegetable oil	1 t. salt
1½ c. cooked, mashed	2 t. cinnamon
carrots or 3 4½ oz. jars	
baby food carrots	

Lemon Frosting

¼ c. butter, at room	1 16 oz. box confectioners'
temperature	sugar, sifted
1 3 oz. package cream cheese,	½ t. vanilla
at room temperature	Juice of 1 lemon

Combine eggs, sugar, oil, and carrots. Sift together dry ingredients; add to egg mixture. Pour into 2 greased 9 x 13 pans; bake at 350° for 20 to 30 minutes. Cool; ice with lemon frosting and cut into bars.

Frosting Cream butter, cream cheese, and sugar; add vanilla and lemon juice, mixing well.

Yields approximately 48 bars/Freezes.
Mrs. Tom Schulze (Linda McDaniel)

Self-Made Millionaires

½ lb. caramels (approximately 25 pieces)	4 1 oz. squares semi-sweet chocolate
2 T. heavy cream	1 t. vanilla
1¼ c. pecan halves	

Melt caramels with cream in a double boiler over hot water. Let cool 10 minutes. Arrange pecan halves in groups of 3 or 4 on a lightly greased cookie sheet. Spoon melted caramels over pecans, leaving tips exposed, and let stand at least 30 minutes. Melt chocolate over hot water. Add vanilla and stir until smooth. Cool and spread over caramel; do not cover tips of pecans.

Yields approximately 24.
Mrs. Frank N. Ikard, Jr. (Carol Foster)

Chocolate Sugarplums

4 c. sifted confectioners' sugar	2 c. chopped pecans
½ c. butter, at room temperature	3 6 oz. packages semi-sweet chocolate chips
1 14 oz. can sweetened condensed milk	½ 4 oz. bar paraffin
1 7 oz. can grated coconut	Toothpicks

Combine confectioners' sugar, butter, milk, coconut, and pecans in large bowl and chill. Roll into 1 inch balls. Melt chocolate chips and paraffin in top of double boiler. Insert toothpick in balls and dip one at a time into chocolate mixture. Place on wax paper to cool. Store in refrigerator or freezer.

Yields approximately 80/Keeps indefinitely.
Mrs. David Gaffey Ford (Laura Lee Hill)

Bookmarks

4   c. fresh peeled peach slices
½   c. packed brown sugar
¼   t. nutmeg

1½ t. cinnamon
3   T. sugar

Combine peaches, brown sugar, nutmeg, and 1 t. of the cinnamon in blender and purée. Spread on a greased jelly roll pan. Bake for 12 hours at 200°. Cut into 6 x 1 inch strips. Combine sugar and remaining cinnamon; dust bookmarks with cinnamon sugar.
Yields 2 dozen.
Mrs. Frank N. Ikard, Jr. (Carol Foster)

Crackerjack Peanuts

2   c. raw Spanish peanuts
½   c. water
1   c. sugar

Place all ingredients in an iron skillet. Stir and simmer until the liquid crystalizes and peanuts are thoroughly coated. Place on ungreased cookie sheet, separating the nuts, and bake at 300° for 20 to 25 minutes. Cool and store in an airtight container.
Mrs. James A. Williams (Priscilla Nichols)

Fiesta Pralines

1   c. sugar
½   c. packed brown sugar
¼   c. milk

1   T. butter
1   c. pecan pieces
1   t. vanilla

Combine first 5 ingredients in a saucepan and bring to a boil. Boil for 1½ minutes, no longer. Remove from heat and add vanilla. Beat until creamy. Drop by spoonfuls onto wax paper. Cool.
So quick to make, you'll still have time for a siesta.
Yields approximately 2 dozen.
Mrs. John H. Tyler, Jr. (Patricia Robinson)

Buttermilk Pralines

2 c. sugar	2 t. butter
1 c. buttermilk	2⅓ c. pecans
1 t. baking soda	1 t. vanilla
½ t. salt	

Mix together all ingredients except vanilla; boil until soft balls form in cold water. Remove from heat; add vanilla. Cool slightly; beat until creamy. Drop by spoonfuls on wax paper.

An essential ending to a Mexican meal.

Yields 2½ to 3 dozen.

Mrs. Robert Zelsman (Catherine Thompson)

Pecan Mints

2 c. sugar	12 large marshmallows
1 c. water	½ to 1 t. peppermint extract
1 T. light corn syrup	5 c. pecan halves
¼ t. salt	

Boil sugar, water, corn syrup, and salt to the soft-ball stage. Remove from heat; beat in marshmallows and peppermint extract until marshmallows dissolve. Stir in pecans; mix well. Pour onto wax paper; break apart immediately.

Yields approximately 20 dozen.

Mrs. Michael T. Roche (Gayle Glass)

Frank Jr.'s Fudge

4 c. sugar	3 T. butter
⅔ c. cocoa	1 t. vanilla
2 c. milk	2 c. pecans, finely chopped

Combine sugar and cocoa in a 3 quart saucepan; gradually add 1 cup milk. Mix thoroughly and add remaining cup of milk. Simmer over

moderate heat for approximately 30 minutes, stirring often. Candy is done when 4 or 5 drops of syrup in a cup of cool water can be picked up with a fork. Add butter and vanilla; heat for 2 minutes. Add pecans and beat until almost too thick to pour. Pour into a greased 7 x 11 pyrex pan. Let cool; cut into squares before candy hardens.
Yields 24 squares.
Mrs. George Covert (Helen Cook)

Pecans Scandia

1   c. sugar
2   egg whites, stiffly beaten
4   c. pecan halves

½   c. butter
Salt to taste

Fold sugar into egg whites; add pecans. Melt butter in a jellyroll pan in a 325° oven; spoon nut mixture over butter; stir and spread out evenly. Bake at 325° for 30 minutes, stirring occasionally. While baking, sprinkle with salt. Cool.
Make plenty to meet the demand.
Yields 4 cups.
Mrs. Jim Abney (Lo Ann Burch)

Frozen Fangos

2   c. sifted confectioners' sugar
1   c. butter
4   eggs
4   oz. semi-sweet chocolate,
      melted

¾   t. peppermint flavoring
1   t. vanilla
½   c. pecans, finely chopped
4 to 6 sticks peppermint candy,
      crushed

Cream sugar and butter. Add eggs, one at a time, beating after each addition. Stir in additional ingredients. Pour into miniature lined baking cups. Freeze until serving time.
To pass with coffee after dinner.
Yields 26.
Mrs. Frank N. Ikard, Jr. (Carol Foster)

Mango Ice Cream

1 c. heavy cream	4 egg whites
2 T. crème de cacao	⅛ t. salt
½ c. puréed mangoes	4 T. sugar
½ t. lemon juice	

Whip cream until almost stiff. Add crème de cacao and continue beating until stiff. Add lemon juice to the puréed mangoes, then fold into whipped cream. Beat egg whites and salt to a soft peak stage. Continue beating, adding 1 tablespoon of sugar at a time. Fold egg whites into cream mixture. Freeze in a 1 gallon ice cream freezer.
A tropical romantic flavor.
Yields 2 quarts.
Mrs. Frank N. Ikard, Jr. (Carol Foster)

Green Gage Plum Sherbet

1 1 lb., 14 oz. can unpeeled Green Gage plums	¾ c. sauterne
1⅔ c. sugar	2 T. lemon juice
	2 c. heavy cream, whipped

Stone plums; purée with liquid in blender. Add sugar, sauterne, and lemon juice. Mix and freeze until mushy. Stir in whipped cream and freeze.
Serves 8 to 10.
Mrs. E. Arnold Menn, Jr. (Sharon Henson)

Peppermint Ice Cream

½ lb. peppermint stick candy, crushed
2 c. milk
1 qt. heavy cream, whipped

Soak candy overnight in milk, covered, in refrigerator. Fold in whipped cream and freeze.
Yields 1½ quarts.
Mrs. Norman M. Barker (Mary Brownlee)

Peach Ice

¾ c. sugar
1   c. water
3   c. fresh peaches, peeled and
     sliced

Juice of 1 lemon
½ c. apricot brandy

Boil sugar and water for 5 minutes. Cool. Purée peaches and combine with syrup. Add lemon juice and apricot brandy. Mix well. Pour mixture in a shallow pan or mold and freeze until mushy. Remove from freezer and beat, but do not allow to melt. Freeze until solid.
Serves 6.
Mrs. Stephen Clark (Kate Eustis)

Butterscotch Bombe

1   c. finely crushed gingersnaps
3   T. butter, melted
1   qt. vanilla ice cream, softened

2   1⅛ oz. chocolate-covered
     English toffee bars, crushed

Praline Sauce
½ c. packed brown sugar
½ c. light cream
¼ c. butter

¼ c. chopped, toasted almonds
1   t. vanilla

Combine gingersnaps and butter. Press into 5 cup mold; freeze. Combine ice cream and candy; spoon into mold, smoothing top. Cover; freeze until firm. To serve, invert on chilled plate. Rub mold with warm damp towl and lift off mold. Cut into wedges; serve with praline sauce.

Praline Sauce   In a small pan, combine brown sugar, cream, and butter; bring to a boil, stirring constantly. Remove from heat; stir in almonds and vanilla.
A variation—individual ice cream balls rolled in the crumbs.
Serves 4 to 6/Freezes.
Mrs. Robert G. Ballard (Kay Tyler)

Lemon Ice with Raspberries

1 T. unflavored gelatin	1 T. grated lemon peel
4½ c. cold water	1 t. vanilla
2 c. sugar	1 10 oz. package frozen
⅛ t. salt	raspberries, thawed
1 c. lemon juice	Fresh mint

Sprinkle gelatin over ¼ cup of the water. Combine sugar, remaining 4¼ cups water, and salt in a saucepan. Simmer, uncovered, for 5 minutes. Remove from heat; cool for 5 minutes. Add softened gelatin; cool to lukewarm. Stir in lemon juice, lemon peel, and vanilla. Freeze until firm, but not solid. Remove from freezer and beat until fluffy, but not melted. Pour into a 1½ quart ring mold; freeze until firm, stirring twice as it freezes. Unmold on a round platter. To serve, fill the center of the ring with raspberries and garnish with mint.
Serves 8.
Mrs. Stephen Clark (Kate Eustis)

Lemon Ice Cream

1½ c. lemon juice (approximately 12 lemons)	1 qt. milk
	1 qt. light cream
2 T. grated lemon rind	½ t. salt
3 c. sugar	

Combine lemon juice, rind, and sugar. Gradually add remaining ingredients, stirring constantly. Freeze in trays or in an ice cream freezer. *Splash with a spoonful of gin and have Lemon Ice Cream with a Twist.*
Yields 3 quarts.
Mrs. Barbara Alford (Bobbie Shaw)

Jailhouse Chocolate Ice Cream

1 3 oz. square unsweetened chocolate	2 c. milk
1½ c. sugar	2 eggs, beaten
¼ c. flour	4 c. heavy cream
⅛ t. salt	2 T. vanilla

Melt chocolate in large, heavy pan. Add sugar, flour, salt, and milk; mix well. Stir in eggs and 3 cups of the cream. Cook over low heat until mixture thickens, stirring often. Whip remaining 1 cup of cream; stir whipped cream and vanilla into chocolate. Freeze in ice cream freezer or freezer compartment.

Crime might pay—served to "guests" in a Texas jail.

Yields approximately 2 quarts.

Mrs. Charles Crites (Mildred "Milly" Holmes)

Grape Ice Cream

Juice of 4 lemons	2 c. evaporated milk
3 c. sugar	1 qt. grape juice
2 c. light cream	Milk

Mix lemon juice and sugar in ice cream freezer can. Pour in cream and evaporated milk, stirring well. Add grape juice and enough milk to reach the fill line. Freeze.

Especially for children.

Yields approximately 2½ quarts.

Mrs. Roy Snodgrass (Joan Pratt)

German Pancake

3	eggs	6	T. butter, melted
½	c. sifted flour		Juice of ½ lemon
½	t. salt		Sifted confectioners' sugar
½	c. milk		

Beat eggs; gradually add flour, salt, and milk, blending after each addition. Spread half of the butter in 12 inch iron skillet and pour in batter. Bake at 450° for 20 to 30 minutes, until browned and puffed. Combine lemon juice with remaining butter and pour over pancake. Sprinkle with confectioners' sugar and serve immediately.

A dessert pancake of heroic proportions.
Serves 4.
Mrs. Leon Bronson Dorsey, Jr. (Cathryn Seymour)

Date Cake Trifle

1	c. sugar	3	eggs, beaten
3	T. flour	1	c. chopped dates
1	t. baking powder	1	c. chopped walnuts
½	t. salt		

Topping

2	oranges, sectioned	1	c. heavy cream, whipped
¾	c. sugar		Maraschino cherries
4	bananas, sliced		

Combine sugar, flour, baking powder, and salt; add eggs and mix well. Stir in dates and walnuts. Bake in greased and floured 8 inch square pan at 250° for 1 hour or until cake pulls away from sides of pan. Cool and break into small pieces. Combine oranges and sugar; chill at least 1 hour. Just before serving, gently toss oranges, bananas, and cake together. Place mixture in individual sherbet dishes; top each with whipped cream and maraschino cherry.

A man's dessert.
Serves 6 to 8.
Mrs. John P. Watson (Barbara Lee Calhoun)

Banana Split Cake

2 c. crushed graham crackers	1 16 oz. can crushed pineapple,
1 c. butter, melted	drained
1 c. sifted confectioners' sugar	2 c. heavy cream, whipped
2 eggs	Cherries, halved
5 bananas, sliced	Pecans

Combine graham crackers and ½ cup of the butter; press in bottom of 9 x 13 baking dish. Combine remaining ½ cup butter, confectioners' sugar, and eggs; beat for 12 minutes. Pour over crust. Place bananas over filling; add pineapple and top with whipped cream. Garnish with cherries and nuts.
Serves 8.
Mrs. Richard F. Brown (Ann Jarvis)

Walnut Roll

7 eggs, separated	Sifted confectioners' sugar
¾ c. sugar	2 c. heavy cream
1½ c. ground walnuts	2 T. sugar
1 t. baking powder	2 t. vanilla

Brush bottom and sides of a 10 x 15 jelly roll pan with oil and line with oiled wax paper. Beat egg yolks with sugar 2 to 3 minutes until mixture is pale and forms a ribbon when the beater is lifted. Stir in walnuts and baking powder. Stiffly beat egg whites and fold in. Spread batter in prepared pan and bake at 350° for 15 to 20 minutes, until golden. Immediately turn upside down onto towel sprinkled with confectioners' sugar; remove paper from cake, and roll lengthwise in the towel; chill. Shortly before serving, remove towel and place cake on wax paper. Whip cream with sugar and vanilla and spread over unrolled cake. Loosely roll cake, lengthwise, only once so that ends overlap. Place on serving platter and sprinkle with confectioners' sugar.
Reputations are built on desserts like this.
Serves 12.
Mrs. Robert H. McIntyre (Danya Nicholson)

Tipsy Squire with Sherry Custard

½ c. shortening
1 c. sugar
2 eggs
2¼ c. sifted flour
3 t. baking powder
½ t. salt

¾ c. milk
1 t. vanilla
1 c. heavy cream, whipped
and sweetened
1 c. toasted slivered almonds

Sherry Custard

1 qt. milk
¾ c. sugar
3 T. cornstarch
⅛ t. salt

3 egg yolks
1 egg
1 t. rum extract
½ c. cream sherry

Cream shortening and sugar; add eggs and beat until lemon-colored and fluffy. Add sifted dry ingredients alternately with milk; beat well. Add vanilla with last addition of milk. Pour into a greased and floured 11 x 7 baking pan. Bake at 350° for 35 to 40 minutes.

Sherry Custard Mix milk with sugar, cornstarch, and salt in a saucepan. Simmer over medium heat, stirring constantly, until slighlty thickened. Beat egg yolks and whole egg. Add 1 cup of hot milk mixture to beaten egg yolks; stir; return to hot milk. Continue cooking, stirring constantly until custard consistency; do not boil. Add rum extract and sherry. Cool. To serve, pour sherry custard over cake squares. Garnish with sweetened whipped cream and toasted almonds.
Serves 8.
Mrs. J. Travis Davis (Kathleen Penn)

Strawberry Crêpes

1   c. sifted flour
2   T. sugar
1 1/2 t. baking powder
1/2 t. salt

2   eggs, slightly beaten
1 1/4 c. milk
3   T. vegetable oil

Filling

2   c. sour cream
3   T. sugar
2   T. Cointreau
2   c. sliced fresh strawberries,
    sweetened

2   T. butter
Confectioners' sugar

Sift flour, sugar, baking powder, and salt together. Combine eggs, milk, and oil, then blend with dry ingredients until just moistened. Pour 2 to 3 tablespoons batter for each crêpe into well-greased, hot crêpe pan. Cook until top is bubbly, edges dry, and underside slightly brown. Turn and cook other side. May be made ahead and stacked between sheets of wax paper and refrigerated or frozen.

Filling   Combine sour cream, sugar, and Cointreau. Spread crêpes with equal amounts of the sour cream mixture and strawberries. Reserve some strawberries for the top. Roll crêpes up and arrange in a shallow casserole. May cover and refrigerate at this point. To serve, melt butter in a large flat skillet. Add the reserved strawberries and heat. Top crêpes with strawberries and heat at 350° for 10 minutes until warm. Sprinkle with confectioners' sugar.

Yields 16 crêpes.
Mrs. John Philip Ferguson (Mitzi Ann Riddle)

Frozen Lime Soufflé

6 to 8 large limes	Pinch salt
6 egg yolks, beaten	¾ c. heavy cream, whipped
¼ c. sugar	2 T. Cointreau, optional
1 c. milk, scalded	Toasted almonds
2 egg whites	Grated coconut

Grate and reserve rind of 4 limes. Squeeze limes to yield 1 cup of juice. Beat egg yolks and sugar until mixture is pale yellow and forms a ribbon; add lime juice. Add milk slowly, stirring constantly. Pour into heavy sauce pan; cook over low heat, stirring often with a wooden spoon, until mixture coats the spoon (do not boil). Strain and add lime rind. Set pan in a bowl of ice water; stir occasionally until sauce thickens. Beat egg whites with salt until stiff. Fold into whipped cream; add Cointreau. Fold whipped cream mixture into lime mixture. Pour into a 1 quart soufflé dish and freeze at least 6 hours. Sprinkle with toasted almonds and coconut.

Cold, smooth soufflé contrasted with crunchy topping.

Serves 6.

Mrs. Edward Robinson, Jr. (Mercedes Jensen)

Cherry Torte

1 egg	1 t. baking soda
1 c. sugar	½ t. salt
1 16 oz. can dark, tart cherries, drained; reserve juice	1 T. cornstarch
	3 T. sugar
1 c. sifted flour	Vanilla ice cream

Mix together egg and 1 cup sugar; stir in cherries. Sift together flour, baking soda, and salt; add to cherry mixture. Pour into greased springform pan. Bake at 350° for 45 minutes. Remove from pan. Combine cherry juice, cornstarch, and 1 to 2 tablespoons sugar in a saucepan; simmer, stirring, until thick and clear. Pour while hot over baked torte. Serve with vanilla ice cream on top.

Serves 6 to 8.

Mrs. Hugh Rushing (Elaine Robinson)

Raisin Pudding with Butter Sauce

2	T. butter, at room temperature	1	c. raisins
1	c. sugar	2	t. vanilla
1	c. milk	½	c. chopped pecans or walnuts
2	c. sifted flour	2	c. packed brown sugar
1	t. baking soda	¼	c. butter
1	t. nutmeg	4	c. boiling water
½	t. salt		Ice cream or whipped cream

Combine butter, sugar, and milk. Sift together flour, soda, nutmeg, and salt. Blend into sugar and milk mixture; batter should be smooth. Add raisins, vanilla, and nuts. Spread in a buttered 2½ quart casserole or 10 x 13 pan. In a saucepan, combine brown sugar, butter, and water. Dissolve over medium heat and pour over raisin pudding. Bake at 375° for 30 minutes. Serve warm with ice cream or whipped cream.
Raisin pudding elevated from the everyday to the extraordinary.
Serves 8 to 10.
Mrs. Terrell James (Dianne Hill)

Cold Lemon Soufflé

2	T. unflavored gelatin	1	T. grated lemon rind
½	c. water	⅔	c. lemon juice
6	eggs	2	c. heavy cream, whipped
1½	c. sugar		

Tie a collar of wax paper around a 1 quart soufflé dish; butter collar and dish well. Sprinkle gelatin over water in a saucepan. Let stand 10 minutes to soften. Place saucepan over low heat until gelatin dissolves and mixture is clear. Cool. Beat eggs and sugar until very thick. Combine rind and juice with gelatin. Pour into egg-sugar mixture; blend well. Place bowl over ice and stir until mixture thickens. Fold 1¾ cups of the whipped cream into lemon mixture. Pour into soufflé dish. Chill at least 3 hours. Top with remaining whipped cream.
Serves 6.
Mrs. Leon Bronson Dorsey, Jr. (Cathryn Seymour)

Lemon and Strawberry Dessert

4 eggs, separated	6 T. lemon juice
¼ t. cream of tartar	2 c. heavy cream
1½ c. sugar	1 t. vanilla
1 t. grated lemon rind	6 fresh strawberries

Beat egg whites with cream of tartar until almost stiff. Gradually add ¾ cup of the sugar; beat until stiff. Pour into 8 or 9 inch pyrex pan. Make a nest about 1 inch deep with a 2 inch rim. Bake at 225° for 1 hour 15 minutes; cool. In a double boiler, beat the egg yolks and ½ cup of the sugar. Add lemon rind and juice. Stir over simmering water for 15 minutes, until mixture is a thick custard; cool. Whip 1 cup of the cream, fold into the lemon custard, and spoon into meringue shell. Chill 24 hours. Before serving, beat remaining 1 cup of cream; add remaining ¼ cup of sugar and vanilla. Drop 6 dollops of whipped cream over custard and place 1 strawberry on each dollop of cream.
Serves 6.
Mrs. Frank N. Ikard, Jr. (Carol Foster)

Pears in Port Wine

1 c. sugar	2 c. port wine
2 c. water	1 c. sour cream
1 stick cinnamon	Crystallized ginger
Thinly sliced peel of 1 lemon	
6 Bartlett pears, peeled, quartered and seeded	

Mix sugar, water, cinnamon, and lemon peel; boil over moderate heat for 15 minutes. Add pears; simmer gently for approximately 20 minutes or until tender, but still firm. Remove pears from syrup to 1 quart jar. Simmer liquid until reduced to a thick syrup. Mix with port; pour over pears. Cool. Chill for 12 hours. Serve pears topped with sour cream and crystallized ginger.
Serves 6.
Mrs. Sam Fason (Maydelle Foster)

Pears and Sherbet in Rum Sauce

2 c. sugar
1½ c. water
⅛ t. salt
4 2 inch cinnamon sticks
½ t. whole cloves

½ t. allspice
4 1 inch slices ginger root
12 firm fresh pears
¾ c. light rum
12 scoops lemon sherbet

Combine sugar, water, salt, and cinnamon sticks in a saucepan. Place cloves, allspice, and ginger root together in a cheese cloth bag; add to saucepan. Boil. Peel pears, leaving them whole, with stems intact. Add a few pears at a time to syrup. Cover and simmer slowly for 10 to 20 minutes or until pears are tender, turning to cook uniformly. Remove spice bag and add rum. Cool pears in the sauce and let stand for at least 24 hours. Before serving, place a scoop of lemon sherbet in each dessert dish. Place whole pear, stem up, in the sherbet. Top with spiced rum sauce.
Elegant.
Serves 12.
Mrs. Robert H. McIntyre (Danya Nicholson)

Frozen Lemon Tart

1 c. vanilla wafer crumbs
3 eggs, separated
¼ c. lemon juice
Grated rind of 1 lemon

Pinch of salt
½ c. sugar
¾ c. evaporated milk, chilled
    and whipped

Line an 8 x 8 inch pyrex dish with half of the vanilla wafer crumbs. Combine egg yolks, lemon juice, rind, salt, and sugar in the top of a double boiler. Cook until thick, stirring constantly. Cool. Beat egg whites until stiff. Fold the whipped evaporated milk and egg whites into the lemon mixture. Spoon into serving dish, top with remaining wafer crumbs, and freeze. Serve frozen.
A lemon cloud on a crumb crust.
Serves 8 to 10/Freezes.
Mrs. James Swearingen (Jonilu Sellers)

Apricot Crisp

1	16 oz. can apricot halves, undrained	1	c. butter, melted
2	T. brown sugar	½	c. chopped pecans
¼	t. cinnamon	1	7 oz. can grated coconut
1	1 lb., 2½ oz. yellow cake mix	2	c. heavy cream, whipped

Arrange apricots and liquid in 3 quart baking dish. Sprinkle with brown sugar, cinnamon, and cake mix. Pour butter over all. Bake for 40 minutes at 350°. Remove from oven and top with pecans and coconut. Return to oven and bake 20 minutes. Turn oven off; allow dish to cool in oven. Serve with whipped cream.
Serves 12 to 15.
Mrs. Carroll McPherson (Martha Bundy)

Rainbow Parfait

Lemon ice cream (not sherbet)   Fresh blueberries
Fresh strawberries, sliced   1   T. rum
Raspberry sherbet   Fresh mint

In individual parfait glasses layer lemon ice cream, strawberries, raspberry sherbet, blueberries, then sprinkle with rum. Garnish with mint.
Mrs. Frank N. Ikard, Jr. (Carol Foster)

Strawberries Marco Polo

Sliced fresh strawberries   Sour cream
Sugar   Brown sugar
Lemon juice

Place strawberries in individual bowls. Sprinkle with sugar and lemon juice. Top with dollop of sour cream. Sprinkle with brown sugar. Top with a strawberry.
Other fresh fruit may be substituted; we like it with seedless green grapes.
Mrs. Kenny Jastrow (Susan Thomas)

Fresh Fruit Shortcake

1 c. butter, at room temperature	1 qt. sweetened strawberries,
½ c. sifted confectioners' sugar	peaches, blueberries, or
Pinch of salt	blackberries
2 c. sifted flour	1 c. heavy cream, whipped

Whip butter. Add sugar, salt, and flour to form a soft dough. On a well floured surface, roll dough ¼ inch thick. Cut into 3 inch rounds. Bake at 350° for 10 to 12 minutes or until brown. To serve, spoon a layer of fruit over each short cake. Repeat layers and top with whipped cream. *A delicate and crisp shortbread base.*
Serves 6.
Mrs. John Berkman (Lynn Langston)

Swedish Apple Dumplings

Pastry

2 c. sifted flour	½ c. shortening
4 t. baking powder	⅔ to ¾ c. milk
½ t. salt	

Filling

6 small apples, peeled and cored	Dash cinnamon
	1½ c. sugar
6 T. sugar	⅓ to ½ c. butter
1 c. water	Light cream

Pastry   Sift flour with baking powder and salt. Cut in shortening; add milk. Stir with a fork; dough should be soft. Roll out on a floured surface. Cut dough into 6 squares, each approximately 6 inches square.

Filling   Place an apple in the center of each square; sprinkle 1 tablespoon of sugar into the core of each apple. Pull corners of dough up to meet and pinch edges together so that apple is completely sealed. Arrange in baking pan. Bring sugar and butter to a boil; pour over apples. Bake at 400° for 15 minutes; reduce heat to 300° for 45 minutes. Serve warm with cream.
Serves 6.
Mrs. Walter Reifslager, Jr. (Janet Sadler)

Brandied Pumpkin Flan

¾ c. sugar
1 c. cooked pumpkin
1 c. milk
1 c. light cream
6 eggs, beaten

½ c. sugar
½ t. salt
2 t. vanilla
⅓ c. plus 2 T. Cognac

Heat sugar in heavy skillet to a light brown syrup. Pour syrup into an 8 inch round dish; rotate dish to cover bottom and sides. Set aside. To make custard, blend pumpkin, milk, and cream in saucepan and heat over low heat, stirring constantly, until bubbles form around side of pan. Add sugar, salt, and vanilla to beaten eggs. Gradually stir in hot milk mixture and ⅓ cup Cognac. Pour into prepared baking dish. Set dish in hot water bath. Bake at 350° for 1 hour. Cool; refrigerate overnight. To serve, run spatula around edge of dish. Invert onto platter; shake gently. At the table, warm 2 tablespoons brandy; ignite, and quickly pour over the flan.
Serves 12.
Mrs. Jerry P. Bordelon (Joyce Graves)

Pumpkin Pudding

1 c. butter, at room
  temperature
3 c. sugar
8 eggs, beaten
1 29 oz. can pumpkin
1 c. light cream
3 T. bourbon
½ t. salt

½ t. nutmeg
½ t. allspice
1 t. cinnamon
1 c. white raisins
1 c. chopped pecans
½ c. flour
4 oz. grated coconut
Whipped cream

Cream butter and sugar. Add eggs, pumpkin, cream, bourbon, salt, nutmeg, allspice, and cinnamon. In another bowl, combine raisins, pecans, and flour. Stir into the pumpkin mixture. Pour into a 9 x 13 pan. Sprinkle with coconut and bake at 250° until set. Cut into squares and top with whipped cream.
Serves 12.
Mrs. J. K. Lyles (Mary Nobles)

Oranges Copenhagen

1 c. sugar	1 c. heavy cream
½ c. water	1 t. vanilla
6 navel oranges	Pistachio nuts, chopped
¾ c. Grand Marnier	

Combine sugar and water in a saucepan. Boil rapidly for 3 minutes. Cool. From 1 of the oranges, remove thin strips of orange rind and cut into 1 inch slivers. Peel and section all 6 oranges, working over a bowl to retain juices. To the orange sections, add half of the Grand Marnier and 6 tablespoons of the sugar syrup. Marinate in refrigerator for 2 hours. Add rind to remaining syrup and boil for 5 minutes; remove rind with slotted spoon, drain, and cool. Whip cream with vanilla. Divide orange segments into 6 champagne glasses. Into each glass sprinkle orange peel, 1 tablespoon of Grand Marnier, and top with whipped cream and pistachio nuts.

Light and unusual.
Serves 6.
Mrs. Leonard Sayers (Rosella O'Neal)

Hot Chocolate Soufflé

3 squares unsweetened or semi-sweet chocolate	¼ t. salt
	½ c. pecan pieces
1 c. sugar	2 t. vanilla
4 eggs, separated	1 c. heavy cream, whipped

Melt chocolate in top of double boiler; add ⅓ cup of the sugar and stir. Beat egg yolks with ⅓ cup of the sugar. Whip egg whites with salt until stiff, adding remaining ⅓ cup of sugar. Combine yolks and whites; fold in chocolate, pecans, and vanilla. Turn into well-buttered, 2 quart soufflé dish. Set in pan of hot water; bake at 375° for 30 to 40 minutes. Serve hot with whipped cream.

Dating from the '40's at Camp Waldemar.
Serves 6 to 8.
Mrs. Richard T. Spencer, Jr. (Ann Alexander)

Hot Fudge Pudding

2 eggs, beaten until light	½ c. butter
1 c. sugar	1 c. chopped pecans
2 T. flour	½ t. vanilla
1 T. cocoa	

Combine eggs, sugar, and flour. Melt cocoa and butter; add to egg mixture. Add nuts and vanilla. Bake in a buttered, 1 quart dish, set in a pan of hot water, at 300° for approximately 2 hours.
Serves 4.
Mrs. Ann Turnbull McLean

Cream Cheese Mousse with Brandy Sauce

1 T. unflavored gelatin	¼ c. lemon juice
1 8 oz. package cream cheese, at room temperature	1 T. rum
	½ t. grated lemon rind
½ c. sugar	3 egg whites, stiffly beaten
¼ c. milk	1 c. heavy cream, whipped

Brandy Sauce

¾ c. sugar	3 egg yolks, beaten
1 T. cornstarch	1 T. brandy
1 c. water	

Soften gelatin in ½ cup water and dissolve over low heat. Blend cream cheese with sugar. Add milk, lemon juice, rum, lemon rind, and gelatin mixture. Chill until thickened. Whip mixture well. Fold in egg whites and whipped cream. Pour into a well oiled 1 quart mold and chill until set.

Brandy Sauce   Cook sugar, cornstarch, and water until thick and clear. Pour hot mixture slowly into egg yolks, beating constantly. Return to heat for a few minutes to thicken sauce. Add brandy and chill.
Serves 8 to 10.
Mrs. Wayland Rivers (Ann Staacke)

Grapenut Pudding

4 eggs	Pinch salt
1 c. sugar	½ c. grapenuts
3 c. milk, scalded	¼ t. nutmeg
1 t. vanilla	

Beat eggs until fluffy; add sugar and slowly stir in scalded milk. Add remaining ingredients, stirring until well mixed; the grapenuts will sink to the bottom. Pour into 2 quart baking dish; sprinkle with nutmeg. Bake in a hot water bath at 350° for 1 hour. Serve warm or chilled.
Serves 4 to 6.
Mrs. Patrick J. Nugent (Luci Johnson)

Egg Nog Dessert

2 T. unflavored gelatin	¼ t. nutmeg
½ c. water	½ c. rum
6 eggs, separated	1 t. rum flavoring
1½ c. sugar	½ t. salt
2 c. milk	2 c. heavy cream, whipped

Crust
22 graham crackers, crushed
½ c. butter
½ c. confectioners' sugar
Nutmeg

Sprinkle gelatin over water. Beat egg yolks; add sugar and milk. Pour into double boiler and cook over hot water for 10 minutes. Remove from heat and stir in gelatin. Add nutmeg, rum, and rum flavoring; chill until the mixture begins to thicken. Beat egg whites with salt until peaks form. Add whipped cream to custard; fold in egg whites. To prepare crust, mix graham crackers, butter, and confectioners' sugar. Press crust into 9 x 13 dish. Fill with dessert mixture; sprinkle with nutmeg and chill overnight.
Serves 12 to 14.
Mrs. Homer Garrison, III (Anne Reese)

Dark Chocolate Mousse

4 squares unsweetened chocolate
¾ c. sugar
¼ c. coffee
5 eggs, separated (at room
   temperature)

1½ t. vanilla or 2 T. Cognac,
   rum, or Kirsch
1 c. heavy cream, whipped
Chopped pistachios or
   chocolate shavings

Combine chocolate, sugar, and coffee in top of double boiler; cook, stirring constantly, over boiling water until chocolate is melted. Remove from heat but leave top in double boiler; add egg yolks, one at a time, beating well after each addition. Remove top of double boiler; cool and stir in flavoring. Beat egg whites until stiff; fold into chocolate. Pour into individual soufflé dishes. Cover and chill at least 12 hours. Serve with a dollop of whipped cream sprinkled with pistachios or chocolate shavings.
Unconscionably rich.
Serves 6 to 8.
Mrs. J. Dudley Youman (Sandy Geyer)

Sam's Pots de Crême

1 6 oz. package semi-sweet
   chocolate chips
1 T. sugar
Pinch salt
1 t. vanilla

1 t. peppermint extract,
   optional
¾ c. light cream, scalded
Whipped cream

Place all ingredients in blender and blend for one minute at high speed. Pour into 6 individual pots de crême cups and chill for several hours. Top with whipped cream.
Easily changes from pudding to sauce served hot over ice cream.
Serves 6.
Mrs. Ashley Bracken (Susan Fry)

Mary Shary's Tipsy Pudding

4 eggs, separated	½ c. bourbon or rum
½ c. sugar	1 c. chopped dates
2 c. milk, scalded	1 c. white raisins
2 T. unflavored gelatin	1 c. chopped pecans
¼ c. cold water	1 c. heavy cream, whipped
1 t. vanilla	

Beat egg yolks with sugar. Slowly add scalded milk, stirring constantly. Put into top of double boiler; cook over water until thick, stirring constantly. Dissolve gelatin in water; add to egg mixture. Cool; add stiffly beaten egg whites, vanilla, and whiskey. Fold in dates, raisins, and pecans. Pour into 1½ quart mold; chill until firm. Serve with whipped cream. May be doubled to serve 20, using a 3 quart bundt pan for the mold.
Served by Mrs. Allan Shivers at the Governor's Mansion, from her mother's recipe.
Serves 10.
Mrs. Charles E. Bates (Linda Steinhauser)

Chocolate Toffee Dessert

1 c. fine vanilla wafer crumbs (20 wafers)	2 4 oz. bars German's sweet chocolate, melted
⅔ c. butter, at room temperature	⅔ c. chopped walnuts
1⅓ c. sifted confectioners' sugar	1 t. vanilla
2 eggs, separated	1 c. heavy cream, whipped

Sprinkle ½ of the crumbs in an 8 inch square pan. Cream butter and sugar; stir in egg yolks, chocolate, walnuts, and vanilla. Beat egg whites until stiff; fold into chocolate mixture. Spread over the crumbs; sprinkle remaining crumbs on top. Chill several hours. Cut into small squares; serve with whipped cream.
Serves 8 to 10.
Mrs. Bethea W. Brindley (Mary Ellen Kennedy)

Bread and Butter Pudding

⅔ c. raisins
10 slices bread, sliced into
   1 inch strips
5 T. butter, melted
4 eggs
4 c. milk

2 c. sugar
¼ t. salt
1 t. cinnamon
1 t. nutmeg
1 t. vanilla

Spread half of the raisins on the bottom of a buttered, 2½ quart casserole. Dip half of the bread strips in butter; arrange on top of raisins. Repeat layers of raisins and bread. Combine remaining ingredients; pour over bread. Bake at 350° for 45 to 60 minutes, depending on depth of dish.
Serves 8.
Mrs. Wayland Rivers (Ann Staacke)

Jane's Sherry Mousse

1 lb. marshmallows
2¼ c. sherry
1 T. unflavored gelatin

1 qt. heavy cream, whipped
Vanilla wafers, finely rolled
Hershey's chocolate candy bar

In a double boiler, melt marshmallows in 2 cups of the sherry. Add gelatin which has been dissolved in remaining sherry. Chill until mixture begins to thicken. Fold whipped cream into gelatin mixture. Butter a 3 quart mold or bundt pan and dust with wafer crumbs. Pour in mixture. Chill overnight. Unmold carefully. Sprinkle generously with shavings of chocolate.
Smooth and delicate.
Serves 12.
Mrs. John C. Phillips (Peggy Smith)

Flan

½ c. sugar
6 eggs, lightly beaten
9 T. sugar

½ t. salt
½ t. vanilla
3 c. milk

Place ½ cup sugar in heavy skillet with 1 tablespoon water; cook over medium heat, stirring frequently until syrupy and brown. Do not burn. Pour syrup into a lightly buttered 2 quart baking dish and cool. Combine eggs, sugar, salt, vanilla, and milk. Pour through a strainer onto caramelized sugar. Place dish in a hot water bath and bake at 325° for 1 hour or until knife inserted in custard comes out clean. Chill. Invert to serve.
A Spanish custard.
Serves 8 to 10.
Mrs. Tom McCrummen (Marian Marley)

Rum Custard Cream

½ c. sugar
2 T. flour
1 egg, beaten

⅔ c. light cream
2 T. dark rum
1 c. heavy cream, whipped

In top of double boiler combine sugar, flour, egg, and light cream. Cook over boiling water for 5 minutes, stirring constantly. Add rum and cook 5 minutes; remove from heat and cool. Chill 1 hour; fold in whipped cream.
Serves 4.
Mrs. Thomas E. Fairey (Judith Gund)

Steamed Chocolate Pudding

Pudding

1	c. flour	1	egg, slightly beaten
2	t. baking powder	1½	squares unsweetened
1	T. melted butter		chocolate, melted
½	c. sugar	½	c. milk

Sauce

2   eggs, separated
1   c. confectioners' sugar
½   c. heavy cream, whipped
1   T. rum, bourbon, or vanilla

Pudding   Sift the flour and baking powder together. Add other ingredients and mix well. Pour the batter into a buttered 1 quart mixing bowl, or pudding mold. Cover the container tightly with foil; set in a deep kettle. Pour boiling water around the mold to ⅔ its height. Cover the kettle and steam over low heat for 1 hour. Unmold pudding and serve hot, accompanied by sauce.

Sauce   Beat egg yolks lightly, adding sugar, whipped cream, and flavoring. Before serving, fold in egg whites, stiffly beaten.

A recipe brought from Scotland by the Thomas family.

Mrs. John Thomas (Martha Helen Hall)

Christmas Pudding

1½ c. fine dry bread crumbs	½ t. salt
1 c. minced suet	Raisins
¾ c. flour, unsifted	Currants
⅔ c. sugar	Sultanas
3 eggs	Citron
1 c. Cognac	Chopped almonds
Grated rind and juice of 1 lemon	1 grated carrot
and 1 orange	1 grated apple
1 t. allspice	

Hard Sauce
½ c. butter, at room temperature
1 c. sugar
Cognac, rum, or bourbon

In a large bowl, mix bread crumbs, suet, flour, sugar, eggs, and Cognac. Stir in lemon and orange rind and juice, allspice, and salt. Add raisins, currants, sultanas, citron, and almonds to carrot and apple to measure 4 cups. Cover and refrigerate overnight. Place in a buttered mold or bowl and seal tightly with oiled wax paper, then aluminum foil; tie securely with string. Place in a hot water bath. Cover and steam for 6 to 8 hours. Serve warm with hard sauce. Pudding can be reheated by steaming.

Hard Sauce Cream butter and sugar until light. Beat in liquor to taste.
An old-fashioned favorite that deserves to be revived.
Serves 12/Freezes.
Mrs. W. T. Archer (Dorothy Newton)

Carmel Caramel

¾ c. sugar	¼ t. salt
2 c. milk	½ t. vanilla
2 eggs	

In a heavy skillet, melt sugar to a light brown syrup. Add milk. Mixture will look ruined, but is not. Cook, stirring constantly, until smooth. Beat eggs, salt, and vanilla together. Slowly pour sugar mixture into eggs, stirring constantly. Pour into buttered individual molds and place molds in a pan of hot water. Bake at 350° for 15 to 20 minutes or until set. Do not let water in pan boil.
Serves 4.
Mrs. Charles F. Herring (Doris Wallace)

Dorothy's Crème Brulée

1 qt. heavy cream	8 egg yolks
1 vanilla bean	Light brown sugar
2 T. sugar	

Heat cream in a double boiler with vanilla bean and sugar. Beat egg yolks until pale yellow. Remove vanilla bean and add cream to eggs, a little at a time, stirring constantly. Strain into a baking dish. Place dish in a hot water bath. Bake at 325° for 30 to 40 minutes or until a knife comes out clean. Cool. Chill for at least 8 hours. Sift brown sugar over the custard to ⅛ inch thickness. Place under broiler until sugar caramelizes. Chill and serve on chilled dessert plates.
Serves 10.
Mrs. R. Kinnan Golemon (Jackie Burst)

Coffee Mousse in Meringue Shell

Shell
4   egg whites
Pinch salt
½ t. lemon juice
¾ c. sugar

Coffee Mousse

2 T. powdered instant coffee
⅓ c. boiling water
1 T. unflavored gelatin
½ c. walnuts

3 eggs, separated
½ c. sifted confectioners' sugar
2 c. heavy cream, whipped

Beat egg whites with salt to soft peaks. Add lemon juice and gradually beat in sugar until sugar dissolves and meringue stands in stiff peaks. Spread half of the meringue on the bottom and sides of a greased 10 inch pie pan. With a teaspoon, arrange mounds of remaining meringue around the rim of the pie. Do not place mounds too close to the rim because meringue will expand while cooking. Bake shell at 300° for 50 to 55 minutes or until crisp but still white. Let cool. Dissolve coffee in water. Let cool. Sprinkle in gelatin to soften. Place mixture over a pan of boiling water and stir until gelatin is dissolved. In a large bowl, beat egg yolks with confectioners' sugar until light in color. Stir in gelatin mixture and chill until thickened slightly. Beat egg whites until they hold peaks. Fold egg whites and whipped cream into gelatin mixture. Spoon mousse into meringue shell and sprinkle with walnuts around edge. Chill until set. Serve the pie the same day it is made.
Would win a beauty prize.
Serves 6 to 8.
Mrs. Charles R. Crites (Mildred "Milly" Holmes)

Etcetera

Sauce Diane

½	c. butter	1	T. lemon juice
2	t. dry mustard	1	T. Worcestershire sauce
¾	lb. mushrooms, sliced	1	t. salt
1½	c. chopped green onion	¼	c. chopped parsley

Melt butter; stir in mustard, mushrooms, and onions. Sauté 8 to 10 minutes. Stir in lemon juice, Worcestershire sauce, salt, and parsley. *The ultimate sauce for a peppered and grilled steak.*
Yields approximately 2 cups.
Mrs. John Philip Ferguson (Mitzi Ann Riddle)

Pico de Gallo

½	c. chopped salad olives	3	fresh green chilies,
	Juice of 1 lime		1 to 2 inches long, minced
2	onions, finely chopped	2	cloves garlic, minced
¾	c. olive or vegetable oil		Salt and pepper
2	tomatoes, finely chopped	2	T. chopped cilantro, optional

Combine ingredients and refrigerate overnight to blend flavors.
Serve over tacos or scrambled eggs.
Yields 1 quart.
Mrs. Dudley McCalla (Maline Gilbert)

Sweet and Sour Sauce for Ham

2	t. cornstarch	¾	c. beef bouillon
1	t. sugar	1	c. sliced, seeded
1	T. red wine vinegar		Tokay grapes
1	T. soy sauce		

Combine cornstarch and sugar. Add vinegar, soy sauce, and bouillon. Cook mixture until clear. Before serving, add grapes.
A sauce that glistens.
Yields 1 cup.
Mrs. Thomas Irvin Lowry (Katherine Sangster)

Sauce Provençale

4 tomatoes, peeled, seeded, and cut into wedges	½ c. dry sherry
½ t. sugar	½ c. butter
2 T. butter	3 cloves garlic, minced
¼ c. chopped green onions	2 T. chopped parsley
	Salt and pepper to taste

Sprinkle tomato wedges with sugar and set aside. Melt 2 tablespoons butter and stir in onions. Add sherry and simmer until liquid is slightly reduced. Add tomatoes and stir, but do not allow them to lose shape. Add butter, garlic, parsley, salt, and pepper. Heat, stirring gently, until butter melts.

Serve over steak.

Yields approximately 6 cups.

Mrs. John Philip Ferguson (Mitzi Ann Riddle)

Blender Béarnaise Sauce

3 egg yolks	2 t. chopped shallots
2 T. tarragon vinegar	½ t. tarragon
1 T. lemon juice	¼ t. chervil
½ t. salt	½ c. butter, at room temperature
¼ t. white pepper	½ c. boiling water

Combine all ingredients, except water, in blender. Cover and whirl until well blended. With blender on, gradually pour water into center. Replace cover and continue to blend approximately 1 minute or until very smooth. Remove to the top of a double boiler and cook over hot water, stirring constantly, for 3 minutes until sauce thickens slightly. May be refrigerated and warmed over hot water, stirring constantly.

Yields 1½ cups.

Mrs. John Moss (Margaret Davis)

Spicy Chili Sauce

4 ribs celery, chopped
2 to 3 medium onions, chopped
½ lb. fresh jalapeño
  peppers, chopped
3 14 oz. cans whole
  tomatoes, drained
1 3 oz. can jalapeño or
  hot cherry peppers, chopped

⅛ t. ground cloves
¼ t. dry mustard
1¼ t. cinnamon
1¼ c. packed brown sugar
1 T. salt
1 c. cider vinegar

Combine celery, onions, jalapeños, and tomatoes; simmer 1 hour. Add canned peppers and cook 30 minutes. Stir in sugar, dry ingredients, and vinegar and simmer 1½ hours.
Chili sauce lovers serve it on omelets, meat, vegetables—anything!
Yields 1 quart/Freezes.
Mrs. Frank Gregg (Beverly Lamb)

Salsa

4 ripe tomatoes, peeled
  and finely chopped
½ c. finely chopped onion
½ c. finely chopped celery
¼ c. finely chopped bell pepper
¼ c. olive oil or vegetable oil
3 T. green chilies, drained
  and finely chopped

2 T. red wine vinegar
1 t. mustard seed
1 t. ground cumin
Salt, garlic powder,
  and Tabasco to taste

Combine all ingredients. Cover and chill several hours or overnight. Serve with tortilla chips or as a condiment.
A Southwestern topping for everything, including eggs and beans.
Yields approximately 2½ cups.
Mrs. John Oscar Robinson (Nancy Newton)

Whipped Orange Sauce

Juice and grated rind of
  2 oranges
4 egg yolks, beaten
1 c. sugar

Juice of ½ lemon
1 c. heavy cream, whipped
Orange slices or grated
  chocolate

Place orange juice and rind, egg yolks, sugar, and lemon juice in the top of a double boiler. Cook until thick. Cool. Fold whipped cream into the sauce. Chill at least 4 hours. Serve over slices of cake or gingerbread and garnish with orange slices or grated chocolate.

Mrs. J.E. Fryer (Phyllis Garland)

Machismo Barbeque Sauce

½ c. butter
½ c. vinegar
½ c. lemon juice

3 jalapeño peppers
Salt and pepper

Combine butter, vinegar, lemon juice and peppers in saucepan; boil 5 minutes. Add salt until briny and plenty of pepper.

The jalapeños lose their fire after being boiled and may be sliced and eaten with impunity.

Yields 1½ cups.

Mrs. Sam Fason (Maydelle Foster)

Wine Marinade

1½ c. peanut oil or
    vegetable oil
¾ c. soy sauce
2 T. Worcestershire sauce
2 T. dry mustard
2 T. salt

1 T. freshly ground pepper
½ t. garlic salt
1 c. dry red wine
2 t. dried parsley flakes
⅓ c. lemon juice

Combine all ingredients in a 1 quart jar. Seal tightly and shake vigorously.
A marinade for steaks, brisket, or beef cubes for kabobs.
Yields approximately 1 quart.
Mrs. Charles Michael Smith (Sally Thomas)

White Sauce Mix

1 c. flour
4 c. instant non-fat dry milk
4 t. salt

1 c. butter, at room
    temperature
1 c. milk

Blend flour, dry milk, and salt. Cut in butter. Store mixture in refrigerator.
For thin sauce: ⅓ cup mix plus 1 cup milk
For medium sauce: ½ cup mix plus 1 cup milk
For thick sauce: 1 cup mix plus 1 cup milk
Cook over low heat, stirring constantly, for 3 to 6 minutes.
Extra convenience plus extra protein.
Mrs. W. R. Long, III (Carol Tyler)

Bread and Butter Pickles

1 gallon cucumbers (approximately 8 3-inch cucumbers), thinly sliced	5 c. sugar
8 to 10 small onions, thinly sliced	½ t. ground cloves
2 bell peppers, grated	1 t. celery seed
½ c. uniodized salt	1½ t. turmeric
1 qt. crushed ice	2 T. mustard seed
	5 c. cider vinegar
	3 small jalapeno peppers, sliced

Combine cucumbers and onions. Add bell peppers, salt, and crushed ice. Chill for 3 hours. Drain. In a saucepan, boil remaining ingredients until sugar is dissolved. Pour over vegetables and mix. Scald, but do not boil. Pack and seal in jars.
Yields 8 to 10 pints.
Mrs. John L. Berkman, Jr. (Lynn Langston)

Easy Crisp Sweet Pickles

2 qt. sour pickles, sliced	½ c. vinegar
6 c. sugar	2 T. pickling spices

In a large bowl, cover pickles with remaining ingredients. Stir every 30 minutes until sugar is dissolved. Pack into jars and seal. Store in refrigerator. Pickles will be crisp in 2 days.
Yields 4 pints.
Mrs. Willard Y. Ferrick (Alice Heiligenthal)

Cabbage Pickle

Salt	Whole allspice
1 head cabbage, sliced into ½ inch wide strips	3 pieces cinnamon stick, finely broken
2 T. sugar	Celery seed
¾ c. cider vinegar	Pepper
¼ c. water	Turmeric
White mustard seed	Dried red pepper pods
Black mustard seed	

Make a strong salt water brine and heat to boiling. Pour over shredded cabbage and allow to stand for 24 hours. Drain. Combine sugar, vinegar, and water. Pour over cabbage to cover, making more vinegar mixture as necessary. Bring to a boil, remove from heat and let cool slightly. Place 1 inch layers of cabbage in sterilized jars, sprinkle each layer with remaining ingredients, except red pepper. Fill jar about ¾ full with cabbage and spices and top with 1 pepper pod per jar. Bring vinegar mixture to a boil and pour to fill jars. Allow to stand 1 week before opening and use within 1 month. Serve chilled.
A recipe over 100 years old.
Yields approximately 4 pints.
Mrs. Stanley Finch (Emily Rice)

Pickled Onions

5 lb. small pickling onions	1½ T. mustard seed
2 c. salt	1 c. sugar
1 qt. vinegar	6 small red or green chili
1½ T. celery seed	peppers

Pour boiling water to cover over onions; let stand 20 minutes. Peel onions and place in enamel pan or crock. Make a brine of salt and 1 gallon boiling water; pour over onions and let stand overnight. Drain and heat brine; pour over onions. Repeat twice. On the third day, rinse onions in cold water and let soak in ice water while preparing pickling liquid. Mix vinegar with 2 cups water, celery seed, mustard seed, and sugar; boil. Drain onions and pack into sterilized jars; add 1 pepper to each jar and fill with hot liquid. Seal jars. Serve chilled.
Not for sissies.
Yields 5 to 6 pints.
Mrs. C. N. Avery, Jr. (Lucille Sharp)

Faye Harris' Peach Preserves

1   lb. sugar to each
     lb. of peaches

Peel and slice peaches. In a large kettle, arrange peaches and sugar in layers, adding 4 to 5 peach kernels, and let stand overnight. Bring peaches to a boil, stirring gently; simmer for 4 to 5 hours until transparent, skimming foam occasionally. Pack in sterilized jars and seal.

½ bushel of peaches fills approximately 8 quart jars.
Mrs. Thomas C. Wommack (Virginia Ford)

Orange Marmalade

3   California oranges   Sugar
3   lemons   Paraffin
(Choose firm, unblemished
    fresh fruit)

First day: Wash and remove ends of fruit, leaving rind on fruit. Slice fruit as thinly as possible, cutting each slice into fourths or smaller. Add 2 parts of water to 1 part of fruit; let stand overnight in glass or enamel container (not aluminum).
Second day: Simmer fruit and water, covered, 15 to 20 minutes, until tender. Fruit is tender when it cuts easily with side of fork and looks clear. Let set, covered, overnight in glass or enamel container (not aluminum).
Third day: Add ¾ cup sugar for each cup of fruit and water. Cook 3 to 4 cups at a time in heavy saucepan. Bring to a rolling boil, stirring often but gently to scrape sugar from sides of pan as it dissolves; reduce heat and cook, stirring occasionally, until juice coats spoon and drops in large thick drops, like jelly, approximately 30 to 45 minutes. When marmalade is thick, pour into sterilized jars or glasses and cover with ¼ to ½ inch thick layer of melted paraffin. When cool, seal with lids.
Clear, pure, and fresh.
Yields 4 pints.
Mrs. Carroll McPherson (Martha Bundy)

Fig Preserves

1	gallon figs, cut into small pieces
8	c. sugar

1	c. light corn syrup
3	lemons, thinly sliced

Combine ingredients and cook until thick. Pour into sterilized jars and seal with paraffin.
Yields 8 pints.
Mrs. John Thomas (Martha Helen Hall)

Mimi's Chutney

1	lb. dried prunes, pitted and finely chopped
5	c. cider vinegar, heated
½	lb. dried apricots
1	lb. pitted dates
1	lb. onions, peeled
3	oranges, seeded
1	lemon, seeded
6½	lb. apples, cored
1	lb. seedless raisins
6	cloves garlic, minced

¼	oz. ginger root, crushed
4	t. salt
2	t. dry mustard
½	t. cayenne
2	t. allspice
2	lbs. dark brown sugar
2	T. pickling spices
5	cloves
8	fresh hot peppers
Cheesecloth	

Soak prunes in vinegar for 1 hour. Coarsely grind apricots, dates, onions, oranges, and lemon. Place prunes with vinegar, apples, raisins, and ground mixture in a large pot. Add garlic, ginger root, salt, mustard, cayenne, allspice, and sugar. Tie pickling spices, cloves, and hot peppers into a cheesecloth bag and add to mixture. Simmer slowly, uncovered, approximately 1½ hours. Remove cheesecloth bag; pour into sterilized jars and seal.
Yields approximately 14 pints.
Mrs. W. T. Archer (Dorothy Newton)

Antebellum Strawberry Preserves

2   T. lemon juice
1   qt. strawberries, hulled
4   c. sugar

Combine all ingredients. Heat to boiling, and cook rapidly for 8 minutes, stirring constantly. Pour berry mixture into shallow glass container; cover with plastic wrap, propping up one side to permit some evaporation. Place in sunshine for 2 to 3 days, stirring occasionally, and bringing inside at night. At the end of this time, the preserves will be thickened. Place in sterilized jars and seal.
Abundant sunshine is needed to make this recipe.
Yields approximately 4½ pints.
Mrs. Robert Jenkins (Carlene Johnson)

Pyracantha Jelly

1   qt. ripe, red
    Pyracantha berries
1   qt. water
1   small grapefruit, juiced

1   small lemon, juiced
1   1¾ oz. package fruit
    pectin (Sure Jell)
5½ c. sugar

Place berries in pan and cover with 1 quart water; boil 20 minutes. Strain and add grapefruit and lemon juices to liquid. Add water, if necessary, to yield 4½ cups. Pour into a heavy saucepan and stir in fruit pectin. Bring to a hard boil, stirring constantly. Add sugar and boil for 1½ minutes, stirring constantly. Remove from heat and skim. Pour into hot, sterilized jars and seal with paraffin.
Yields 8½ pints
Mrs. Maury Hughes, Jr. (Phoebe Foster)

Mango Chutney

9 c. green mangoes, sliced	¼ c. mustard seed
1 c. kosher or rock salt	3¼ c. cider vinegar
1½ c. packed light brown sugar	1 to 2 c. water
5¾ c. sugar	2 lemons, thinly sliced
4 cloves garlic	⅛ c. crushed red pepper
¼ lb. ginger root, chopped	1 lb. raisins

Soak mangoes in salt overnight; drain and rinse many times. Combine remaining ingredients with mangoes and simmer approximately 1 hour until mangoes are clear. Pour into sterilized jars and seal.
Yields approximately 18 pints.
Mrs. William Terry Bray (Judy Wallace)

Italian Prune Conserve

4 c. fresh Italian prunes	½ t. allspice
6 c. sugar	½ c. lemon juice
¾ t. cinnamon	3 oz. liquid pectin
¾ t. ground cloves	

Pit prunes and chop them in the blender. Combine all ingredients, except pectin, in a large kettle; mix well. Bring to a rolling boil, stirring frequently. Boil rapidly for 1 minute, stirring constantly. Remove from heat; add pectin. Stir and skim at intervals for approximately 5 minutes. Pour into sterilized jars. Cover at once with thin layer of melted paraffin; add another layer when the conserve is cold.
Try at Thanksgiving as an accompaniment to turkey.
Yields approximately 10 6-ounce glasses.
Mrs. James N. Ludlum (Dorothy Standifer)

Pear Preserves

4   qt. hard pears, sliced
¼   c. lemon juice
6   c. sugar

Slivered peel of 1 lemon
1   t. ground ginger

Peel, core, and sliver pears. Place in a large pot and sprinkle with lemon juice and sugar. Let stand, covered, 8 hours or overnight. Bring to a rolling boil; add ginger and lemon peel. Simmer 2 to 2½ hours, stirring occasionally, until pears are clear. Syrup should be fairly thick. Pack into hot, sterilized jars.
Yields 4 to 5 pints.
Mrs. Vernon L. Elledge (Sharon Prentice)

Cranberry-Orange Relish

1   lb. fresh or frozen
    cranberries
1   c. orange juice
2   c. sugar

½   t. nutmeg
½   t. ground cardamon
2   oranges, peeled and
    coarsely chopped

Mix all ingredients in a saucepan and bring to a boil, stirring occasionally. Reduce heat and simmer for 10 minutes or until cranberries are tender, stirring continuously. Cool. Pour into sterilized jars and seal. Serve chilled.
Chopped pecans are a nice addition.
Yields 2 pints.
Mrs. Charles R. Crites (Mildred "Milly" Holmes)

Krishnan's Curry Powder

1	cinnamon stick	½	t. coriander
3	whole cloves	1	t. turmeric
¼	t. caraway seeds	2	T. chili powder

Grind cinnamon stick, cloves, and caraway seeds in a mortar, pepper mill, or blender. Combine with remaining ingredients. Store in tightly sealed jar. Keeps indefinitely.
Be original—make your own.
Mrs. W. R. Long, III (Carol Tyler)

Prunes Plumped in Red Wine

Pitted prunes
Red Wine
1   t. pickling spice per c. of wine
Cheesecloth

Fill a jar with prunes. Heat red wine with pickling spices, tied in a cheesecloth bag, and pour over prunes. Cover. Let stand at least two days; remove cheesecloth bag before serving.
The perfect accompaniment to roast leg of pork, page 110.
Mrs. Walter Bremond, III (Zenobia Myers)

Granola

5	c. rolled oats	¼	c. soy flour
1	c. slivered almonds	1	c. non-fat dry powdered milk
1	c. sesame seeds	1	c. wheat germ
1	c. hulled sunflower seeds	1	c. honey
1	c. grated coconut	1	c. vegetable oil

Combine dry ingredients. Add honey and oil; mix well. Bake on 2 jelly roll pans at 325° until brown, 15 to 20 minutes. Stir often and watch carefully as it burns easily. Store tightly covered.
An after-school snack as well as breakfast food.
Yields 12 cups.
Mrs. Sam Fason (Maydelle Foster)

Hot Fruit Compote

1½	c. sugar	1	8¼ oz. can crushed pineapple, undrained
¾	c. water		
	Juice of 1 lemon	2	bananas, diced
8	Jonathan or winesap apples, peeled and sliced		

Boil sugar and water until sugar dissolves; stir in lemon juice and apples. Simmer gently until apples are almost tender; add pineapple. When apples are done, add bananas. Bake in a 2 quart soufflé dish at 350° for 20 to 30 minutes.
Change from a pork accompaniment to a dessert by adding cream or baked meringue.
Serves 6 to 8.
Mrs. Laurens B. Fish, Jr. (Julia Corley)

Glacéed Nuts and Fruits

2 c. sugar
1 c. boiling water
⅛ t. cream of tartar

Combine all ingredients in saucepan and bring to a boil. Boil *without stirring* until syrup begins to discolor (310°). Remove pan from heat and place in cold water to stop boiling instantly. Take pan from cold water and place pan in hot water during dipping process. To dip nuts or fruits, spear separately on a long pin, dip in syrup, place on oiled wax paper to cool.
An edible centerpiece or after dinner coffee accompaniment.
Mrs. Milner Thorne (Polly Perry)

Antipasto

2 16 oz. cans pitted black olives, drained and sliced
2 16 oz. cans stuffed green olives, drained and sliced
2 20 oz. jars dill pickle slices, drained
2 medium heads cauliflower, parboiled
3 c. marinated artichoke hearts
2 16 oz. cans whole green beans, drained
3 4½ oz. jars small onions, drained
5 10 oz. cans sliced mushrooms, drained
2 c. vegetable oil or olive oil
1½ c. white vinegar
6 14 oz. bottles catsup
3 2 oz. cans anchovy fillets
5 6½ oz. cans solid pack tunafish, drained and rinsed
2 bell peppers, parboiled
2 c. chopped pimientos

Chop all ingredients. In a large stainless steel or enamel kettle, combine all but the last 4 ingredients. Simmer for 10 minutes. Add anchovies, tuna, bell peppers, and pimientos; simmer for 5 minutes. Pack the antipasto in pint jars; place in hot water bath for 15 minutes and seal. Let stand at least 24 hours before using. Salt antipasto to taste before serving.
Yields 20 pints.
Mrs. William Terry Bray (Judy Wallace)

Mike and Charlie's Avocado Butter

1 c. butter, at room temperature	2 T. chopped parsley
½ c. mashed avocado	2 t. Worcestershire sauce
2 T. lemon juice	1 t. garlic salt

Beat butter in mixer until very soft. Add remaining ingredients and blend well. Cover and refrigerate. Serve over grilled trout or redfish. Also good over steak.
Too good to be true.
Yields approximately 1½ cups.
Mrs. Charles E. Bates (Linda Steinhauser)

Strawberry Butter

1 c. butter, at room temperature (do not substitute)	1 cup ripe, fresh strawberries or 1 10 oz. box frozen strawberries, undrained, at room temperature
½ t. salt	
2 or 3 T. confectioners' sugar	

Whip butter in blender 1 minute. Add remaining ingredients (use 2 tablespoons sugar with frozen strawberries and 3 tablespoons sugar with fresh strawberries); whip 2 minutes. Refrigerate. Serve with bread, toast, or pancakes.
Yields 2 cups.
Mrs. William F. Weldon (Morey McGonigle)

College Inn Orange Butter

1 c. butter, at room temperature (do not substitute)	½ c. sifted confectioners' sugar
Grated rind and juice of 2 oranges	

Combine ingredients and blend in mixer. Serve with hot biscuits, French toast, waffles, or pancakes.
Yields 1½ cups.
Mrs. Vernon L. Elledge, Jr. (Sharon Prentice)

Mint Cooler

2   c. sugar
2   c. water
Juice of 6 oranges
Juice and rind of 2 lemons

1½ c. frest mint
6   qt. ginger ale
Crushed ice

Boil sugar and water together, uncovered, for 10 minutes; remove from heat and add fruit juices and 1 cup of the mint. Cover tightly; let stand for at least 1 hour. Strain; chill in a covered jar. This will keep indefinitely. Mix 1 part of this mixture with 4 parts ginger ale. Pour over crushed ice and garnish with mint.
Yields 7½ quarts.
Mrs. Charles F. Herring (Doris Wallace)

Mint Tea

1   c. tea leaves
2½ qt. water
3   c. sugar
Approximately 35 sprigs mint

Grated rind of 3 lemons
Juice of 9 lemons
3   c. pineapple juice

Steep tea in 1½ quarts of boiling water for 8 minutes. Boil sugar in remaining 1 quart water until a light syrup forms; add mint and lemon rinds. Steep 10 minutes. Add tea; steep 10 minutes. Strain; add lemon juice, pineapple juice, and enough additional water to make 2 gallons.
A hot weather refresher.
Yields 2 gallons.
Mrs. Sam. A. Wilson (Sonia Wolf)

Chocolate Iced Coffee

4   qt. strong coffee, chilled
1   c. sugar
1   tray ice cubes
½ t. peppermint extract

½ gallon chocolate ice
    cream, softened
2   c. heavy cream,
    whipped

Pour coffee into punchbowl. Add sugar and ice cubes; mix. Stir in peppermint extract and ice cream. Float whipped cream on top.
Serves 48.
Mrs. Sam A. Wilson (Sonia Wolf)

Frozen Irish Coffee

½   c. milk
¼   c. Irish whiskey
1   qt. coffee ice cream

1   t. instant coffee powder
½   c. heavy cream, whipped
4   cinnamon sticks

Mix milk and whiskey in blender; add ice cream and instant coffee powder. Blend until smooth. Pour into tall chilled glasses. Top each with whipped cream and a cinnamon stick. May substitute ½ cup strong brewed coffee for milk and instant coffee powder.
A summer version of a winter favorite.
Serves 4.
Mrs. Duke Matthews Covert (Lynne Carole Shapiro)

Café au Cacao

1   gallon cold coffee
1   gallon chocolate ice cream,
     softened
1½ c. dark crème de cacao
1   c. heavy cream, whipped

Combine coffee, ice cream, and crème de cacao; mix well. Fold in whipped cream.
A combination after-dinner drink and dessert.
Yields approximately 25 cups.
Mrs. Shannon Ratliff (Gay Kokernot)

Kahlua

3   c. sugar
¼   c. Yuban instant coffee
2   c. boiling water

2   c. Cognac
1   vanilla bean

Combine sugar and instant coffee. Stir in boiling water and mix until sugar and coffee dissolve. Pour into a glass container; add Cognac and vanilla bean. Seal tightly and allow to stand in a dark place 3 to 4 weeks. In small bottles this is a lovely gift.
Before a very warm fire.
Yields approximately 1 quart.
Mrs. Walter Demond (Ann Elizabeth Moss)

Winter Warmer

2   qt. apple juice
2   c. canned orange juice
1½ c. pineapple juice
1   c. lemon juice

1   stick cinnamon
1   t. whole cloves
Sugar to sweeten, if desired

Combine ingredients and simmer for 30 minutes. Strain and serve hot.
Houstonians will recognize this Christmas time treat from the Bank of the Southwest, where it is served with gingerbread.
Mrs. Charles R. Crites (Mildred "Milly" Holmes)

Very Old-Fashioneds

1   qt. bourbon
1   c. light rum
1   c. sugar
2   T. Angostura bitters

1   17 oz. jar mixed salad
     fruits, undrained
Maraschino cherries

Combine all ingredients, except cherries. Cover and refrigerate 1 week. Serve over ice garnished with maraschino cherry.
For very cold days.
Serves 10.
Mrs. Frank N. Ikard, Jr.(Carol Foster)

Wassail

1   c. sugar
4   cinnamon sticks
3   lemon slices
½   c. water
2   c. pineapple juice

2   c. orange juice
6   c. claret
½   c. lemon juice
1   c. dry sherry
Lemon slices

Boil sugar, cinnamon sticks, lemon slices, and water for 5 minutes. Combine remaining ingredients and heat. Stir in hot syrup and mix well. Serve hot, garnished with lemon slices.
Saxon word for "Be well."
Yields 3 quarts.
Mrs. Frank N. Ikard, Jr. (Carol Foster)

Cynthia's Punch

1   6 oz. can frozen orange juice concentrate, thawed
1   6 oz. can frozen lemonade concentrate, thawed
2   6 oz cans frozen limeade concentrate, thawed
1   1 qt. 14 oz. can pineapple juice
2   c. cranberry juice
4   c. cold water
2   1 qt. bottles ginger ale, chilled
1   1 pt. bottle club soda
1   8 inch frozen fruit ring

Mix fruit juices and water. Pour mixture into punch bowl and chill. Before serving, add ginger ale and soda and mix well. Float fruit ring on top.

Fruit Ring

1   orange, sliced
2   limes, sliced
1   lemon, sliced
2   qt. fruit juice or water

Halve orange slices. Place lime, lemon, and orange slices in an 8 inch ring mold and fill with fruit juice or water. Freeze. Unmold and float in punch.
Serves 20 to 25.
Mrs. Terrell James (Dianne Hill)

Percolator Punch

9   c. unsweetened pineapple juice
9   c. cranberry juice cocktail
4½ c. water
1   c. packed brown sugar
4½ t. whole cloves
4   cinnamon sticks, broken into pieces
¼   t. salt

Combine juices, water, and sugar in 30 cup coffee percolator. Place cloves, cinnamon, and salt in basket; plug in percolator and let it perk as you would for coffee.
Serves 30.
Mrs. Howard N. Richards (Katherine Ross)

Garden Party Punch

1	6 oz. can frozen lemonade concentrate	2	fifths dry champagne, chilled
1	1 qt. 14 oz. can unsweetened pineapple juice, chilled		Whole fresh strawberries, fresh peach slices, and lime slices
1	fifth sauterne chilled		

Combine lemonade, pineapple juice, and sauterne. Just before serving, add champagne and fruit. Pour over a block of ice or ice ring mold and garnish with additional fresh fruit.
Yields 25 punch cups.
Mrs. Charles E. Bates (Linda Steinhauser)

Tumbleweed Ice

1½ T. Kahlua
1½ T. dark crème de cacao
3   scoops vanilla ice cream

Whirl in blender until smooth. Serve in brandy snifter.
Serves 1.
Mrs. Wayland Rivers (Ann Staacke)

Champagne Cup

1	10 oz. package frozen straw-berries, partially thawed	½	c. Cognac
1	10 oz. package frozen peaches, partially thawed	12	scoops orange sherbet
1	c. pineapple chunks	1	bottle champagne
		12	fresh strawberries, with stems

Combine strawberries, peaches, and pineapple; pour Cognac over fruit and toss gently. Refrigerate at least 1 hour. Divide fruit between 12 champagne glasses, add a scoop of sherbet, and fill with champagne. Garnish with whole strawberry.
Equally good without sherbet as a champagne cocktail.
Serves 12.
Mrs. Charles E. Bates (Linda Steinhauser)

Peach Daiquiri

1   6 oz. can frozen lemonade,
     undiluted
¾   c. vodka (1 lemonade can full)
4   large peaches, peeled
     and seeded

Place all ingredients in blender; add crushed ice to fill container and blend until smooth. Serve in tulip shaped glasses.
Vodka instead of rum makes a tarter, peachier drink.
Serves 4 to 6.
Mrs. Charles Crites (Mildred "Milly" Holmes)

Strawberry Daiquiri

1   6 oz. can frozen limeade,   ¾   c. light rum (1 limeade
     undiluted   can full)
1   10 oz package frozen straw-   Fresh strawberries
     berries, partially thawed   Fresh mint

Place limeade, frozen strawberries, and rum in blender; add water to fill container and blend until smooth. Freeze at least 12 hours. Remove from freezer 5 minutes before serving. Garnish with fresh strawberries and mint.
Serves 4 to 6.
Mrs. Walter E. Demond (Ann Elizabeth Moss)

Gracias en Julio

1½ oz. white rum
3   oz. cranberry juice
Juice of ¼ lime
Sugar to taste

Mix rum, cranberry juice, and lime juice. Add sugar, if desired. Serve over ice.
Translates as "Thanksgiving in July."
Serves 1.
Mrs. Thomas D. Kirksey (Gene Weisinger)

Sangria

1 bottle dry red wine	Spiral of orange peel or
Juice of 1 lemon	cucumber rind
Juice of 1 orange	6 to 8 ice cubes
1 10 oz. package frozen peaches	1 10 oz. bottle soda water

Combine wine with juices and peaches; let stand until peaches defrost. Refrigerate 2 to 3 hours. Pour into a tall pitcher and add peel or rind, ice cubes and soda water.
Serves 6.
Mrs. Philip F. Patman (Katherine Ashley Sellers)

Cola de Lagarto (Alligator's Tail)

Ice cubes	½ oz. crème de menthe
2 oz. vodka	1 1 x 1 x 6 inch strip of
½ oz. fresh lime juice	watermelon and rind
Dry white wine	

Place the ice cubes in a Tom Collins glass; add vodka and lime juice. Fill the glass with wine and gently stir in crème de menthe. With a sharp knife, zig-zag the flesh side of watermelon to resemble an alligator's tail. Garnish drink with the melon.
Yields 1 cocktail.
Mrs. Charles E. Bates (Linda Steinhauser)

Velvet Hammer

3 oz. Cointreau
1 oz. white crème de menthe
Vanilla ice cream

Pour the liqueurs into blender; add enough ice cream to fill container. Blend. Pour into stemmed glasses or brandy snifters.
Serves 6.
Mrs. George Covert (Helen Cook)

Bundy Marys

1	46 oz. can tomato juice	Generous dashes of seasoned salt,
3	10½ oz. cans condensed	garlic salt, lemon-pepper
	beef bouillon, undiluted	marinade, celery salt, dill
1½ c. lemon juice		weed
4 to 6 T. Worcestershire sauce		Vodka
10 drops Tabasco		

Combine all ingredients except vodka in a 1 gallon container. Shake well and refrigerate. Before serving, add 1½ ounces of vodka to each glass, fill with the mix, and stir.
Yields approximately 3 quarts/Keeps up to 3 weeks in the refrigerator; should be made at least 12 hours ahead.
Mrs. Howard N. Richards (Katherine Ross)

Claret Cup

1   6 oz. can frozen lemonade,
     undiluted
1   c. claret
¼   c. rum
1   16 oz. bottle ginger ale

Combine all ingredients and serve over ice.
Serves 6.
Mrs. Jack W. Scarbrough (Betty Richer)

Wine Spritzer

1   c. burgundy
½   c. pineapple juice
½   c. apricot nectar

Mix ingredients and serve over ice.
Yields 2 cups.
Mrs. John A. Moss (Margaret Davis)

French 75

8½ T. confectioners' sugar
8½ lemons, juiced
1½ qt. gin
5½ qt. champagne

Dissolve sugar in lemon juice and add gin. Store mixture in refrigerator. When ready to serve, combine gin mixture with champagne in a punch bowl with an ice ring. (Gin mixture can be kept in refrigerator.) For smaller servings, mix 2 cups gin mixture with 1 fifth of champagne.
A rollicking party punch.
Yields 75 3-ounce drinks.
Mrs. Charles F. Herring (Doris Wallace)

Index

Acorn Squash, Holiday 184
Acorn Squash, Pineapple 185
Aggression Cookies 258
Alcoholic Beverages—see
  Beverages, Alcoholic
Alligator's Tail (Cola de
  Lagarto) 313
Almond-Poppy Seed Noodles for
  Herbed Beef Stew 100
Anacuchos 91
Anchovy Butter for
  Vegetables 192
Angel Pie 232
Antebellum Strawberry
  Preserves 300
Antipasto 305
Appetizers
  Antipasto 305
  Artichoke Balls 1
  Artichoke and Cheese Canapé 1
  Artichoke Squares 4
  Beer Cheese 78
  Black-eyed Pea Dip 12
  Braunschweiger Loaf 16
  Camille's Mantequilla de
    Pobre 7
  Caviar Dip 21
  Caviar Pie 20
  Chafing Dish Artichokes 1
  Cheese Dip for Vegetables 10
  Cheese Toasties 5
  Chicken Curry Balls 15
  Chili Dip 11
  Chutney Cream Cheese
    Spread 10
  Crabmeat Epicurean 6
  Cucumber Sandwiches 16
  Del Rio Steak Tartare 20
  Devil Sticks 3
  Deviled Spinach Eggs 12
  Eggplant Caviar 13
  Empanadas 7
  Fringe Benefit Bean Dip 158
  George Covert's Marinated
    Shrimp 19
  Goose Liver Roll 15
  Ham Salad Baked in Rolls 18
  Hot Clam-Cheese Dip 2
  Hot Crabmeat Dip 8
  Jalapeño Pie 3
  Jamaican Bacon 2
  Kinser Cheeseball 10
  Lamb Riblets 2
  Liptauer Cheese 9
  Marinated Carrots 14
  Mediterranean Loaf 17
  Mushroom Caviar 13
  Party Pâté 14
  Sautéed Shrimp 4

  Shrimp Roll 19
  Shrimp Spread 18
  Smoked Oyster Loaf 17
  Sombrero Dip 11
  South American Appetizer 3
  Spinach Dip 5
  Spicy Picadillo 8
  Stuffed Mushrooms 6
  Texas Crabgrass 181
  Texas Picadillo 9
  Vegetable Dip 11
  Versatile Crab 4
  Wild Rice Salad or Appetizer 60
Apples
  Apple Spice Cake 215
  Applesauce Squares 256
  French Apple Pie 231
  Hot Fruit Compote 304
  Swedish Apple Dumplings 277
Apple Spice Cake 215
Applesauce Squares 256
Apricots
  Apricot Confections 250
  Apricot Crisp 276
  Apricot Pie in Spice Crust 233
  Roast Pork with Apricot
    Glaze 109
Apricot Confections 250
Apricot Crisp 276
Apricot Glaze for Roast Pork 109
Apricot Pie in Spice Crust 233
Argyle Salad Dressing 45
Arkansas Cheese Bread 212
Artichokes
  Artichoke and Cheese Canapé 1
  Artichoke Balls 1
  Artichoke Soup 37
  Artichoke Squares 4
  Artichokes alla Ricco's 153
  Chafing Dish Artichokes 1
  Mushroom, Ham, and Artichoke
    Salad 50
  Scalloped Artichokes 153
  Spinach and Artichokes 179
  Turkey Artichoke Casserole 134
  Vegetable Platter with Crab
    Dressing 54
Artichoke and Cheese Canapé 1
Artichoke Balls 1
Artichoke Soup 37
Artichoke Squares 4
Artichokes alla Ricco's 153
Asparagus
  Cool, Cool Asparagus Soup 36
  Fresh Asparagus 154
  Opulent Asparagus 154
  Sweet Pickled Asparagus 53
  Vegetable Platter with Crab
    Dressing 54

Avery Corn Pudding 166
Avocados
  Avocado Bowl 46
  Avocado Cream for Summer
    Salmon Mousse 71
  Avocado Mayonnaise for
    Gazpacho Salad 46
  Camille's Mantequilla de
    Pobre 7
  Chilled Avocado Soup 38
  Elegant Avocado Aspic 47
  Gazpacho Salad with Avocado
    Mayonnaise 46
  Green Goddess Salad
    Dressing 43
  Guacamole Mousse 47
  Mike and Charlie's Avocado
    Butter 306
  Sesame Salad 53
  Summer Fresh Tomato and
    Avocado Soup 36
  Vegetable Platter with Crab
    Dressing 54
Avocado Bowl 46
Avocado Cream for Summer
  Salmon Mousse 71
Avocado Mayonnaise for
  Gazpacho Salad 46

Bacon
  Bacon Slaw 57
  Bacon-Stuffed Yellow
    Squash 186
  Breaded Breakfast Bacon 115
  Brunch Casserole 79
  Jamaican Bacon 2
  South American Appetizer 3
Bacon Slaw 57
Bacon-Stuffed Yellow
  Squash 186
Baked and Broiled Chicken 123
Baked Barley 155
Baked Spinach and
  Tomatoes 180
Baked Squash 185
Bananas
  Banana Birthday Cake 215
  Banana Split Cake 269
  Hot Fruit Compote 304
Banana Birthday Cake 215
Banana Split Cake 269
Barbeque Sauces
  Barbeque Sauce 108
  Machismo Barbeque Sauce 294
  Venison Marinade 145
Barbeque Sauce 108
Barbequed Dove 151
Barbequed Redfish 143
Barley, Baked 155

Bayou Rice 176
Beans—see also Green Beans
  Chinese Vegetables 193
  Frijoles Borrachos 156
  Green Beans in Casserole 159
  Green Beans with Horseradish
    Sauce 156
  Lentil Soup 31
  Lima Beans Sauté 157
  Louisiana Red Beans and
    Sausage 111
  Mexican Black Bean Soup 26
  Pinto Bean Soup 32
  Raunch Beans 158
  Susan Diggle Horton's Green
    Beans 157
  Teresita's Black Beans 158
  Vegetables with Anchovy
    Butter 192
Beárnaise, Blender 292
Beaumont Inn Grapefruit
  Salad 66
Beef
  Anacuchos 91
  Beef à la Deutsch 89
  Beef Jerky 96
  Beef Tenderloin 87
  Beef Tenderloin Stuffed with
    Mushrooms 87
  Brisket and Sauerkraut 89
  Broiled Flank Steak 97
  Cabbage Rolls 101
  Carne Asada 93
  Chilies Rellenos 104
  Chipped Beef Deluxe 98
  Cold Pepper Roast 93
  Corned Beef Blackburn 94
  Cornish Pasties 101
  Del Rio Steak Tartare 20
  Flank Steak with Onions 96
  French Beef 92
  Herbed Beef Stew with Almond-
    Poppy Seed Noodles 100
  Lasagne 103
  Lasagne Napoli 102
  Lemon Barbequed Steak 90
  Liver Teriyaki 105
  Meat Loaf 94
  Meat Pie Robertson 99
  Oriental Beef 96
  Oven Barbequed Beef
    Brisket 108
  Pepper Steak Caballero 90
  Pineapple Beef Teriyaki 88
  Pot Roast 91
  Rice Dressing 177
  Rouläden 99
  Sautéed Liver with Herbs 106
  Savory Meat Balls 102

Spaghetti with Beef and Wine
  Sauce 104
Spicy Picadillo 8
Stefado with Wild Rice 98
Stew in a Pumpkin 95
Texas Picadillo 9
Tuscan Roast 88
Beef à la Deutsch 89
Beef Jerky 96
Beef Tenderloin 87
Beef Tenderloin Stuffed with
  Mushrooms 87
Beer Cheese 78
Beets
  Fresh Beets in Orange
    Sauce 160
  Sweet and Sour Beets 159
  Vegetable Platter with Crab
    Dressing 54
Bell Peppers, Rice Filled 178
Best Vegetable Soup (The) 32
Beverages, Alcoholic
  Alligator's Tail 313
  Bundy Marys 314
  Café au Cacao 308
  Champagne Cup 311
  Claret Cup 314
  Cola de Lagarto (Alligator's
    Tail) 313
  French 75 315
  Frozen Irish Coffee 308
  Garden Party Punch 311
  Gracias en Julio 312
  Kahlua 308
  Peach Daiquiri 312
  Sangria 313
  Strawberry Daiquiri 312
  Tumbleweed Ice 311
  Velvet Hammer 313
  Very Old-Fashioneds 309
  Wassail 309
  Wine Spritzer 314
Beverages, Non-Alcoholic
  Chocolate Iced Coffee 307
  Cynthia's Punch 310
  Mint Cooler 307
  Mint Tea 307
  Percolator Punch 310
  Winter Warmer 309
Bing Cherry Salad 65
Black-eyed Pea Dip 12
Blender Beárnaise Sauce 292
Blueberries
  Blueberry Cobbler 240
  Blueberry Pie 235
  Rainbow Parfait 276
Blueberry Cobbler 240
Blueberry Pie 235
Blue Cheese Dressing 44

Blushing Peach Fried Pies 240
Bookmarks 261
Borsch, Russian 25
Bran Rolls 201
Brandied Pumpkin Flan 278
Braunschweiger Loaf 16
Breads
  Arkansas Cheese Bread 212
  Bran Rolls 201
  Carrot Mincemeat Bread 209
  Cheese and Pepper Bread 202
  Cinnamon Puffs 200
  Cottage Cheese Pancakes 213
  Cracked Wheat Bread 202
  Cranberry Coffee Cake 204
  Cranberry Nut Bread 210
  Crisp Waffles 212
  Double Boiler Bread 210
  Edwina's Angel Rolls 198
  Honey Walnut Bread 211
  Hungarian Coffee Cake 204
  Laurens' Sour Dough
    Pancakes 199
  Lemon Bread 211
  Lou Neff's Cheese Bread 196
  Molassas Muffins 206
  Monkey Bread 197
  Naturally Good Rye Bread 195
  Oatmeal Bread 197
  Orange Bread 208
  Orange Honey French
    Toast 206
  Orange Muffins 207
  Peach Nut Bread 209
  Persimmon Bread 208
  Pineapple Coconut Coffee
    Cake 205
  Rolled Butter Rolls 201
  Sally Lunn 200
  Sarah Penn Harris' Wheat
    Bread 195
  Sausage Coffee Cake 205
  Semester Muffins 207
  Sour Dough Bread 199
  Sour Dough Starter 198
  Swedish Bread 203
  Whole Wheat Bread 196
Bread and Butter Pickles 296
Bread and Butter Pudding 284
Breaded Breakfast Bacon 115
Breast of Chicken in Mustard
  Sauce 126
Brisket and Sauerkraut 89
Broccoli
  Broccoli Bisque 33
  Broccoli with Mushrooms 160
  Chinese Vegetables 193
  Red, White, and Green Salad 52
  Tomato-Broccoli Stackup 161

Broccoli Bisque 33
Broccoli with Mushrooms 160
Broiled Flank Steak 97
Brown Corn Soup 34
Brownies, Rum-Fudge 257
Brunch Casserole 79
Bundy Marys 314
Burgundy Venison Stew 147
Butterflied Leg of Lamb 119
Buttermilk-Date Cake 219
Buttermilk Pie 238
Buttermilk Pralines 262
Butters
  Anchovy Butter for
    Vegetables 192
  Butter Sauce for Raisin
    Pudding 273
  College Inn Orange Butter 306
  Mike and Charlie's Avocado
    Butter 306
  Strawberry Butter 306
Butterscotch Bars 255
Butterscotch Bombe 265

Cabbage
  Bacon Slaw 57
  Cabbage Pickle 296
  Cabbage Rolls 101
  German Cabbage Salad 62
  Gumbochu 161
  Hot Cabbage Crisp 162
  Red Cabage 162
Cabbage Pickle 296
Cabbage Rolls 101
Café au Cacao 308
Cakes
  Apple Spice Cake 215
  Banana Birthday Cake 215
  Buttermilk-Date Cake 219
  Chocolate Angel Food Cake with
    Peppermint Filling 223
  Chocolate Pound Cake 222
  Curtis' Grand Finale
    Cheesecake 226
  Fig Preserve Cake 218
  Fresh Coconut Cake 218
  Gingerless Gingerbread 228
  Ice Box Gingerbread 224
  Italian Cream Cake 217
  Lucille's Date-Nut Fruit
    Cake 229
  Marble Cake 225
  Oatmeal Cake 220
  Pecan Cake 221
  Pineapple Cake 216
  Pineapple Walnut Cake 216
  Pound Cake 227
  Pumpkin Spice Cake 221
  Praline Cheese Cake 227

Rodeo Cake 222
Sock-It-To-Me Cake 224
Upside Down Cake 229
Vanilla Wafer Cake 220
White Chocolate Cake 225
White Fruit Cake 228
California Cheese Casserole 79
California Chicken Casserole 129
Camille's Mantequilla de Pobre 7
Canapés—see Appetizers
Candy
  Bookmarks 261
  Buttermilk Pralines 262
  Chocolate Sugarplums 260
  Crackerjack Peanuts 261
  Fiesta Pralines 261
  Frank Jr.'s Fudge 262
  Frozen Fangos 263
  Pecan Mints 262
  Pecans Scandia 263
  Self-Made Millionaires 260
Caper Sauce for Confetti Chicken
    Mold 73
Carbonara 85
Carmel Caramel 288
Carne Asada 93
Carrots
  Carrot Bars 259
  Carrot Mincemeat Bread 209
  Carrot Ring 164
  Carrots in Cheese Sauce 164
  Carrots Lyonnaise 165
  Carrots Parmesan 165
  Carrots Veronique 163
  Copper Carrots 54
  Garden Patch 191
  Ginger Glazed Carrots 163
  Marinated Carrots 14
  Vegetable Platter with Crab
    Dressing 54
  Vegetables with Anchovy
    Butter 192
Carrot Bars 259
Carrot Mincemeat Bread 209
Carrot Ring 164
Carrots in Cheese Sauce 164
Carrots Lyonnaise 165
Carrots Parmesan 165
Carrots Veronique 163
Cauliflower
  Garden Patch 191
  Red, White, and Green Salad 52
  Sarah's Marinated Mushroom-
    Cauliflower Salad 49
  Snow Pea Salad 51
Caviar Dip 21
Caviar Pie 20
Celery
  Vegetables with Anchovy

  Butter 192
Celestial Potato Soup 41
Chafing Dish Artichokes 1
Chalupas 83
Champagne Cup 311
Charcoal Broiled Shrimp 140
Charcoal Lemon Chicken 121
Charlie Potatoes 173
Cheese
  Beer Cheese 78
  California Cheese Casserole 79
  Cheese and Pepper Bread 203
  Cheese Dip for Vegetables 10
  Cheese Stuffed Potatoes 172
  Cheese-Stuffed Zucchini 187
  Cheese Toasties 5
  Chutney Cream Cheese
    Spread 10
  Kinser Cheeseball 10
  Liptauer Cheese 9
  Lou Neff's Cheese Bread 196
  Swiss Fondue 78
  Tomato-Cheese Tart 80
Cheese and Pepper Bread 203
Cheese Dip for Vegetables 10
Cheese Stuffed Potatoes 172
Cheese-Stuffed Zucchini 187
Cheese Toasties 5
Cheesecake
  Cheesecake Squares 255
  Curtis' Grand Finale
    Cheesecake 226
  Praline Cheesecake 227
Cheesecake Squares 255
Cherry Torte 272
Chess Pie, Lemon 237
Chess Pie, Meringue 238
Chicken
  Baked and Broiled Chicken 123
  Breast of Chicken in Mustard
    Sauce 126
  California Chicken
    Casserole 129
  Charcoal Lemon Chicken 121
  Chicken à l'Orange 133
  Chicken and Artichokes 128
  Chicken and Sausage Loaf 132
  Chicken Chinoiserie 131
  Chicken Curry Balls 15
  Chicken Élan 132
  Chicken Enchiladas with Sour
    Cream 134
  Chicken in Pastry 121
  Chicken in the Limelight 125
  Chicken Lasagne 127
  Chicken Livers Parisienne 127
  Chicken Spaghetti for 25 130
  Chicken Tetrazzini 124
  Chicken-Wild Rice Salad 61

Confetti Chicken Mold 73
Cream of Chicken Soup 30
Green Tomato Enchiladas 135
Herb Stuffed Broilers 124
Hop Po Gai Ding (Chicken with
  Walnuts) 128
Hot Chicken Salad 130
London Chicken 122
Moroccan Chicken 126
Oven Barbequed Chicken 133
Paëlla 138
Party Chicken Salad 129
Red and Green Chicken 123
Roast Chicken with Rice
  Dressing 122
Victor Szebehely's Hungarian
  Chicken 131
Chicken à l'Orange 133
Chicken and Artichokes 128
Chicken and Sausage Loaf 132
Chicken Chinoiserie 131
Chicken Curry Balls 15
Chicken Élan 132
Chicken Enchiladas with Sour
  Cream 134
Chicken in Pastry 121
Chicken in the Limelight 125
Chicken Lasagne 127
Chicken Livers
  Party Pâté 14
Chicken Livers Parisienne 127
Chicken Livers Parisienne 127
Chicken Salads
  Chicken-Wild Rice Salad 61
  Hot Chicken Salad 130
  Party Chicken Salad 129
Chicken Spaghetti for 25 130
Chicken Tetrazzini 124
Chicken-Wild Rice Salad 61
Chicken with Walnuts (Hop Po
  Gai Ding) 128
Chilaquiles 82
Chili
  Chili Dip 11
  Drake Chili 24
  Gregg Chili 23
  Pedernales River Chili 23
Chili Dip 11
Chilies Rellenos 104
Chilled Avocado Soup 38
Chilled Cucumber Soup 37
Chinese Vegetables 193
Chipped Beef Deluxe 98
Chocolate
  Chocolate Angel Food Cake with
    Peppermint Filling 223
  Chocolate Chip Squares 252
  Chocolate Covered Butter
    Cookies 243

Chocolate Crinkles 243
Chocolate Iced Coffee 307
Chocolate Peppermint
  Squares 254
Chocolate Pound Cake 222
Chocolate Sauce 223
Chocolate Sauce for Ice Cream
  Pie 237
Chocolate Sugarplums 260
Chocolate Toffee Dessert 283
Dark Chocolate Mousse 282
  Frozen Fangos 263
  Frank Jr.'s Fudge 262
  Hattie Ford's Chocolate
    Meringue Pie 242
  Hot Chocolate Soufflé 279
  Hot Fudge Pudding 280
  Ice Cream Pie 237
  Jailhouse Chocolate Ice
    Cream 267
  Marble Cake 225
  Rocky Road Fudge Pie 241
  Rodeo Cake 222
  Rum Fudge Brownies 257
  St. Patrick's Day Meringues 250
  Sam's Pots de Crème 282
  Self-Made Millionaires 260
  Steamed Chocolate
    Pudding 286
  White Chocolate Cake 225
Chocolate Angel Food Cake with
  Peppermint Filling 223
Chocolate Chip Squares 252
Chocolate Covered Butter
  Cookies 243
Chocolate Crinkles 243
Chocolate Iced Coffee 307
Chocolate Peppermint
  Squares 254
Chocolate Pound Cake 222
Chocolate Sauce 223
Chocolate Sauce for Ice Cream
  Pie 237
Chocolate Sugarplums 260
Chocolate Toffee Dessert 283
Chowder—see Soups
Christmas Pudding 287
Christmas Rum Pie 241
Chutney
  Chutney Cream Cheese
    Spread 10
  Mango Chutney 301
  Mimi's Chutney 299
Chutney Cream Cheese
  Spread 10
Cinnamon Crisps 244
Cinnamon Puffs 200
Citrus Salad with Mint
  Dressing 63

Clams
  Hot Clam-Cheese Dip 2
  "Real Texas" New England
    Clam Chowder 28
  Spaghetti Mario 141
Claret Cup 314
Clear Tomato Soup 35
Coconut
  Chocolate Sugarplums 260
  Coconut Chews 247
  Coconut Cream Pie 242
  Fresh Coconut Cake 218
  Italian Cream Cake 217
  Walnut Bars 253
Coconut Chews 247
Coconut Cream Pie 242
Coffee
  Café au Cacao 308
  Chocolate Iced Coffee 307
  Coffee Mousse in Meringue
    Shell 289
  Kahlua 308
Coffee Cakes
  Cranberry Coffee Cake 204
  Hungarian Coffee Cake 204
  Pineapple Coconut Coffee
    Cake 205
  Sausage Coffee Cake 205
Coffee Mousse in Meringue
  Shell 289
Cola de Lagarto (Alligator's
  Tail) 313
Cold Lemon Soufflé 273
Cold Pepper Roast 93
College Inn Orange Butter 306
Condiments for Curry 118
Confetti Chicken Mold 73
Cookies
  Aggression Cookies 258
  Applesauce Squares 256
  Apricot Confections 250
  Butterscotch Bars 255
  Carrot Bars 259
  Cinnamon Crisps 244
  Cheesecake Squares 255
  Chocolate Chip Squares 252
  Chocolate Covered Butter
    Cookies 243
  Chocolate Crinkles 243
  Chocolate Peppermint
    Squares 254
  Coconut Chews 247
  Date-Nut Balls 258
  Date Nut Bars 259
  English Toffee Cookies 248
  Frosted Cashew Clusters 246
  Health Nut Cookies 244
  Lemon Bars 257
  Lou Neff's Sand Tarts 247

Melting Moments 253
Miss Casey's Cookies 256
Nut Dainties 250
Oat Cakes 246
Oatmeal Tollhouse Cookies 252
Post Toastie Macaroons 248
Potato Chip Cookies 245
Raisin Nut Cookies 245
Rich Butter Cookies 248
Rolled Butter Cookies 249
Rum Butter Sweets 249
Rum-Fudge Brownies 257
St. Patrick's Day Meringues 250
Sesame Cookies 244
Scotch Shortbread 254
Thumbprint Cookies 251
Walnut Bars 253
Cool, Cool Asparagus Soup 36
Copper Carrots 54
Coquilles Saint Jacques 139
Corn
  Avery Corn Pudding 166
  Brown Corn Soup 34
  Corn Pudding 166
  Jones Corn Soup 34
  Zucchini and Corn 187
Corn Pudding 166
Corned Beef Blackburn 94
Cornish Pasties 101
Cottage Cheese Pancakes 213
Crab
  Crab Dressing for Vegetable
    Platter 54
  Crab Salad 72
  Crabmeat Epicurean 6
  Crabmeat in Ramekins 136
  Hot Crabmeat Dip 8
  Shellfish au Gratin 138
  Texas Crabgrass 181
  Versatile Crab 4
Crab Dressing for Vegetable
  Platter 54
Crab Salad 72
Crabmeat Epicurean 6
Crabmeat in Ramekins 136
Cracked Wheat
  Cracked Wheat Bread 202
  Tabooli Salad 58
Cracked Wheat Bread 202
Crackerjack Peanuts 261
Cranberry Coffee Cake 204
Cranberry Nut Bread 210
Cranberry-Orange Relish 302
Cranberry Pie 234
Cranberry Salad 67
Cranberry Salad, Frozen 234
Cream Cheese Mousse with
  Brandy Sauce 280
Cream of Chicken Soup 30

Cream of Cucumber Soup 30
Cream of Split Pea Soup 29
Crème Brulée 288
Creole Eggs 76
Crêpes
  Crêpes Florentine 86
  Strawberry Crêpes 271
Crêpes Florentine 86
Crisp Waffles 212
Cucumber Salad 56
Cucumber Salad Mold 56
Cucumber Sandwiches 16
Cucumber Sauce for Summer
  Salmon Mousse 71
Cucumber Soup, Chilled 37
Cucumber Soup, Cream of 30
Currant Jelly Sauce for
  Lamb 116
Curry
  Chicken Curry Balls 15
  Condiments for Curry 118
  Krishnan's Curry Powder 303
  Lamb Curry Williams 118
  Senegalese Soup 39
Curtis' Grand Finale
  Cheesecake 226
Custards
  Brandied Pumpkin Flan 278
  Carmel Caramel 288
  Crème Brulee 288
  Flan 285
  Rum Custard Cream 285
Cynthia's Punch 310

Dark Chocolate Mousse 282
Dates
  Buttermilk-Date Cake 219
  Date Cake Trifle 268
  Date-Nut Balls 258
  Date Nut Bars 259
  Lucille's Date-Nut Fruit
    Cake 229
Date Cake Trifle 268
Date-Nut Balls 258
Date Nut Bars 259
Del Rio Steak Tartare 20
Dessert Sauces
  Brandy Sauce for Cream Cheese
    Mousse 280
  Chocolate Sauce 223
  Chocolate Sauce for Ice Cream
    Pie 237
  Hard Sauce for Christmas
    Pudding 287
  Praline Sauce for Butterscotch
    Bombe 265
  Rum Sauce for Pears and
    Sherbet 275
  Sherry Custard for Tipsy

Squire 270
  Whipped Orange Sauce 294
Desserts—see also Cakes,
    Cookies, Candies, Ice Creams,
    Pies
  Apricot Crisp 276
  Banana Split Cake 269
  Brandied Pumpkin Flan 278
  Bread and Butter Pudding 284
  Carmel Caramel 288
  Cherry Torte 272
  Chocolate Toffee Dessert 283
  Christmas Pudding 287
  Coffee Mousse in Meringue
    Shell 289
  Cold Lemon Soufflé 273
  Cream Cheese Mousse with
    Brandy Sauce 280
  Crème Brulée 288
  Dark Chocolate Mousse 282
  Date Cake Trifle 268
  Egg Nog Dessert 281
  Flan 285
  Fresh Fruit Shortcake 277
  Frozen Lemon Tart 275
  Frozen Lime Soufflé 272
  German Pancake 268
  Grapenut Pudding 281
  Hot Chocolate Soufflé 279
  Hot Fudge Pudding 280
  Jane's Sherry Mousse 284
  Lemon and Strawberry
    Dessert 274
  Mary Shary's Tipsy
    Pudding 283
  Oranges Copenhagen 279
  Pears and Sherbet in Rum
    Sauce 275
  Pears in Port Wine 274
  Pumpkin Pudding 278
  Rainbow Parfait 276
  Raisin Pudding with Butter
    Sauce 273
  Rum Custard Cream 285
  Sam's Pots de Crème 282
  Strawberries Marco Polo 276
  Strawberry Crêpes 271
  Steamed Chocolate
    Pudding 286
  Swedish Apple Dumplings 277
  Tipsy Squire with Sherry
    Custard 270
  Walnut Roll 269
Devil Sticks 3
Deviled Spinach Eggs 12
Dips—see also Appetizers
  Camille's Mantequilla de
    Pobre 7
  Cheese Dip for Vegetables 10

Chili Dip 11
Hot Clam-Cheese Dip 2
Sombrero Dip 11
Spicy Picadillo 8
Spinach Dip 5
Texas Crabgrass 181
Texas Picadillo 9
Vegetable Dip 11
Dot Carter's Venison Backstrap
  Sauté 146
Double Boiler Bread 210
Dove, Barbequed 151
Drake Chili 24
Dressings—see also Stuffings
  Rice Dressing 177
  Rice Dressing for Roast
    Chicken 122
Dressings, Salad—see Salad
  Dressings
Drinks—see Beverages
Duck, or Roast Goose 149
Duke of Windsor Sandwich 114
Dunkin' Quail 148

Easy Crisp Sweet Pickles 296
Edwina's Angel Rolls 198
Egg and Cheese Strata 76
Egg Nog Dessert 281
Eggplant
  Eggplant Caviar 13
  Eggplant with Mushroom
    Stuffing 167
  Moussaka 120
  Ratatouille 167
Eggplant Caviar 13
Eggplant with Mushroom
  Stuffing 167
Eggs
  Brunch Casserole 79
  Creole Eggs 76
  Deviled Spinach Eggs 12
  Egg and Cheese Strata 76
  Eggs Olé 75
  Green Eggs with Jordan Parsley
    Dressing 43
  Huevos Rancheros 75
  Migas 77
  Russian Eggs 77
  Savory Eggs 76
  Vegetable Platter with Crab
    Dressing 54
Eggs Olé 75
Elegant Avocado Aspic 47
Empanadas 7
Enchiladas
  Chicken Enchiladas with Sour
    Cream 134
  Green Tomato Enchiladas 135
English Toffee Cookies 248

Fail-Safe Pie Crust 230
Fay Harris' Peach Preserves 298
Fettucini 83
Fiesta Pralines 261
Fiesta Venison 145
Fig Preserve Cake 218
Fig Preserves 299
Fire and Ice Tomatoes 48
Fish—see Seafood
Flan 285
Flank Steak with Onions 96
Fork-Tender Venison 144
Frank Jr.'s Fudge 262
French Apple Pie 231
French Beef 92
French Epicurean Peas 171
French Fried Mushrooms 169
French Fried Onions 170
French 75 315
Fresh Asparagus 154
Fresh Beets in Orange Sauce 160
Fresh Coconut Cake 218
Fresh Fruit Shortcake 277
Fresh Tomato Veal Cutlets 107
Fried Quail for Saturday
  Breakfast 149
Frijoles Borrachos 156
Frosted Cashew Clusters 246
Frozen Cranberry Salad 62
Frozen Fangos 263
Frozen Fruit Salad 64
Frozen Irish Coffee 308
Frozen Lemon Tart 275
Frozen Lime Soufflé 272
Fruit
  Glacéed Nuts and Fruits 305
  Hot Fruit Compote 304
  Prunes Plumped in Red
    Wine 303
Fruit Cake
  Lucille's Date-Nut Fruit
    Cake 229
  White Fruit Cake 228
Fruit Salads
  Beaumont Inn Grapefruit
    Salad 66
  Bing Cherry Salad 65
  Citrus Salad with Mint
    Dressing 63
  Cranberry Salad 67
  Frozen Cranberry Salad 62
  Frozen Fruit Salad 64
  Green Gage Plum Salad 67
  Mango Salad 66
  Mint Julepeach Salad 63
  Orange Salad 62
  Raspberry Salad 64
  Spicy Orange Salad 65
Fudge

Frank Jr.'s Fudge 262
Hot Fudge Pudding 280
Rocky Road Fudge Pie 241
Rum-Fudge Brownies 257

Game—see also Dove, Quail,
  Duck, Venison
Barbequed Dove 151
Burgundy Venison Stew 147
Dot Carter's Venison Backstrap
  Sauté 146
Dunkin' Quail 148
Fiesta Venison 145
Fork-Tender Venison 144
Fried Quail for Saturday
  Breakfast 149
Jack Corley's Venison
  Annandale 147
Quail with Cherry Sauce 148
Roast Goose or Duck 149
Sautéed Quail 150
Stuffed Pheasant 150
Venison Marinade 145
Venison Scallopini 144
Venison Shoulder Roast 146
Garden Party Punch 311
Garden Patch 191
Gazpacho 40
Gazpacho Salad with Avocado
  Mayonnaise 46
George Covert's Marinated
  Shrimp 19
German Cabbage Salad 62
German Cheese Schnitzel 106
German Pancake 268
German Potato Salad 55
German Potatoes 175
Ginger Glazed Carrots 163
Gingerbread, Gingerless 228
Gingerbread, Ice Box 224
Gingerless Gingerbread 228
Glacéed Nuts and Fruits 305
Glazed Pork Ribs 109
Gnocchi, Spinach 182
Goose
  Roast Goose or Duck 149
Goose Liver Roll 15
Gracias en Julio 312
Granola 304
Grape Ice Cream 267
Grapenut Pudding 281
Greek Lemon Soup 25
Green Beans
  Chinese Vegetables 193
  Green Beans in Casserole 159
  Green Beans with Horseradish
    Sauce 156
  Green Bean Salad 52
  Susan Diggle Horton's Green

Beans 157
Vegetable Platter with Crab
  Dressing 54
Vegetables with Anchovy
  Butter 192
Green Bean Salad 52
Green Beans in Casserole 159
Green Beans in Horseradish
  Sauce 156
Green Gage Plum Salad 67
Green Gage Plum Sherbet 264
Green Goddess Salad
  Dressing 43
Green Pea Ring 171
Green Peppers—see Bell Peppers
Green Summer Soup 35
Green Tomato Enchiladas 135
Green Tomato Pie 82
Gregg Chili 23
Guacamole Mousse 47
Gumbo 28
Gumbochu 161

Ham
  Brunch Casserole 79
  Del Rio Steak Tartare 20
  Duke of Windsor Sandwich 114
  Ham Loaf with Horseradish
    Sauce 115
  Ham Rolls Continental 112
  Ham Salad Baked in Rolls 18
  Marinated Baked Ham 112
  Mushroom, Ham, and Artichoke
    Salad 50
  Roast Leg of Pork 110
  Sweet and Sour Sauce for
    Ham 291
Ham Loaf with Horseradish
  Sauce 115
Ham Rolls Continental 112
Ham Salad Baked in Rolls 18
Hamburger Meat—see Beef
Hattie Ford's Chocolate Meringue
  Pie 242
Health Nut Cookies 244
Herb Stuffed Broilers 124
Herbed Beef Stew with Almond-
  Poppy Seed Noodles 100
Holiday Acorn Squash 184
Hominy
  Posole 114
  Spanish Hominy 168
Honey Walnut Bread 211
Hop Po Gai Ding (Chicken with
  Walnuts) 128
Hors d'Oeuvres—see Appetizers
Hot Cabbage Crisp 162
Hot Chicken Salad 130
Hot Chocolate Soufflé 279

Hot Clam-Cheese Dip 2
Hot Crabmeat Dip 8
Hot Fruit Compote 304
Hot Fudge Pudding 280
Hot Mustard 92
Hot Sour Cream Potatoes 174
Huevos Rancheros 75
Hungarian Coffee Cake 204

Ice Box Gingerbread 224
Ice Creams and Sherbets
  Butterscotch Bombe 265
  Grape Ice Cream 267
  Green Gage Plum Sherbet 264
  Jailhouse Chocolate Ice
    Cream 267
  Lemon Ice Cream 266
  Lemon Ice with Raspberries 266
  Mango Ice Cream 264
  Peach Ice 265
  Peppermint Ice Cream 264
  Rainbow Parfait 276
Ice Cream Pie 237
Italian Broiled Shrimp 141
Italian Cream Cake 217
Italian Prune Conserve 301
Italian Rice 176
Italian Salad Dressing 43

Jack Corley's Venison
  Annandale 147
Jailhouse Ice Cream 267
Jalapeño Pie 3
Jamaican Bacon 2
Jambalaya Lafitte 137
Jelly, Pyracantha 300
Jane's Sherry Mousse 284
Jones Corn Soup 34
Jordan Parsley Dressing 43
Joy's Molded Spinach Salad 59

Kahlua 308
Kinser Cheeseball 10
Knackwurst and Sauerkraut 113
Korean Salad 57
Krishnan's Curry Powder 303

Lamb
  Butterflied Leg of Lamb 119
  Lamb Avgolemono 119
  Lamb Chops Madeira in Choux
    Paste 116
  Lamb Curry Williams 118
  Lamb Riblets 2
  Leg of Lamb with Pork
    Tenderloin 116
  Moussaka 120
  Shish Kebob 117
Lamb Avgolemono 119

Lamb Chops Madeira in Choux
  Paste 116
Lamb Curry Williams 118
Lamb Riblets 2
Lasagne 103
Lasagne, Chicken 127
Lasagne Napoli 102
Laurens' Sour Dough
  Pancakes 199
Layered Picnic Salad 52
Leek and Mushroom Quiche 80
Leg of Lamb with Pork
  Tenderloin 116
Lemon-Alaska Pie 236
Lemon and Strawberry
  Dessert 274
Lemon Barbequed Steak 90
Lemon Bars 257
Lemon Bread 211
Lemon Chess Pie 237
Lemon Ice Cream 266
Lemon Ice with Raspberries 266
Lemon Pie, Slice-O- 232
Lemon Soufflé, Cold 273
Lemon Tart, Frozen 275
Lentil Soup 31
Lima Beans Sauté 157
Liptauer Cheese 9
Liver
  Chicken Livers Parisienne 127
  Liver Teriyaki 105
  Party Pâté 14
  Sautéed Liver with Herbs 106
Liver Teriyaki 105
Lobster
  Shellfish au Gratin 138
London Chicken 122
Lou Neff's Cheese Bread 196
Lou Neff's Sand Tarts 247
Louisiana Red Beans and
  Sausage 111
Lucille's Date-Nut Fruit
  Cake 229

Macaroons, Post Toastie 248
Machismo Barbeque Sauce 294
Mango Chutney 301
Mango Ice Cream 264
Mango Salad 66
Maple Pecan Pie 239
Marble Cake 225
Marinade, Wine 295
Marinade, Venison 145
Marinated Baked Ham 112
Marinated Carrots 14
Mary Shary's Tipsy Pudding 283
Meat—see Beef, Chicken, Game,
  Ham, Lamb, Pork, Turkey, and
  Veal

Meat Loaf 94
Meat Pie Robertson 99
Mediterranean Loaf 17
Melting Moments 253
Meringue Chess Pie 238
Mexican Food
  California Cheese Casserole 79
  Camille's Mantequilla de
    Pobre 7
  Chalupas 83
  Chilaquiles 82
  Chicken Enchiladas with Sour
    Cream 134
  Chilies Rellenos 104
  Empanadas 7
  Frijoles Borrachos 156
  Huevos Rancheros 75
  Green Tomato Enchiladas 135
  Mexican Black Bean Soup 26
  Mexican Congealed Salad. 48
  Mexican Spinach Soup 33
  Mexican Squash 184
  Migas 77
  Pico de Gallo 291
  Pinto Bean Soup 32
  Salsa 293
  Sombrero Dip 11
  Taco Salad 68
  Tortilla Soup 27
Mexican Black Bean Soup 26
Mexican Congealed Salad 48
Mexican Spinach Soup 33
Mexican Squash 184
Migas 77
Mike and Charlie's Avocado
  Butter 306
Mike and Charlie's Quiche 81
Mimi's Chutney 299
Minestrone, Oven-Baked 3
Mincemeat
  Carrot Mincemeat Bread 209
Mint Cooler 307
Mint Dressing for Citrus Salad 63
Mint Julepeach Salad 63
Mint Tea 307
Miss Casey's Cookies 256
Molasses Muffins 206
Monkey Bread 197
Moroccan Chicken 126
Moussaka 120
Muffins
  Cinnamon Puffs 200
  Molasses Muffins 206
  Orange Muffins 207
  Semester Muffins 207
Mushrooms
  Chinese Vegetables 193
  French Fried Mushrooms 169
  Garden Patch 191

Leek and Mushroom Quiche 80
Mushroom Caviar 13
Mushroom, Ham, and Artichoke
  Salad 50
Mushroom Pie 168
Mushroom Stuffing for Beef
  Tenderloin 87
Mushroom Stuffing for
  Eggplant 167
Mushroom Tossed Salad 49
Mushrooms au Gratin 169
Sarah's Marinated Mushroom-
  Cauliflower Salad 49
Spinach and Mushroom Salad
  with Mustard Dressing 59
Stuffed Mushrooms 6
Mushroom Caviar 13
Mushroom, Ham, and Artichoke
  Salad 50
Mushroom Pie 168
Mushroom Tossed Salad 49
Mushrooms au Gratin 169
Mustard
  Hot Mustard 92
  Mustard Dressing for Spinach
    and Mushroom Salad 59

Naturally Good Rye Bread 195
Noodles
  Almond-Poppy Seed
    Noodles 100
  Fettucini 83
Nut Dainties 250

Oatmeal
  Aggression Cookies 258
  Oat Cakes 246
  Oatmeal Bread 197
  Oatmeal Cake 220
  Oatmeal Tollhouse Cookies 252
Oat Cakes 246
Oatmeal Bread 197
Oatmeal Cake 220
Oatmeal Tollhouse Cookies 252
Okra and Tomatoes 170
Onions
  French Fried Onions 170
  Onion Pie 81
  Onion-Sauced Tomatoes 189
  Pickled Onions 297
  Sautéed Cherry Tomatoes and
    Small Onions 190
Onion Pie 81
Onion-Sauced Tomatoes 189
Opulent Asparagus 154
Oranges
  Chicken à l'Orange 133
  College Inn Orange Butter 306
  Cranberry-Orange Relish 302

Orange Bread 208
Orange Cashew Rice 178
Orange Honey French
  Toast 206
Orange Marmalade 298
Orange Muffins 207
Orange Salad 62
Oranges Copenhagen 279
Spicy Orange Salad 65
Whipped Orange Sauce 294
Orange Bread 208
Orange Cashew Rice 178
Orange Honey French Toast 206
Orange Marmalade 298
Orange Muffins 207
Orange Salad 62
Oranges Copenhagen 279
Oriental Beef 96
Oven-Baked Minestrone 38
Oven Barbequed Beef
  Brisket 108
Oven Barbequed Chicken 133
Overnight Salad 55
Oysters
  Gumbo 28
  Jambalaya Lafitte 137
  Smoked Oyster Loaf 17

Paëlla 138
Pancakes
  Cottage Cheese Pancakes 213
  German Pancake 268
  Laurens' Sour Dough
    Pancakes 199
Party Chicken Salad 129
Party Pâté 14
Pasta-see Lasagne, Noodles, and
  Spaghetti
Pasta al Pesto 85
Pastry—see Pie Crusts
Pâté
  Braunschweiger Loaf 16
  Goose Liver Roll 15
  Party Pâté 14
Peaches
  Bookmarks 261
  Blushing Peach Fried Pies 240
  Faye Harris' Peach
    Preserves 298
  Peach Daiquiri 312
  Peach Ice 265
  Peach Nut Bread 209
  Peaches and Cream Pie 233
Peach Daiquiri 312
Peach Ice 265
Peach Nut Bread 209
Peaches and Cream Pie 233
Peanuts, Crackerjack 261
Pear Preserves 302

Pears and Sherbet in Rum
Sauce 275
Pears in Port Wine 274
Peas
Cream of Split Pea Soup 29
French Epicurean Peas 171
Green Pea Ring 171
Green Summer Soup 35
Layered Picnic Salad 52
Overnight Salad 55
Potage Paul 40
Pecans
Buttermilk Pralines 262
Date-Nut Balls 258
Date Nut Bars 259
Fiesta Pralines 261
Maple Pecan Pie 239
Nut Dainties 250
Pecan Cake 221
Pecan Crunch Pie 236
Pecan Crust 230
Pecan Mints 262
Pecan Pie 231
Pecans Scandia 263
Raisin Pecan Pie 239
Self-Made Millionaires 260
Pecan Cake 221
Pecan Crunch Pie 236
Pecan Crust 230
Pecan Mints 262
Pecan Pie 231
Pecans Scandia 263
Pedernales River Chili 23
Pepper Shrimp 139
Pepper Steak Caballero 90
Peppermint Ice Cream 264
Percolator Punch 310
Persimmon Bread 208
Pheasant, Stuffed 150
Pickled Shrimp Salad 69
Pickled Onions 297
Pickles
Bread and Butter Pickles 296
Cabbage Pickle 296
Easy Crisp Sweet Pickles 296
Pickled Onions 297
Pico de Gallo 291
Pie Crusts
Fail-Safe Pie Crust 230
Pecan Crust 230
Sesame Seed Pastry 230
Spice Crust for Apricot Pie 233
Pies
Angel Pie 232
Apricot Pie in Spice Crust 233
Blueberry Cobbler 240
Blueberry Pie 235
Blushing Peach Fried Pies 240
Buttermilk Pie 238

Christmas Rum Pie 241
Coconut Cream Pie 242
Cranberry Pie 234
French Apple Pie 231
Hattie Ford's Chocolate
Meringue Pie 242
Ice Cream Pie 237
Lemon-Alaska Pie 236
Lemon Chess Pie 237
Maple Pecan Pie 239
Meringue Chess Pie 238
Peaches and Cream Pie 233
Pecan Crunch Pie 236
Pecan Pie 231
Pumpkin Chiffon Pie 235
Raisin Pecan Pie 239
Rocky Road Fudge Pie 241
Slice-O-Lemon Pie 232
Strawberry Pie 234
Sweet Potato Chiffon Pie 238
Pineapple
Hot Fruit Compote 304
Pineapple Acorn Squash 185
Pineapple Beef Teriyaki 88
Pineapple Cake 216
Pineapple Coconut Coffee
Cake 205
Pineapple Walnut Cake 216
Upside Down Cake 229
Pineapple Acorn Squash 185
Pineapple Beef Teriyaki 88
Pineapple Cake 216
Pineapple Coconut Coffee
Cake 205
Pineapple Walnut Cake 216
Pinto Beans
Frijoles Borrachos 156
Pinto Bean Soup 32
Raunch Beans 158
Pinto Bean Soup 32
Piquant Salad Dressing 44
Plums
Green Gage Plum Salad 67
Green Gage Plum Sherbet 264
Poppy Seed Dressing 45
Pork—see also Ham, Sausage
Breaded Breakfast Bacon 115
Chilies Rellenos 104
Empanadas 7
Glazed Pork Ribs 109
Leg of Lamb with Pork
Tenderloin 116
Paëlla 138
Pork Scallopini 111
Posole 114
Roast Leg of Pork 110
Roast Pork with Apricot
Glaze 109
Tourtière 110

Pork Scallopini 111
Port Aransas Boiled Shrimp 137
Portuguese Soup 24
Posole 114
Post Toastie Macaroons 248
Pot Roast 91
Potage Paul 40
Potato Chip Cookies 245
Potatoes
Celestial Potato Soup 41
Charlie Potatoes 173
Cheese Stuffed Potatoes 172
German Potato Salad 55
German Potatoes 175
Hot Sour Cream Potatoes 174
Sesame Hash Browned
Potatoes 174
Poultry—see Chicken and Turkey
Pound Cakes
Chocolate Pound Cake 222
Pound Cake 227
Pralines
Buttermilk Pralines 262
Fiesta Pralines 261
Praline Cheesecake 227
Praline Sauce for Butterscotch
Bombe 265
Praline Cheese Cake 227
Preserves
Antebellum Strawberry
Preserves 300
Cranberry-Orange Relish 302
Faye Harris' Peach
Preserves 298
Fig Preserves 299
Italian Prune Conserve 301
Mango Chutney 301
Mimi's Chutney 299
Orange Marmalade 298
Pear Preserves 302
Prunes
Italian Prune Conserve 301
Prunes Plumped in Red
Wine 303
South American Appetizer 3
Prunes Plumped in Red
Wine 303
Puddings—see also Desserts
Bread and Butter Pudding 284
Christmas Pudding 287
Grapenut Pudding 281
Hot Fudge Pudding 280
Mary Shary's Tipsy
Pudding 283
Pumpkin Pudding 278
Raisin Pudding with Butter
Sauce 273
Steamed Chocolate
Pudding 286

Pumpkin
  Brandied Pumpkin Flan 278
  Pumpkin Chiffon Pie 235
  Pumpkin Pudding 278
  Pumpkin Spice Cake 221
  Stew in a Pumpkin 95
  Pumpkin Chiffon Pie 235
  Pumpkin Pudding 278
  Pumpkin Spice Cake 221
  Punch—see Beverages
  Pyracantha Jelly 300

Quail
  Dunkin' Quail 148
  Fried Quail for Saturday
    Breakfast 149
  Quail with Cherry Sauce 148
  Sautéed Quail 150
  Quail with Cherry Sauce 148
Quiches
  Green Tomato Pie 82
  Leek and Mushroom Quiche 80
  Meat Pie Robertson 99
  Mike and Charlie's Quiche 81
  Mushroom Pie 168
  Onion Pie 81
  Spinach Cheese Pie 183
  Tomato-Cheese Tart 80

Rainbow Parfait 276
Raisin Nut Cookies 245
Raisin Pecan Pie 239
Raisin Pudding with Butter
  Sauce 273
Ranch Soup 26
Raspberries
  Lemon Ice with Raspberries 266
  Rainbow Parfait 276
  Raspberry Salad 64
Raspberry Salad 64
Ratatouille 167
Raunch Beans 158
"Real Texas" New England Clam
  Chowder 28
Red and Green Chicken 123
Red Cabbage 162
Red Ceviche Acapulco 72
Redfish, Barbequed 143
Redfish Court Bouillon 140
Redfish, Stuffed, with Shrimp
  Sauce 142
Red French Dressing 45
Red, White and Green Salad 52
Relish, Cranberry-Orange 302
Rice
  Bayou Rice 176
  Chicken-Wild Rice Salad 61
  Italian Rice 176
  Orange Cashew Rice 178

Rice Dressing 177
Rice Dressing for Roast
  Chicken 122
Rice Filled Bell Peppers 178
Rice Indienne 175
Rice Ring 61
Rice Salad 60
Stefado with Wild Rice 98
Wild Rice Salad or Appetizer 60
Wild Rice with Pecans 177
Rice Dressing 177
Rice Dressing for Roast
  Chicken 122
Rice Filled Bell Peppers 178
Rice Indienne 175
Rice Ring 61
Rice Salad 60
Rich Butter Cookies 248
Roast Chicken with Rice
  Dressing 122
Roast Goose or Duck 149
Roast Leg of Pork 110
Roast Pork with Apricot
  Glaze 109
Rocky Road Fudge Pie 241
Rodeo Cake 222
Rolled Butter Cookies 249
Rolled Butter Rolls 201
Rolls
  Bran Rolls 201
  Edwina's Angel Rolls 198
  Rolled Butter Rolls 201
Rouläden 99
Rum Butter Sweets 249
Rum Custard Cream 285
Rum-Fudge Brownies 257
Rum Pie, Christmas 241
Rum Sauce for Pears and
  Sherbet 275
Russian Borsch 25
Russian Eggs 77

St. Patrick's Day Meringues 250
Salad Dressings
  Argyle Salad Dressing 45
  Blue Cheese Dressing 44
  Green Goddess Dressing 43
  Italian Dressing 43
  Jordan Parsley Dressing 43
  Piquant Salad Dressing 44
  Poppy Seed Dressing 45
  Red French Dressing 45
  Tart Garlic Dressing 44
Salade Niçoise 68
Salads—see also Chicken Salads,
  Fruit Salads, Seafood Salads,
  Vegetable Salads
  Avocado Bowl 46
  Bacon Slaw 57

Beaumont Inn Grapefruit
  Salad 66
Bing Cherry Salad 65
Chicken-Wild Rice Salad 61
Citrus Salad with Mint
  Dressing 63
Confetti Chicken Mold 73
Copper Carrots 54
Crab Salad 72
Cranberry Salad 67
Cucumber Salad 56
Cucumber Salad Mold 56
Elegant Avocado Aspic 47
Fire and Ice Tomatoes 48
Frozen Cranberry Salad 62
Frozen Fruit Salad 64
Gazpacho Salad with Avocado
  Mayonnaise 46
German Cabbage Salad 62
German Potato Salad 55
Green Bean Salad 52
Green Gage Plum Salad 67
Guacamole Mousse 47
Joy's Molded Spinach Salad 59
Korean Salad 57
Layered Picnic Salad 52
Mango Salad 66
Mexican Congealed Salad 48
Mint Julepeach Salad 63
Mushroom, Ham, and Artichoke
  Salad 50
Mushroom Tossed Salad 49
Orange Salad 62
Overnight Salad 55
Pickled Shrimp Salad 69
Raspberry Salad 64
Red Ceviche Acapulco 72
Red, White and Green Salad 52
Rice Ring 61
Rice Salad 60
Salade Nicoise 68
Sarah's Marinated Mushroom-
  Cauliflower Salad 49
Sauerkraut Slaw 59
September Salad with Sweet
  French Dressing 50
Sesame Salad 53
Shrimp Mousse 70
Snow Pea Salad 51
Spicy Orange Salad 65
Spinach Salad 58
Spinach and Mushroom Salad
  with Mustard Dressing 59
Summer Salmon Mousse 71
Sweet and Sour Tomato
  Salad 51
Sweet Pickled Asparagus
  Salad 53
Tabooli Salad 58

Taco Salad 68
Vegetable Platter with Crab
 Dressing 54
Wild Rice Salad 60
Sally Lunn 200
Salsa 293
Sam's Pots de Crème 282
Sand Tarts, Lou Neff's 247
Sandwiches
 Cucumber Sandwiches 16
 Duke of Windsor Sandwich 114
 Ham Salad Baked in Rolls 18
 Mediterranean Loaf 17
Sangria 313
Sarah Penn Harris' Wheat
 Bread 195
Sarah's Marinated Mushroom-
 Cauliflower Salad 49
Sauces—see also Butters, Dessert
 Sauces, Barbeque Sauces,
 Marinades, Spaghetti Sauces
 Avocado Cream for Summer
  Salmon Mousse 71
 Bechamel Sauce 123
 Blender Béarnaise Sauce 292
 Caper Sauce for Confetti
  Chicken Mold 73
 Cucumber Sauce for Summer
  Salmon Mousse 71
 Currant Jelly Sauce for
  Lamb 116
 Horseradish Sauce for Ham
  Loaf 115
 Hot Mustard 92
 Pico de Gallo 291
 Salsa 293
 Sauce Diane 291
 Sauce Provençale 292
 Shrimp Sauce for Stuffed
  Redfish 142
 Spicy Chili Sauce 293
 Sweet and Sour Sauce for
  Ham 291
 White Sauce Mix 295
Sauce Diane 291
Sauce Provençale 292
Sauerkraut Slaw 59
Sausage
 Chicken and Sausage Loaf 132
 Empanadas 7
 Jambalaya Lafitte 137
 Knackwurst and Sauerkraut 113
 Lasagne 103
 Louisiana Red Beans and
  Sausage 111
 Paëlla 138
 Rice Dressing 177
 Sausage and Lentils 113
 Sausage Coffee Cake 205

Sausage and Lentils 113
Sausage Coffee Cake 205
Sautéed Cherry Tomatoes and
 Small Onions 190
Sautéed Liver with Herbs 106
Sautéed Quail 150
Sautéed Shrimp 4
Savory Eggs 76
Savory Meat Balls 102
Scalloped Artichokes 153
Scalloped Turnips 191
Scallops, Sea
 Coquilles Saint Jacques 139
Scotch Shortbread 254
Seafood
 Barbequed Redfish 143
 Charcoal Broiled Shrimp 140
 Coquilles Saint Jacques 139
 Crab Salad 72
 Crabmeat Epicurean 6
 Crabmeat in Ramekins 136
 Hot Clam-Cheese Dip 2
 Hot Crabmeat Dip 8
 Italian Broiled Shrimp 141
 Jambalaya Lafitte 137
 Paëlla 138
 Pepper Shrimp 139
 Pickled Shrimp Salad 69
 Port Aransas Boiled Shrimp 137
 Red Ceviche Acapulco 72
 Redfish Court Bouillon 140
 Sautéed Shrimp 4
 Shellfish au Gratin 138
 Shrimp Creole 136
 Shrimp Mousse 70
 Shrimp Roll 19
 Shrimp Spread 18
 Spaghetti Mario 141
 Stuffed Redfish with Shrimp
  Sauce 142
 Summer Salmon Mousse 71
 Versatile Crab 4
Seafood Salads
 Crab Salad 72
 Pickled Shrimp Salad 69
 Red Ceviche Acapulco 72
 Salade Niçoise 68
 Shrimp Mousse 70
 Summer Salmon Mousse 71
Self-Made Millionaires 260
Semester Muffins 207
Senegalese Soup 39
September Salad with Sweet
 French Dressing 50
Sesame Cookies 244
Sesame Hash Browned
 Potatoes 174
Sesame Salad 53
Sesame Seed Pastry 230

Sesame Spinach 181
Shellfish au Gratin 138
Sherbets—see Ice Creams
Shish Kebob 117
Shortbread, Scotch 258
Shrimp
 Charcoal Broiled Shrimp 140
 George Covert's Marinated
  Shrimp 19
 Italian Broiled Shrimp 141
 Jambalaya Lafitte 137
 Pepper Shrimp 139
 Pickled Shrimp Salad 69
 Port Aransas Boiled Shrimp 137
 Sautéed Shrimp 4
 Shellfish au Gratin 138
 Shrimp Creole 136
 Shrimp Mousse 70
 Shrimp Roll 19
 Shrimp Sauce for Stuffed
  Redfish 142
 Shrimp Spread 18
Shrimp Creole 136
Shrimp Mousse 70
Shrimp Roll 19
Shrimp Sauce for Stuffed
 Redfish 142
Shrimp Spread 18
Slice-O-Lemon Pie 232
Smoked Oyster Loaf 17
Snow Pea Salad 51
Sock-It-To-Me Cake 224
Sombrero Dip 11
Soups
 Artichoke Soup 37
 Broccoli Bisque 33
 Brown Corn Soup 34
 Celestial Potato Soup 41
 Chilled Avocado Soup 38
 Chilled Cucumber Soup 37
 Clear Tomato Soup 35
 Cool, Cool Asparagus Soup 36
 Cream of Chicken Soup 30
 Cream of Cucumber Soup 30
 Cream of Split Pea Soup 29
 Drake Chili 24
 Gazpacho 40
 Green Summer Soup 35
 Greek Lemon Soup 25
 Gregg Chili 23
 Gumbo 28
 Jones Corn Soup 34
 Lentil Soup 31
 Mexican Black Bean Soup 26
 Mexican Spinach Soup 33
 Oven-Baked Minestrone 38
 Pedernales River Chili 23
 Pinto Bean Soup 32
 Portuguese Soup 24

Potage Paul 40
Ranch Soup 26
"Real Texas" New England
  Clam Chowder 28
Russian Borsch 25
Senegalese Soup 39
Sour Cream Soup 31
Summer Fresh Tomato and
  Avocado Soup 36
Tortilla Soup 27
Vegetable Soup, The Best 32
Vichysquash 39
Sour Cream Soup 31
Sour Cream Zucchini 188
Sour Dough Bread 199
Sour Dough Pancakes,
  Laurens' 199
Sour Dough Starter 198
South American Appetizer 3
Spaghetti
  Carbonara 85
  Chicken Spaghetti for 25 130
  Chicken Tetrazzini 124
  Pasta al Pesto 85
  Spaghetti Armando 84
  Spaghetti Mario 141
  Spaghetti with Beef and Wine
    Sauce 104
Spaghetti Armando 84
Spaghetti Mario 141
Spaghetti with Beef and Wine
  Sauce 104
Spanish Hominy 168
Spice Cake, Pumpkin 221
Spicy Chili Sauce 293
Spice Crust for Apricot Pie 233
Spicy Orange Salad 65
Spicy Picadillo 8
Spinach
  Baked Spinach and
    Tomatoes 180
  Crêpes Florentine 86
  Deviled Spinach Eggs 12
  Joy's Molded Spinach Salad 59
  Korean Salad 59
  Lasagne Napoli 102
  Mexican Spinach Soup 33
  Overnight Salad 55
  Sesame Spinach 181
  Spinach and Artichokes 179
  Spinach au Gratin 179
  Spinach Balls 180
  Spinach Cheese Pie 183
  Spinach and Mushroom Salad
    with Mustard Dressing 59
  Spinach Dip 5
  Spinach Gnocchi 182
  Spinach Salad 58
  Texas Crabgrass 181

Spinach and Artichokes 179
Spinach au Gratin 179
Spinach Balls 180
Spinach Cheese Pie 183
Spinach and Mushroom Salad
  with Mustard Dressing 59
Spinach Dip 5
Spinach Gnocchi 182
Spinach Salad 58
Split Peas
  Cream of Split Pea Soup 29
Squash
  Bacon-Stuffed Yellow
    Squash 186
  Baked Squash 185
  Cheese-Stuffed Zucchini 187
  Garden Patch 191
  Holiday Acorn Squash 184
  Mexican Squash 184
  Pineapple Acorn Squash 185
  Ratatouille 167
  Sour Cream Zucchini 188
  Squash with Water
    Chestnuts 186
  Vegetable Mélange 192
  Vegetables with Anchovy
    Butter 192
  Vichysquash 39
  Zucchini and Corn 187
  Zucchini Provençale 188
Squash with Water
  Chestnuts 186
Steak—see Beef
Steamed Chocolate Pudding 286
Stefado with Wild Rice 98
Stew
  Herbed Beef Stew with Almond
    Poppy Seed Noodles 100
  Stew in a Pumpkin 95
Stew in a Pumpkin 95
Strawberries
  Antebellum Strawberry
    Preserves 300
  Fresh Fruit Shortcake 277
  Lemon and Strawberry
    Dessert 274
  Rainbow Parfait 276
  Strawberries Marco Polo 276
  Strawberry Butter 306
  Strawberry Crêpes 271
  Strawberry Daiquiri 312
  Strawberry Pie 234
Strawberries Marco Polo 276
Strawberry Butter 306
Strawberry Crêpes 271
Strawberry Daiquiri 312
Strawberry Pie 234
Stuffed Baked Sweet
  Potatoes 173

Stuffed Mushrooms 6
Stuffed Pheasant 150
Stuffed Redfish with Shrimp
  Sauce 142
Stuffings—see also Dressings
  Mushroom Stuffing for Beef
    Tenderloin 87
  Mushroom Stuffing for
    Eggplant 167
Substitute for Fresh Basil 84
Summer Fresh Tomato and
  Avocado Soup 36
Summer Salmon Mousse 71
Susan Diggle Horton's Green
  Beans 157
Swedish Apple Dumplings 277
Swedish Bread 203
Sweet and Sour Beets 159
Sweet and Sour Sauce for
  Ham 291
Sweet and Sour Tomato Salad 51
Sweet Breads
  Carrot Mincemeat Bread 209
  Cinnamon Puffs 200
  Cranberry Nut Bread 210
  Double Boiler Bread 210
  Honey Walnut Bread 211
  Lemon Bread 211
  Orange Bread 208
  Orange Honey French
    Toast 206
  Peach Nut Bread 209
  Persimmon Bread 208
Sweet French Dressing for
  September Salad 50
Sweet Pickled Asparagus 53
Sweet Potato Chiffon Pie 238
Sweet Potato Soufflé 172
Sweet Potatoes, Stuffed
  Baked 173
Swiss Fondue 78

Tabooli Salad 58
Taco Salad 68
Tart Garlic Dressing 44
Teresita's Black Beans 158
Texas Chili Tradition 23
Texas Crabgrass 181
Texas Picadillo 9
Thumbprint Cookies 251
Tipsy Squire with Sherry
  Custard 270
Tomatoes
  Baked Spinach and
    Tomatoes 180
  Camille's Mantequilla de
    Pobre 7
  Clear Tomato Soup 35
  Fire and Ice Tomatoes 48
  Gazpacho 40

Green Tomato Enchiladas 135
Green Tomato Pie 82
Okra and Tomatoes 170
Onion-Sauced Tomatoes 189
Ratatouille 167
Red, White and Green Salad 52
Sautéed Cherry Tomatoes and
Small Onions 190
Summer Fresh Tomato and
Avocado Soup 36
Sweet and Sour Tomato
Salad 51
Tomato-Broccoli Stackup 161
Tomato-Cheese Tart 80
Vegetable Mélange 192
Vegetable Platter with Crab
Dressing 54
Winedale Cold Stewed
Tomatoes 189
Tomato-Broccoli Stackup 161
Tomato-Cheese Tart 80
Tortilla Soup 27
Tourtière 110
Tumbleweed Ice 311
Tuna Fish
Antipasto 305
Salade Niçoise 68
Turkey
Duke of Windsor Sandwich 114
Turkey Artichoke Casserole 134
Turkey Artichoke Casserole 134
Turnip and Onion Casserole 190
Turnips, Scalloped 191
Tuscan Roast 88

Upside Down Cake 229

Vanilla Wafer Cake 220
Veal
Fresh Tomato Veal Cutlets 107
German Cheese Schnitzel 106
Veal Scaloppine alla
Vanessa 107
Veal Scaloppine alla Vanessa 107
Vegetables
Artichokes alla Ricco's 153
Artichoke Squares 4
Avery Corn Pudding 166
Baked Barley 155
Baked Spinach and
Tomatoes 180
Baked Squash 185
Bacon-Stuffed Yellow
Squash 186
Bayou Rice 176
Broccoli with Mushrooms 160
Carrots in Cheese Sauce 164
Carrots Lyonnaise 165
Carrots Parmesan 165

Carrot Ring 164
Carrots Veronique 163
Charlie Potatoes 173
Cheese Stuffed Potatoes 172
Cheese-Stuffed Zucchini 187
Chinese Vegetables 193
Corn Pudding 166
Eggplant with Mushroom
Stuffing 167
French Epicurean Peas 171
French Fried Mushrooms 169
French Fried Onions 170
Fresh Asparagus 154
Fresh Beets in Orange
Sauce 160
Frijoles Borrachos 156
Garden Patch 191
German Potatoes 175
Ginger Glazed Carrots 163
Green Beans in Casserole 159
Green Beans with Horseradish
Sauce 156
Green Pea Ring 171
Gumbochu 161
Holiday Acorn Squash 184
Hot Cabbage Crisp 162
Hot Sour Cream Potatoes 174
Italian Rice 176
Lima Beans Sauté 157
Mexican Squash 184
Mushrooms au Gratin 169
Mushroom Pie 168
Okra and Tomatoes 170
Onion-Sauced Tomatoes 189
Opulent Asparagus 154
Orange Cashew Rice 178
Pineapple Acorn Squash 185
Ratatouille 167
Raunch Beans 158
Red Cabbage 162
Rice Dressing 177
Rice Filled Green Peppers 178
Rice Indienne 175
Sautéed Cherry Tomatoes and
Small Onions 190
Scalloped Artichokes 153
Scalloped Turnips 191
Sesame Hash Browned
Potatoes 174
Sesame Spinach 181
Sour Cream Zucchini 188
Spanish Hominy 168
Spinach and Artichokes 179
Spinach au Gratin 179
Spinach Balls 180
Spinach Cheese Pie 183
Spinach Gnocchi 182
Squash with Water
Chestnuts 186

Stuffed Baked Sweet
Potatoes 173
Susan Diggle Horton's Green
Beans 157
Sweet and Sour Beets 159
Sweet Potato Soufflé 172
Teresita's Black Beans 158
Texas Crabgrass 181
Tomato-Broccoli Stackup 161
Turnip and Onion
Casserole 190
Vegetable Mélange 192
Vegetable Platter with Crab
Dressing 54
Vegetables with Anchovy
Butter 192
Wild Rice with Pecans 177
Winedale Cold Stewed
Tomatoes 189
Zucchini and Corn 187
Zucchini Provençale 188
Vegetable Dip 11
Vegetable Mélange 192
Vegetable Platter with Crab
Dressing 54
Vegetable Salads—see Salads
Vegetable Soup, The Best 32
Vegetables with Anchovy
Butter 192
Velvet Hammer 313
Venison
Burgundy Venison Stew 147
Dot Carter's Venison Backstrap
Sauté 146
Drake Chili 24
Fiesta Venison 145
Fork-Tender Venison 144
Gregg Chili 23
Jack Corley's Venison
Annandale 147
Ranch Soup 26
Venison Marinade 145
Venison Scallopini 144
Venison Shoulder Roast 146
Venison Marinade 145
Venison Scallopini 144
Venison Shoulder Roast 146
Versatile Crab 4
Very Old-Fashioneds 309
Vichysquash 39
Victor Szebehely's Hungarian
Chicken 131
Vinaigrette Dressing for Shrimp
Mousse 70
Vinegar Dressing for Spinach
Salad 57

Waffles, Crisp 212
Walnut Bars 253
Walnut Roll 269
Wassail 309
Whipped Orange Sauce 294
White Chocolate Cake 225
White Fruit Cake 228
White Sauce Mix 295
Whole Wheat Bread 196
Wild Rice
  Chicken-Wild Rice Salad 61
  Stefado with Wild Rice 98
  Wild Rice Salad or Appetizer 60
  Wild Rice with Pecans 177
Wild Rice Salad or Appetizer 60
Wild Rice with Pecans 177
Wine Marinade 295
Wine Spritzer 314

Winedale Cold Stewed
  Tomatoes 189
Winter Warmer 309

Yeast Breads
  Bran Rolls 201
  Cheese and Pepper Bread 202
  Cinnamon Puffs 200
  Cracked Wheat Bread 202
  Edwina's Angel Rolls 198
  Laurens' Sour Dough
    Pancakes 199
  Lou Neff's Cheese Bread 196
  Monkey Bread 197
  Naturally Good Rye Bread 195
  Oatmeal Bread 197
  Rolled Butter Rolls 201
  Sally Lunn 200

  Sarah Penn Harris' Wheat
    Bread 195
  Sour Dough Bread 199
  Sour Dough Starter 198
  Swedish Bread 203
  Whole Wheat Bread 196

Zucchini
  Cheese-Stuffed Zucchini 187
  Garden Patch 191
  Ratatouille 167
  Sour Cream Zucchini 188
  Vegetables with Anchovy
    Butter 192
  Zucchini and Corn 187
  Zucchini Provençale 188
Zucchini and Corn 187
Zucchini Provençale 188

A cookbook you can trust: recipes for THE COLLECTION have been tested for quality and edited for clarity and ease of preparation.

Proceeds from the sale of this book are returned to the community through Junior League projects in education, health, welfare, and the arts.

PHOTOGRAPHY/ *Carole McIntosh Sikes*

GRAPHIC DESIGN/ *Guy D. Kingsbery*

For additional copies of THE COLLECTION, send $8.95, plus $1.25 to cover postage and handling, plus 45¢ sales tax for Texas residents.
Total:
☐ $10.65 per copy for Texas residents
☐ $10.20 per copy for out-of-state.
Send to:
  THE COLLECTION
  The Junior League of Austin
  P.O. Box 165
  Austin, Texas 78767
Make check payable to THE COLLECTION.
(Price and sales tax subject to change without notice)

THE COLLECTION
The Junior League of Austin
P.O. Box 165
Austin, Texas 78767

Name _____

Street _____

City _____ State _____ Zip _____

Send me _____ copies of THE COLLECTION at $8.95 per copy, plus $1.25 to cover postage and handling, plus 45¢ sales tax for Texas residents. Enclosed is my check for $_____.

☐   ($10.65 per copy for Texas residents)
☐   ($10.20 per copy for out-of-state)

Make check payable to THE COLLECTION.

THE COLLECTION
The Junior League of Austin
P.O. Box 165
Austin, Texas 78767

Name _____

Street _____

City _____ State _____ Zip _____

Send me _____ copies of THE COLLECTION at $8.95 per copy, plus $1.25 to cover postage and handling, plus 45¢ sales tax for Texas residents. Enclosed is my check for $_____.

☐   ($10.65 per copy for Texas residents)
☐   ($10.20 per copy for out-of-state)

Make check payable to THE COLLECTION.

THE COLLECTION
The Junior League of Austin
P.O. Box 165
Austin, Texas 78767

Name _____

Street _____

City _____ State _____ Zip _____

Send me _____ copies of THE COLLECTION at $8.95 per copy, plus $1.25 to cover postage and handling, plus 45¢ sales tax for Texas residents. Enclosed is my check for $_____.

☐   ($10.65 per copy for Texas residents)
☐   ($10.20 per copy for out-of-state)

Make check payable to THE COLLECTION.